Knowledge and Belief

The Problems of Philosophy
Their Past and Present

General Editor: Ted Honderich
Grote Professor of the Philosophy of
Mind and Logic
University College, London

Each book in this series is written to bring into view and to deal with a great or significant problem of philosophy. The books are intended to be accessible to undergraduates in philosophy, and to other readers, and to advance the subject, making a contribution to it.

The first part of each book presents the history of the problem in question, in some cases its recent past. The second part, of a contemporary and analytic kind, defends and elaborates the author's preferred solution.

*Also available in paperback

Knowledge and Belief

Frederick F. Schmitt

London and New York

For
Marcia Baron

First published 1992
by Routledge
11 New Fetter Lane, London EC4P 4EE

Simultaneously published in the USA and Canada
by Routledge
a division of Routledge, Chapman and Hall, Inc.
29 West 35th Street, New York, NY 10001

© 1992 Frederick F. Schmitt
Set in 10/12pt Times by Selectmove
Printed and bound in Great Britain by
T J Press (Padstow) Ltd, Padstow, Cornwall

British Library Cataloguing in Publication Data
Schmitt, Frederick F.
Knowledge and belief. – (The problems of philosophy: their past and
present)
I. Title II. Series
121

Library of Congress Cataloging in Publication Data
Schmitt, Frederick F.
Knowledge and belief/Frederick F. Schmitt.
p.   cm. -- (The Problems of philosophy)
Includes bibliographical references and index.
1. Belief and doubt.   2. Skepticism.   3. Justification (Theory of
knowledge)   I. Title.   II. Series: Problems of philosophy
(Routledge (Firm))
BD215.S34   1991
121′.6--dc20   91–30982

ISBN 0–415–03317–9

Contents

Acknowledgments

I am indebted to a great many philosophers for inspiration and criticism. I had the good fortune to study with Alvin Goldman, and his influence will be apparent throughout. I am indebted to his specific theories and to his general approach to epistemology. My own reliabilism about justification arose, as did others', from reflection on Goldman's then unpublished reliabilist accounts of perceptual and inferential knowledge. Goldman's work and that of another epistemologist to whom I am deeply indebted, Fred Dretske, have radically changed the character of epistemology in recent years, and I hope this book will contribute to that change. It will be evident that I owe a great debt to Bill Alston, Hilary Kornblith, and Marshall Swain. Their views have shaped much of what I have written here. Over the years I have been powerfully influenced by Robert Audi, Bill Lycan, and George Pappas. They have given me more support than I could possibly repay. Though their generous attempts to reform me have failed, the outcome must be blamed entirely on a defect in my character. I have received help from so many people that it would be impossible to remember them all. Here is a short list: Paul Boghossian, Charles Caton, Richard Feldman, Robert Fogelin, John Heil, Steve Jacobson, Jaegwon Kim, Philip Kitcher, Robert Kraut, John Kvanvig, Keith Lehrer, Louis Loeb, Patrick Maher, Tim McCarthy, Joe Mendola, David Fate Norton, Michael Resnik, Amelie Rorty, Jay Rosenberg, David Shatz, David Shwayder, Larry Sklar, Michael Slote, Ernest Sosa, Steve Wagner, Nick White, Fred Will, and Michael Williams. My special thanks for inspiration and unflagging intellectual support go to Marcia Baron and Hugh Chandler. I'm grateful to Larry Hardin for getting me into this business in the first place. Dick Schacht, Ted Honderich and the infinitely patient editors at Routledge, Stratford Caldecott,

Anita Roy, and Adrian Driscoll have made the book possible. I am grateful to Glenna Cilento, Cheri Zander, and especially Lisa Henrichs for fine secretarial work.

Quotations from David Hume (1978) *A Treatise of Human Nature*, ed. L.A. Selby-Bigge, 2nd edn, ed. P.H. Nidditch, are reprinted by permission of Oxford University Press.

Abbreviations

Acad.	Cicero (1933) *Academica*, in *Cicero*, vol. 19, trans. H. Rackham, Cambridge, Massachusetts: Loeb Classical Library, Harvard University Press.
AT	Descartes, R. (1964–76) *Oeuvres de Descartes*, 12 vols, ed. C.H. Adam and P. Tannery, Paris: Vrin/C.N.R.S.
C	Kant, I. (1929) *Critique of Pure Reason*, trans. N. Kemp-Smith, London: Macmillan.
CB	Descartes, R. (1976) *Descartes' Conversation with Burman*, trans. J. Cottingham, Oxford: Oxford University Press.
CSM	—— (1984) *The Philosophical Writings of Descartes*, 2 vols, trans. J. Cottingham, R. Stoothoff, and D. Murdoch, Cambridge: Cambridge University Press.
E	Locke, J. (1894) *An Essay Concerning Human Understanding*, ed. A.C. Fraser, Oxford: Oxford University Press.
EI	Reid, T. (1969) *Essays on the Intellectual Powers of Man*, ed. B.A. Brody, Cambridge, Massachusetts: MIT Press.
Es.	Hume, D. (1987) *Essays Moral, Political, and Literary*, rev. edn, ed. E. Miller, Indianapolis: Liberty Classics.
Et.	Sextus Empiricus (1985) *Sextus Empiricus: Selections from the Major Writings on Scepticism, Man, and God*, ed. P.P. Hallie, trans. S.G. Etheridge, Indianapolis: Hackett.
EU	Hume, D. (1974) *Enquiries Concerning Human Understanding and Concerning the Principles of Morals*, ed. L.A. Selby-Bigge, 3rd edn, ed. P.H. Nidditch, Oxford: Oxford University Press.
L	—— (1969) *The Letters of David Hume*, 2 vols, ed. J.Y.T. Grieg, Oxford: Oxford University Press.

LS Long, A.A. and Sedley, D.N. (1987) *The Hellenistic Philosophers*, vol. I: *Translations of the Principal Sources with Philosophical Commentary*, Cambridge: Cambridge University Press.

M Sextus Empiricus (1933) *Against the Professors* in *Sextus Empiricus*, vol. 4, trans. R.G. Bury, Cambridge, Massachusetts: Loeb Classical Library, Harvard University Press.

PH —— (1933) *Outlines of Pyrrhonism* in *Sextus Empiricus*, vol. 1, trans. R.G. Bury, Cambridge, Massachusetts: Loeb Classical Library, Harvard University Press.

PL Descartes, R. (1970) *Descartes: Philosophical Letters*, trans. A. Kenny, Oxford: Oxford University Press.

T Hume, D. (1978) *A Treatise of Human Nature*, ed. L.A. Selby-Bigge, 2nd edn, ed. P.H. Nidditch, Oxford: Oxford University Press.

Introduction: Knowledge, Justification, and True Belief

Plato set the agenda for the theory of knowledge: to say why knowledge is regarded as more valuable than true belief, despite the fact that it is no better as a guide to action (*Meno* 97a–98c). One who correctly believes that this is the road to Larissa will get there just as surely as one who knows it to be so. Now, knowledge is a guide to action in virtue of entailing true belief.[1] Plato's question, then, is what knowledge adds to true belief that enhances the value of true belief. His answer is that it adds the condition that the subject has tied down the reason for the belief. Having tied down the reason may mean that one has a good reason or believes for that reason – in which case Plato is proposing that knowledge is justified true belief.[2] Or it may mean that one has a good reason of a special sort, capable of sustaining belief or justification over time – an interpretation suggested by Plato's analogy between true beliefs and the statues of Daedalus that flee when no one is looking. In this case, Plato is anticipating Bertrand Russell's (1912: 132) observation, repeated by Edmund Gettier (1963), that justified true belief is not sufficient for knowledge. Plato may have in mind the requirement of indefeasible justification – that the subject has enough justification to outweigh any counterevidence he or she may come to possess. On this view knowledge is indefeasibly justified true belief – a widely held view in epistemology, and I believe a correct one.[3]

On either reading of his analysis of knowledge, Plato's account of the surplus value of knowledge over true belief is incomplete: it assumes without explanation the surplus value of justified true belief over true belief. And a complete account of the surplus value of knowledge over true belief needs an account of the relation of justified belief to true belief. Indeed, much historically important epistemology focuses on just this relation.[4] For the

1

surplus value of knowledge resides largely in the value of the justified belief it entails, rather than in the value of *indefeasibly* justified true belief over and above justified true belief. To see this, we need only reflect that, apart from the conclusion that we have no justified belief or true belief, we would regard the skeptical conclusion that we have no knowledge as a curiosity rather than a calamity. It would merely be puzzling to conclude that we have no indefeasibly justified true belief, only defeasibly justified true belief. Accordingly, the central topic of epistemology has always been justified belief. We will maintain this focus and delve into the relation of justified belief to true belief.

The most straightforward, and perhaps the only plausible, way to tie justified belief to true belief is to think of it as belief that contributes to the end of true belief. It is customary to think of justified belief as epistemically permissible or right belief, analogous to morally permissible or right action. And just as morally permissible action is naturally regarded as action that contributes to a good end – e.g., pleasure – so justified belief may be regarded as belief that contributes to an epistemically good end. At any rate, I do not think justified belief can be compared with morally permissible action unless we regard it in this way, since it is not merely belief that is permissible in the sense of meeting side constraints (e.g., consistency) or in the sense of doing no harm, as morally permissible action might be taken to do; it makes a positive contribution to the epistemically good end. Of course belief is not action, or even typically under voluntary control, but, as I will argue in chapter IV, this fact need not prevent us from seeing justified belief as epistemically permissible belief, nor from assimilating justified belief to belief that contributes to an epistemically good end. The epistemically good end is plausibly identified with true belief, to distinguish epistemically justified belief from morally, prudentially, aesthetically, politically, or legally justified belief, which are distinguished by their own characteristic ends.[5]

The idea that justified belief is belief that contributes to the end of true belief is most straightforwardly developed by identifying it with *reliable belief* – belief of a sort that is generally true.[6] In particular, justified belief is belief sanctioned by a principle that generally sanctions true beliefs – a dominant view in ancient epistemology, or so I will argue in chapter I. It is natural, however, to see justified belief as a *means* to true belief – or more exactly,

2

as belief that *results* from a means to true belief. This view is most simply developed by *reliabilism*: justified belief is *reliably formed belief*, or belief that results from the exercise of a reliable cognitive belief-forming process, a process that tends to yield true beliefs (in the actual and nearby counterfactual worlds).[7] Reliabilism was, I will argue in chapters II and III, a dominant view in seventeenth- and eighteenth-century epistemology, and it has recently been endorsed by many epistemologists, receiving its most extensive defense in Alvin Goldman's *Epistemology and Cognition* (1986). I will develop a version of reliabilism here, one that differs from earlier versions in ascribing features to justification only on the basis of a conception of the value of true belief and associated pragmatic conditions of evaluation. I will sketch a solution to what many regard as the most serious problem facing reliabilism, the generality problem (chapter VI), and I will respond to internalist counterexamples to reliabilism (chapter VII).

Reliable processes are an indispensable means to a large number and high proportion of true beliefs. We may see this by observing, to begin with, that all or nearly all of our beliefs result from cognitive processes.[8] It follows by arithmetic that we must usually exercise reliable cognitive processes if our beliefs are to be true in large numbers and in high proportion. Equally, human ecological psychology entails that we must usually exercise reliable cognitive processes if our beliefs about the sorts of things that interest us are to be true in high proportion.[9] For the things that interest us are mostly the fine features of our physical and social environment or generalizations about these features. These environmental features are so complex and ephemeral that we have no chance of believing truths about them in high proportion unless we use either perceptual processes that are specially suited to the task of identifying the features of surrounding objects, or else deductive and inductive processes suited to generalizing about these features. We can hope to believe truths about these features only by exercising reliable perceptual and inferential processes. Exercising reliable processes is therefore indispensable for achieving the epistemic end of true belief. Reliabilism identifies justified belief with this means to the epistemic end.

While reliabilism ties justified belief straightforwardly to true belief, many epistemologists reject its thoroughgoing *externalism* – its implication that justified belief is simply a relation between the subject's belief and her environment (or the truth-values of various beliefs).[10] A chief source of opposition to externalism is its neglect of the subject's own evaluations and perspective – her beliefs about her justification. There are apparent counterexamples to reliabilism intended to show the relevance of epistemic beliefs.[11] We will consider the force of these proposed counterexamples in detail in chapter VII. What is important here is the suggestion that justification has an entirely different character from that attributed by reliabilism, an *internalist* character. Justified belief must be *possessed* by the subject, not merely in the (nearly) uncontroversial sense that her justifying reason is a mental state belonging to her, but in the sense that the subject must have access to or constitute the conditions of justified belief.[12] According to *accessibility internalism*, the subject must have access to the conditions of justified belief in the sense that she must be able to tell by reflection alone that her belief is justified (or satisfies the conditions of justified belief). H.A. Prichard proposes a bold requirement of this sort for *knowledge*: "Whenever we know something, we either do, or at least can, by reflecting directly know that we are knowing it" (1950: 86). According to *perspectival internalism*, the subject constitutes the conditions of justified belief; that is, a belief is justified just in case it is sanctioned by the subject's epistemic perspective, her set of beliefs about justified belief. Both perspectival and accessibility internalism spring from the idea that epistemically people stand above the determinations of nature. Accessibility internalism avers that people have a more powerful access to their own justification than they do to nature, including much of their own cognition. And perspectival internalism proposes that people lay down their own epistemic laws, laws that determine which of their beliefs are justified, in a way that they do not lay down the laws of nature or cognition: in justification, thinking it makes it so. We will examine accessibility and perspectival internalism in detail in chapters IV and V.

Here it will suffice to note that both accessibility and perspectival internalism rule out reliabilism. Accessibility internalism rules it out because one can tell that one's belief is reliably formed only by relying on sensation; reflection is not enough. To be sure, Descartes thought otherwise, but for reasons we will develop below, we can no longer share his optimism about our powers of reflection. Perspectival internalism rules out reliabilism because reliably formed beliefs need not be deemed justified by the subject, and vice versa; reliably formed belief is neither necessary nor sufficient for belief sanctioned by the subject's perspective. The conflict between reliabilism and internalism raises questions about both views. Is internalism consistent with the idea that the epistemic end is true belief, and if not, can it offer an alternative way to distinguish epistemic from moral, prudential, and other kinds of justification? Along these same lines, can internalism offer an account of the value of epistemically justified belief analogous to that offered by reliabilism? Can reliabilism accommodate, or else defuse, the apparent counterexamples that suggest internalism? These questions will be the focus of our discussion.

As I noted a moment ago, reliabilism and accessibility internalism (or more accurately, a close cousin) were not always regarded as inconsistent with one another. The question of their consistency was indeed a key factor in the development of one historically important kind of skepticism, the kind Hume calls *antecedent skepticism*:[13]

> There is a species of scepticism, *antecedent* to all study and philosophy, which is much inculcated by Des Cartes and others, as a sovereign preservative against error and precipitate judgement. It recommends an universal doubt, not only of all our former opinions and principles, but also of our very faculties; of whose veracity, say they, we must assure ourselves, by a chain of reasoning, deduced from some original principle, which cannot possibly be fallacious or deceitful. But neither is there any such original principle, which has a prerogative above others, that are self-evident and convincing: or if there were, could we advance a step beyond it, but by the use of those very faculties, of which we are supposed to be already diffident.
>
> (*EU* 149–50)

Antecedent skepticism assumes no claims about the world. It raises doubts by adverting to what is prima facie possibly the case. For example, I might doubt that there are bodies because it is prima facie possible that I am deceived into believing that bodies exist by a powerful and malevolent demon bent on deceiving me, and thus it is prima facie possible that the sensory process that yields my belief in bodies is unreliable. The doubts that undermine justified belief

according to antecedent skepticism are not themselves justified –
indeed, they are wholly unfounded. They do not supply a reason
to think that my sensory process is unreliable; they simply raise
the prima facie possibility that it is unreliable. Justified belief is
undermined when it turns out that I have no *guarantee* of the
reliability of my sensory process. Antecedent skepticism thus rests
on the assumption, not only that justified belief requires exercising
a reliable process, but that it requires a *guarantee* of the reliability
of the process. To explain the force of antecedent skepticism,
we must combine reliabilism and accessibility internalism (nearly
enough). I am not justified in my sensory belief because I am not
able to rule out the prima facie possibility of unreliability, and thus
I am not able to tell in a suitable way that my sensory process is
reliable.

To be sure, reliabilism contributes to the intuitive force of
antecedent skepticism only *through* accessibility internalism. Antecedent skepticism arises because accessibility internalism requires
a guarantee that the conditions of justified belief are satisfied, and
there is no guarantee if the conditions include reliability. It is not
that reliabilism leads to antecedent skepticism because a guarantee
that *p* entails *p*, so that a guarantee of reliability entails reliability,
though beliefs are not reliable. Nor is it that reliabilism leads to
antecedent skepticism because telling that *p* entails knowing that
p, which entails *p*, and thus telling reliability entails reliability. It is
rather that accessibility internalism leads to antecedent skepticism
only if reliability is among the conditions of justified belief and
hence one of the conditions the satisfaction of which must be
guaranteed. Of course reliabilism and accessibility internalism
are inconsistent with one another only in conjunction with the
assumption that we are justified in our beliefs, and the difficulty
to which they give rise is accordingly that they jointly entail a
consequence we all hope to avoid – skepticism. If we cannot abide
skepticism, then we will have to relinquish one view or the other.

Internalists may insist that the force of antecedent skepticism
derives from the skeptical threat posed by accessibility internalism
alone, without reliabilism.[14] The internalist may deny that the
antecedent skeptical challenge depends on reliabilism by ascribing
the challenge to a version of accessibility internalism on which we
must be able to tell (or do something that falls short of telling in
not entailing the truth of what one tells), not that the conditions of

justified belief are satisfied, but only that our processes are reliable, so that skepticism threatens even if the conditions of justified belief do not include reliability. But this approach would leave us with the question why justified belief should require that we be able to tell that our processes are reliable if reliability is not a condition of justified belief. There is no reason to require that we be able to tell that our processes are reliable unless reliability is such a condition.

In addition to antecedent skepticism, says Hume,

> There is another species of scepticism, *consequent* to science and enquiry, when men are supposed to have discovered, either the absolute fallaciousness of their mental faculties, or their unfitness to reach any fixed determination in all those curious subjects of speculation, about which they are commonly employed. Even our very senses are brought into dispute, by a certain species of philosophers; and the maxims of common life are subjected to the same doubt as the most profound principles or conclusions of metaphysics and theology.
>
> (*EU* 150)

Consequent skepticism thus raises doubts on the basis of claims about the world. The most potent forms of consequent skepticism rely on reliabilism without the aid of any internalism, or so I will argue in chapters I and III.

In my view, reliabilism and consequent skepticism play a far more extensive role in the history of epistemology than many have assumed, and accessibility internalism and antecedent skepticism a far less extensive role. The emphasis on antecedent skepticism derives from an exaggeration of the importance of Cartesian skepticism in the history of epistemology. The flavor of the attitude to history that I oppose may be savored in this manifesto of Laurence BonJour's:

> When viewed from the general standpoint of the Western epistemological tradition, externalism represents a quite substantial departure. It seems safe to say that until very recent times, no serious philosopher of knowledge would have dreamed of suggesting that a person's beliefs might be epistemically justified merely in virtue of facts or relations that are external to his subjective conception. Descartes, for example would surely have been quite unimpressed by the suggestion that his

problematic beliefs about the external world were justified if only they were in fact reliably caused, whether or not he had any reason for thinking this to be so. Clearly his conception, and that of generations of philosophers who followed, was that such a relation could play a justificatory role only if the believer himself possessed adequate reasons for thinking that the relation obtained. Thus the suggestion embodied in externalism would have been regarded as simply irrelevant to the main epistemological issue, so much so that the philosopher who suggested it would have been taken either to be hopelessly confused or to be simply changing the subject (as already noted, this *may* be what some externalists intend to be doing).

(BonJour 1985: 36–7)

BonJour's view of epistemological history as uniformly internalist is echoed in many remarks by internalists. Richard Fumerton puts the claim in similar terms:

> The externalist . . . wants to redefine epistemology in order to ensure that nature doesn't cheat us out of knowledge and justified belief. But in the context of a *philosophical* inquiry, this is the move one must reject . . . . The internalist may be unable to answer some of the fundamental questions the way he would have liked, but at least he doesn't change the meaning of those questions before trying to answer them.

(Fumerton 1987: 188)

Remarks like these are so often repeated that they have misled even externalists into thinking they are changing the subject of epistemology.

BonJour makes two fundamental mistakes here. One is assuming that Cartesian skepticism arises from internalism alone – from accessibility or perspectival internalism, or from some condition that conforms to them. In practice, however, BonJour abandons this assumption when he pursues his own epistemological project in *The Structure of Empirical Knowledge* (1985). As one would expect, he proposes an internalist account of justified belief (a coherentist account, to be specific). It then occurs to him that, as a proponent of the Cartesian epistemological project, he must attempt to answer skepticism. He assumes quite correctly that

8

doing so demands demonstrating in a suitable way that certain of our beliefs are likely to be true. This, however, implicitly abandons his assumption that Cartesian skepticism arises from internalism alone, since it relies on the requirement that justified beliefs are likely to be true. For if accessibility internalism is the source of skepticism, as it seems to be for BonJour, then the skeptical challenge must arise from the constraint that the conditions of justified belief be accessible, and hence from the reliabilist condition that justified beliefs are likely to be true. Nor is there any other warrant for the demand to show that justified beliefs are likely to be true. It will not do, for example, to appeal to the idea that the epistemic end is true belief. That idea leads straight to reliabilism, and any attempt to divert its path will derail the case for such a demand. For example, BonJour's way of expressing the idea is to impose the condition that a belief is justified just in case the subject has reason to believe it is likely to be true – a condition that, in his view, entails coherentism. But this condition cannot be a motive for trying to show that justified beliefs are likely to be true, since showing that the condition obtains requires only showing that the subject's beliefs are coherent, not that they are likely to be true. To put it differently, if justified belief is by definition coherent belief, then the worst skeptical challenge we can face is one that raises doubts about whether our beliefs are coherent. That has nothing to do with showing that our beliefs are likely to be true. BonJour's pure internalism is inconsistent with his Cartesian project.

BonJour and Fumerton make a second mistake: supposing that recent internalism is more closely related to the epistemological views of the past than externalism is – so closely that externalism changes the subject of epistemology. It is my contention to the contrary that accessibility internalism and antecedent skepticism emerge in ancient epistemology rather late, in Pyrrhonian skepticism, and then only in a scattered and underdeveloped form combined with consequent skepticism. They appear in full force only briefly, in Cartesian skepticism, which should be viewed as an extreme internalist moment in the substantially externalist history of skepticism. And, as I have already urged, antecedent skepticism itself arises only from the combination of accessibility internalism with reliabilism. The charge that a pure externalism changes the subject and redefines epistemology gets history backwards.

Epistemologists of the past have subscribed to a pure externalism, but no one until recently ever subscribed to a pure accessibility internalism.[15]

CHAPTER I

Greek Skepticism

1 Plato's skepticism in the Theaetetus

One of the earliest and most influential discussions of skepticism is to be found in Plato's *Theaetetus*.[1] Plato's primary topic in the first half of the *Theaetetus* is the Protagorean claim that knowledge is perception. Plato objects to the claim by offering a skeptical challenge resting on the assumption that knowledge is *perfectly reliable true belief* (or if you prefer, cognition, rather than belief). First, there is evidence that, for Plato, knowledge *entails* perfectly reliable true belief: "So perception (*aisthesis*) is always of what is, and, as being knowledge, it is unerring (*apseudes*)" (152c).[2] Plato's first clause proposes that perception already entails true belief, and his second clause adds that it must also be unerring if it is to count as knowledge. Since he apparently intends the second clause to add something to the first, it would seem that he has in mind the requirement that knowledge entails, not merely true belief, but reliable belief as well – a suggestion consistent with the meaning of *apseudes* as truthful in the manner of an oracle. Second, there is evidence that, for Plato, perfectly reliable belief entails knowledge: "Well then, if I'm unerring (*apseudes*), and don't trip up in my thinking (*dianoia*) about the things that are, or come to be, how could I fail to have knowledge of the things I'm a perceiver of?" (160d). It would seem again that *apseudes* should be translated as "reliable." Plato is claiming that if he is unerring and he does not trip up in his thinking, then he has knowledge. Presumably, not tripping up in his thinking is simply believing what is true. Hence, if "unerring" meant simply "true," Plato's addition of not tripping up in his thinking would be redundant. More importantly, if "unerring" meant "true," he would be claiming preposterously, and in contradiction of his own famous observation in the *Meno*,

11

that true belief is sufficient for knowledge. It is best, then, to read him as claiming that perfectly reliable true belief entails knowledge. Thus, we may conclude that for Plato knowledge is perfectly reliable true belief – belief sanctioned by a criterion of truth, that is, by a perfectly reliable criterion.[3] (I will suppress the qualifier "perfectly" from here on in.) So far, then, Plato assumes an externalist analysis of knowledge as true belief sanctioned by a criterion of truth. Given this assumption, the question whether knowledge is perception turns on whether perceptual criteria are reliable.

In Plato's view, the claim that they are reliable stands or falls with Protagorean relativism about truth, that "a man is the measure of all things: of those which are, that they are, and of those which are not, that they are not" (152a). For perceptual beliefs are invariably true just in case Protagorean relativism is true. Plato can therefore simultaneously challenge Protagorean relativism and the reliability of perceptual criteria. As I interpret his challenge, it rests on the observation that dreaming, disorders, and madness involve false beliefs (157e–158b). Yet the criteria we employ in dreaming, madness, and disorders just are the perceptual criteria – the very criteria we employ in waking. Since these criteria are unreliable, our perceptual criteria are unreliable. But, remember, knowledge is perception only if perceptual criteria are reliable. It follows that knowledge is not perception.

There is a natural temptation for the post-Cartesian reader to interpret Plato's skeptical challenge here as an internalist challenge like Descartes' dream and madness challenges in *Meditation* I. Plato's skeptical challenge, it is tempting to suppose, is that we have no *guarantee* of reliability, and not merely that our criteria are in fact unreliable. Despite our earlier case for reading Plato as identifying knowledge with mere true belief sanctioned by a perfectly reliable criterion, it is natural to read him as imposing a stronger requirement on knowledge – that we be able to tell in a suitable way that our criterion is reliable:

SOCRATES: . . . what evidence (*apodeixai*) would one be able to point to, if someone asked at this very moment whether we're asleep and dreaming everything that we have in mind, or awake and having a waking discussion with each other?

THEAETETUS: Yes, Socrates, it certainly is difficult to see what evidence one should use to prove it; because all the features of the two states correspond exactly, like counterparts. The discussion we've just had could equally well have been one that we seemed, in our sleep, to be having with each other; and when, in a dream, we seem to be telling dreams, the similarity between the two sets of occurrences is extraordinary.

(158b–c)

It is natural to offer an internalist interpretation of this challenge, along these lines. It is prima facie possible that the criteria we employ in waking are unreliable, since these criteria would be unreliable if employed in dreaming, and it is prima facie possible that we are now employing them in dreaming, despite our judgment that we are awake. But if our waking criteria are prima facie possibly unreliable, then we have no guarantee of their reliability – no suitable premises from which to argue for their reliability. If we try to appeal to premises that describe our waking experience, these premises could just as well be true even if our experience were not a waking experience at all but a dreaming experience. And we cannot use our waking criteria to select our premises, since then our proof of the reliability of our waking criteria would depend on the criteria themselves – and thus be ruled out by prohibitions on circularity. Consequently we do not know the propositions sanctioned by our waking criteria.

On this internalist interpretation, Plato's challenge rests on the internalist requirement that we have a suitable proof of the reliability of our waking criteria independent of these criteria. The internalist interpretation differs from the externalist interpretation with which we began in ascribing to Plato an argument that our waking criteria are prima facie possibly unreliable, rather than actually unreliable. On the internalist interpretation Plato argues that for any waking experience, there is some *prima facie possible* dreaming experience *exactly* similar to it. But on the externalist interpretation, he argues instead that for any waking state there is some *actual* dreaming state that is *sufficiently* similar to it. For he must show that our waking criteria are unreliable, and this requires showing that our waking criteria sanction beliefs we have while we dream (call them "dream beliefs"). On the externalist interpretation, our waking criteria must apply in our actual dreaming state. To show that they do apply, Plato must show that our waking criteria are individuated in such a way as to sanction dream beliefs – waking criteria must be individuated broadly. (By contrast, the proponent of the internalist interpretation is free to endorse either a broad or a narrow individuation, since, on the internalist interpretation, the skeptical challenge does not depend on the unreliability of waking criteria.) Thus, on the externalist interpretation, waking states must be shown sufficiently similar to dreaming states. Presumably Plato must argue that the mental similarity between waking and dreaming states outweighs any relevant nonmental dissimilarity in deciding the individuation of criteria.

I believe we must resist the temptation to offer an internalist interpretation. The internalist interpretation requires that Plato treat both the waking experience and the dreaming experience in ways that he does not do. For one thing, the internalist interpretation requires that Plato treat the waking experience as exactly similar to the prima facie possible dreaming experience. And that requires that he distinguish sharply the waking experience from its physiological and environmental correlates. But he does not sharply distinguish these. In an important comparative study of Greek and Cartesian skepticism, Myles Burnyeat (1982) has suggested that the Greeks do not sharply distinguish experience from its bodily or environmental correlates. Burnyeat offers this suggestion as an explanation of why we find no attempt among the Greeks to raise Descartes' demon challenge. Such a challenge requires us to imagine or conceive experience without body. What enables Descartes to raise the challenge is his sharp distinction between mind and body. Now, raising the challenge does not require denying an identity between mind and body. In fact Descartes raises the demon challenge in *Meditation* I, long before he has established the actual or even metaphysically possible ("real") distinction between mind and body in *Meditation* VI. But Descartes does need the prima facie possibility that mind and body are distinct to raise the challenge. We must at least be able to imagine or conceive the distinction in reason. Burnyeat suggests that the Greeks fail to conceive such a distinction.

In making this suggestion, Burnyeat places himself in a venerable tradition that traces Cartesian skepticism to Cartesian mind–body metaphysics – a tradition inaugurated by Gassendi, and developed by Reid and Kant when they locate the source of Cartesian skepticism in Descartes' alleged indirect theory of perception. Now I have grave doubts about the claims of this tradition, for reasons which will be mentioned in subsequent chapters. Nevertheless, Burnyeat does seem to be right that the Greeks do not conceive of the distinction between mind and body in such a way that they are inclined to entertain the prima facie possibility of experience just like the experience we actually have, but in the absence of the subject's own body. Here I want to add to Burnyeat's point the observation that in the *Theaetetus* Plato fails to make even the weaker numerical distinction between experience and its physiological and environmental correlates, quite apart from the prima facie possibility that experience exists without the subject's body. (That distinction, as we will see, is one that the later Academic skeptics do make.) Consequently, Plato fails to imagine the possibility of waking experience *exactly like* dreaming experience. He does not single out waking experience and claim that dreaming experience can be exactly similar to it. Indeed, he does not compare waking and dreaming *experience* at all but rather waking and dreaming *states*. The waking and dreaming states may include bodily states. Accordingly, Plato does not say that waking and dreaming states are exactly alike, but only that they "correspond exactly, like counterparts." There is an exact *correspondence* between waking and dreaming states, but the similarity between them is said to be extraordinary, not exact. Waking and dreaming states differ in their bodily components and environmental correlates, and these must be taken into account in judging their similarity.

A second point against the internalist interpretation is that Plato does not merely argue that for any waking state there is some prima facie possible dreaming state extraordinarily similar to it. He is not content to observe that the conversation between Socrates and Theaetetus could equally well have been one that they seemed in a dream to be having with each other. He observes as well that their waking state is extraordinarily similar to dreams in which they "seem to be telling dreams." Plato seems to be imagining that there is some *actual* dreaming state sufficiently similar to their waking experience. The designation "the two sets of occurrences" makes sense only if the dreaming state to which it refers is an actual and not merely possible entity (or type of entity), since a merely possible dreaming state would have no character independent of the specification that it be like the waking state. Moreover, it is conversationally appropriate for Theaetetus to say that the dreaming state is extraordinarily similar to the waking state only if the dreaming state is not similar by hypothesis. The proponent of the internalist interpretation might retort that Plato observes that there are sufficiently similar actual dreaming states merely to establish that an exactly similar dreaming state is *prima facie possible*. But there is nothing to indicate that Plato's observation of extraordinarily similar actual dreaming states is merely instrumental. And such an observation would hardly be needed to establish the prima facie possibility of an exactly similar dreaming state. It is true that Socrates begins with a comparison of his waking state with a possible dreaming state like it. But the point of the comparison is not to establish that there is a prima facie possible dreaming state just like his waking state. Look closely at the final clause in Theaetetus' rejoinder in the passage at issue: "when, in a dream, we seem to be telling dreams, the similarity between the two sets of occurrences is extraordinary." It is most natural to read Plato as comparing waking states with actual dreaming states. Socrates' observation that his waking state is like some possible dreaming state is apparently designed to indicate that the waking state is rather like actual dreaming states. The observation helps isolate features of the waking state that also belong to actual dreaming states.[4]

If, as I have argued, Plato offers an externalist rather than internalist skeptical challenge in the *Theaetetus*, this would explain why we do not find in Plato anything like the demon challenge raised by Descartes as a sequel to his dream challenge. Descartes, as I will interpret him in the next chapter, raises the prima facie possibility that sense is unreliable because he is dreaming. The Cartesian dream challenge is intended to raise the prima facie possibility that his sensory criteria are unreliable. The demon challenge is a natural extension of the dream challenge, differing mainly in raising the prima facie possibility of more pervasive unreliability, involving even the prima facie possibility of the nonexistence of the physical world, including one's own body. Now Burnyeat, I have noted, has plausibly suggested that the Greeks do not conceive of experience like our actual experience without its bodily and environmental correlates, and that is why none of the Greeks poses the demon challenge in its full power. But this fact does not yet explain why (with the possible exception of Galen) we find *no* form of demon challenge in the Greeks, not even a form that exempts the body from the demon's deception. An externalist interpretation of Plato's dream challenge would explain the absence of any form of demon challenge. For the demon challenge is not a natural extension of an externalist dream challenge, as it is of an internalist dream challenge. The demon challenge cannot be an externalist challenge. An externalist dream challenge requires that similar dreams be actual, since it requires that waking criteria sanction actual false dream beliefs. But similar demon experiences are not actual – there are no deceiving demons. Moreover, even if demon experiences were actual, the overall states in which they are embedded are rather more dissimilar to the waking state than are dreaming states – so much so that they may not be sufficiently similar to the waking state to fall under waking criteria. In short, the demon challenge *cannot* be interpreted externally.

In response to the externalist interpretation, it might be objected that at one point Plato raises a skeptical question that can only be interpreted internally. After noting that the length of time spent in disorders and madness is less than that spent in a normal and sane state, Socrates asks: "Well, is what's true to be determined by the length or shortness of a period of time?" (158d). This might be taken to foreshadow the Pyrrhonian challenge of *isosthenia*: there are different criteria of truth for normal and abnormal states, or for sane and mad states, and these criteria contradict one another; yet there is no proof that one is reliable and the other not. As I will explain below, this challenge does rest on an internalist condition. But I do not think it can be attributed to Plato. For Plato clearly intends the skeptical challenge arising from disorder and madness to parallel the dream challenge. But his dream challenge cannot be intended as a challenge of *isosthenia*. For if it were such a challenge, there would be no reason to emphasize, as he does, the similarity of waking and dreaming states. The claim of similarity is needed only for the conclusion that waking and dreaming criteria are the *same*. But the challenge of *isosthenia* does not require that the criteria be the same. On the contrary, it requires that they be different. (The Pyrrhonian skeptical modes accordingly emphasize the *dissimilarity* of waking and dreaming states, and the contrary

17

conclusions we reach in these states, rather than their similarity.)
It is true that Plato does not argue for the similarity of normal
and abnormal states, or of sane and mad states, as he does for
the similarity of waking and dreaming states. He may, however,
assume that the reader has gotten the point from the example of
dreaming – hence the cursory treatment of disorders and madness.

It remains to explain why Plato asks whether truth is to be
decided by length of time. I would suggest that he is asking
whether length of time is a factor that individuates criteria.[5] If
length of time were an individuating factor, then the criterion
one employs in an abnormal state would be a distinct criterion
from that employed in a normal state, and thus the unreliability
of the abnormal criterion would not count against the reliability
of the normal criterion. Socrates rejects length of time as an
individuating factor when he asks "But have you any other clear
way of showing which of these judgments are true?" (158e). Here
Plato rejects length of time and all other factors as individuating
waking and dreaming criteria, or normal and abnormal, or sane
and mad criteria.

Why is length of time not an individuating factor? The answer,
I would guess, is that it is not a factor that affects the frequency of
truths among the beliefs sanctioned by criteria. On average, our
waking or dreaming, normal or abnormal, sane or mad beliefs are
just as frequently true (or false) over short as over long spans of
time. This answer assumes that criteria are individuated, not only
by the psychological similarity of the mental states they involve (the
intrinsic similarity of waking and dreaming experiences), but also
by the distribution of truth-values among the beliefs they sanction,
and in particular by the nearness of the frequency of true beliefs
among these beliefs. The question which factors are individuating
is a vexed one to which we will return in chapter VI.

For now, we cannot escape noticing that individuating criteria by
the distribution of truth-values threatens Plato's dream, disorder,
and madness skepticism, since dreaming, disorders, and madness
are factors that affect the frequency of truths among beliefs
and so should distinguish the criteria. But once the criteria are
distinguished, Plato can no longer raise the skeptical challenge
on grounds of unreliability. One response to this threat to Plato's
skeptical challenge is to insist that only purely cognitive factors
are individuating, and thus the difference between dreaming and

waking *cannot* matter, since there is no purely cognitive difference between them; there are only physiological and environmental differences. This is not, however, a response that Plato would accept, or even one available to him, if he does not sharply distinguish mentality from its physiological or environmental correlates.[6] In any event, the implausibility of an externalist dream skepticism should not undermine attributing an externalist challenge to Plato, since there is little reason to believe that Plato accepts the dream skepticism purveyed by Socrates.

2 Academic skepticism

Plato's successors in the Academy, Arcesilaus and Carneades, pose two sorts of skeptical challenges. The less important for our purposes is the challenge from the *opposition of propositions*: for any proposition, there are equally justifying arguments for that proposition and at least one of its contraries. Carneades is said to have illustrated this method during his embassy to Rome, where he argued for justice one day and equally against it the next day. The skeptical challenge from the opposition of propositions should not, however, be confused with the skeptical challenge from *isosthenia*, or opposition of appearances, employed in the oppositional modes of the Pyrrhonists. As we will see, the oppositional modes do not involve giving equal arguments for contrary propositions. Moreover, the Pyrrhonists apply *isosthenia* to all topics, while the Academics restrict the opposition of propositions to theoretical topics like justice. The opposition of propositions, unlike *isosthenia*, is a challenge of underdetermination of propositions by reasons, and it may be understood as an externalist challenge based on the claim that a reliable criterion will not favor a proposition over a contrary for which there are equally justifying reasons.[7]

The second Academic skeptical challenge is not so easily interpreted as externalist, and we will accordingly make it the focus of our attention. It is the challenge from *akatalepsis* or lack of cognition. This challenge differs from the opposition of propositions in claiming that we do not have sufficient reason to believe a proposition, while the opposition of propositions claims that we have equal reason to believe the contrary of any proposition. But the doxastic outcome of both challenges is supposed to be the suspension of judgment (*epoche*). The Academics prescribe *epoche* because they think that we should avoid error (*LS* I 438; *Acad.* I 45).

The Academics pose their challenge of *akatalepsis* in reply to the Stoic solution to the problem of the criterion of truth for sensory beliefs. The problem is to distinguish the true sensory impressions from the false. An impression (*phantasia*) is a vision that is expressible by a proposition (*lekton*) and can therefore be true or false. The Stoic criterion of truth is the cognitive impression (*kataleptike phantasia*). A criterion here has considerably narrower extent than the Platonic criteria we earlier discussed: it encompasses only exactly similar impressions. Thus, criteria generally sanction few beliefs, since exactly similar impressions are rare (indeed, as we will see, the Stoics deny that we ever have exactly similar impressions of distinct objects). The cognitive impression is allegedly perfectly reliable, having a character that corresponds to the object from which it arises. There is, as we will see, a sense in which it cannot be confused with the impression of any other (numerically distinct) object.

The cognitive impression is to be distinguished from the resulting cognition (*katalepsis*), which is an act rather than a passive impression. And the cognition, as Julia Annas (1980) has argued, is again to be distinguished from knowledge (*episteme*), which requires fitting the cognition into the body of reasonable beliefs.[8] In the simile of Zeno, the founder of Stoicism, the impression is like an open hand, assent a closing hand, cognition the clenching of the fist, and knowledge the firm grasp of the clenched fist by the other hand (*LS* I 253–4; *Acad.* II 145). The last comparison harkens back to Plato's suggestion in the *Meno* that knowledge is true belief tied down by reasons.[9]

The Academic challenge from *akatalepsis* is designed to show that we do not have cognitive impressions, and thus have no criterion of truth, no cognition, and no knowledge. It is not, however, designed to show that we do not have justified belief (unlike the challenge from opposition of propositions). The Stoics evidently allow a standard of the reasonable (*to eulogon*) that falls short of knowledge, a standard that will guide us even when we suspend judgment (*LS* I 451; *M* VII 158), and this standard tends to sanction more true than false propositions. The Academics, too, seem to allow justified belief. Carneades says that the wise man may "grasp nothing yet opine" (*LS* I 454; *Acad.* II 78). He allows opinions of increasing strength: opinions that are probable (*pithanos*), consistent with other probable opinions ("undiverted") and thoroughly explored and with features explained.[10] According to Sextus Empiricus, Carneades explicitly identifies probability with the actual relative frequency of truth (*LS* I 451–3; *M* VII 166–84). The argument from *akatalepsis*, then, attacks only knowledge, not justified belief.

The admission of justified belief that falls short of knowledge threatens to take the bite out of the Academic recommendation of *epoche*, since it threatens to admit any opinion that is probable. For the recommendation of *epoche* then amounts to no more than the uncontroversial recommendation that we suspend judgment on propositions when we lack justifying reasons. The recommendation of epoche may, however, retain its impact if the Academics admit, not opinions simpliciter, but only different strengths of judgment proportioned to probabilities. The Academics may then recommend that we never make judgments simpliciter but only with specific degrees of strength pegged to the degree of justification supplied by our reasons. For our purposes we need not carry the discussion of *epoche* further. As Cicero observes (*LS* I 454; *Acad.* II 78), the question whether to recommend *epoche* (and whether *epoche* is psychologically possible) is logically independent of the skeptical question whether we have knowledge or justified belief, which is our concern here.

Let us turn to the skeptical challenge from *akatalepsis*. The Academics deny that there are any cognitive impressions, impressions with an intrinsic character that corresponds to its object in such a way that it cannot be confused with the impression of any other numerically distinct object. For any given impression of an object, there are objects similar to the object of the impression that give rise to an exactly similar impression – e.g., twins or eggs. Thus, according to Cicero,

There are four headings to prove there is nothing which can be known, cognized or grasped, which is the subject of this whole controversy. The first of these is that some false impression does exist. The second, that it is not cognitive. The third, that impressions between which there is no difference cannot be such that some are cognitive and others not. The fourth, that no true

21

impression arises from sensation which does not have alongside it another impression no different from it which is not cognitive . . . . If someone looking at Publius Servilius Geminus thought he was looking at Quintus, he was experiencing an impression of an incognitive kind because there was no mark distinguishing the true from the false. With that difference removed, what mark could he have of the kind which would not be false for recognizing Gaius Cotta who was twice consul with Geminus?

(*LS* I 245; *Acad.* II 83–4)

Cicero's point is that someone looking at Publius Servilius Geminus does not have a cognitive impression. Cicero seems to say also that no one can have a cognitive impression of Gaius Cotta, since the impression of Cotta has "alongside it another impression no different from it which is not cognitive."

Our primary task in interpreting the Academics is to decide between two interpretations of the Stoic claim that there are cognitive impressions. Do the Stoics claim that there are impressions for which there are in fact no other exactly similar impressions of distinct objects, or do they instead claim more boldly that there are impressions for which there *could be* no other exactly similar impressions of distinct objects. The former claim can clearly be understood *externally*, but the latter can only be understood *internally*, if "could" is taken epistemically rather than metaphysically. The above passage from Cicero suggests the latter claim, since the exact similarity of the impressions of Publius and Quintus is supposed to entail that the dissimilar impression of Cotta is not cognitive, presumably because it entails that there *could* be an impression similar to that of Cotta. Cicero attributes an objection of this sort to Arcesilaus:

We may take [Arcesilaus] to have asked what would happen if the wise man could not cognize anything and it was the mark of the wise man not to opine. Zeno, I imagine, replied that the wise man would not opine since there was something cognitive. What then was this? Zeno, I suppose, said: an impression. What kind of impression? Zeno then defined it as an impression stamped and reproduced from something which is, exactly as it is. Arcesilaus next asked whether this was still valid if a true impression was just like a false one. At this point Zeno was sharp enough to see that if an impression from what is were such that

22

an impression from what is not could be just like it, there was no cognitive impression.

(*LS* I 242; *Acad*. II 77–8)

Cicero's assumption that a cognitive impression is one for which there cannot be an exactly similar false impression is corroborated by Sextus: "A cognitive impression is one which arises from what is and is stamped and impressed exactly in accordance with what is, of such a kind as could not arise from what is not" (*LS* I 243; *M* VII 247). According to Cicero and Sextus, then, the Stoics demand that for any cognitive impression, there could not be a similar but false impression. This suggests that the Stoics require not merely a perfectly reliable criterion, but a *guarantee* of perfect reliability. It would appear that the Stoics assume an internalist requirement and that the Academics challenge the existence of knowledge so understood.

However, further reports raise doubts about such an internalist interpretation and suggest instead an externalist interpretation. Consider the Stoic response to the Academic challenge, reported by Cicero in the continuation of the first passage above:

You say that such a degree of similarity does not exist in things . . . we will allow that for sure. Yet it can certainly appear to exist and therefore deceive the sense, and if a single likeness has done that, it will have made everything doubtful. With that criterion removed which is the proper instrument of recognition, even if the man you are looking at is just the man you think you are looking at, you will not make the judgment with the mark you say you ought to, viz., one of a kind of which a false mark could not be . . . . You say that everything is in a class of its own and that nothing is the same as something else. That is certainly a Stoic thesis and not a very plausible one – that no hair or grain of sand is in all respects of the same character as another hair or grain. These claims can be refuted, but I don't want to fight. It makes no difference to the matter in hand whether a visual object is no different in every one of its parts, or even if it does differ, is incapable of being distinguished.

(*LS* I 245–6; *Acad*. II 84–5)

At one point in this passage, the Stoic response seems to be straightforwardly externalist. The Stoics are said to respond that numerically distinct objects are never actually similar, so that cognitive impressions of numerically distinct objects are always dissimilar. If this is their response, then the Stoics are defending the claim that cognitive impressions are reliable. (Of course their defense assumes that whenever numerically distinct objects are dissimilar, they will, under certain conditions, appear so.) Elsewhere in the passage, however, Cicero traces the Stoic claim that numerically distinct objects are never similar to the principle of the identity of indiscernibles, and this principle is supposed to hold necessarily (since distinct objects can exist only as "peculiarly qualified individuals"). Since the principle of the identity of indiscernibles holds necessarily, it entails that there could be no similar objects, and hence for any cognitive impression there could be no similar impression of a twin. If this is the Stoic response, then the Stoics are defending the claim that cognitive impressions are *necessarily reliable*. However, even if the Stoics intend such a claim, their analysis of a cognitive impression is still externalist. For, though the claim entails a guarantee of reliability, the guarantee is not *epistemic*, as required by internalism, but *metaphysical*. The principle of the identity of indiscernibles entails only that it is metaphysically impossible for there to be similar objects, not that we have a proof that similar objects are impossible in answer to the prima facie possibility of unreliability. There is some question, though, why the Stoics would insist that criteria be metaphysically necessarily reliable. Such a requirement is hardly warranted by the Stoic aim of true cognition. I would therefore prefer not to attribute the requirement that criteria be metaphysically necessarily reliable.

It seems to me most charitable to both the Stoics and the Academics to read the Stoics as requiring something more than the reliability of criteria but less than an epistemic guarantee of reliability. To read the Stoics as requiring only reliability is to render the Academic challenge to the Stoics irrelevant. The Academics do not argue against the reliability of criteria; they do not claim that for every criterion, there is an actual exactly similar but false impression. The existence of *some* false exactly similar impressions is supposed to entail that there are *no* cognitive impressions. On the other hand, to read the Stoics as requiring an epistemic guarantee of reliability is to render their own defense by appeal to the identity of indiscernibles hopelessly inadequate. And the Academics do not merely claim that for some (or all) alleged cognitive impressions there *could* be a similar false impression. They attempt to cite an *actual* similar false impression.[11] A charitable reading must find a requirement intermediate between these extremes.

A closer look reveals that the Academics assume that a cognitive impression requires, not merely the reliability of the criterion, but the reliability of the *kind* of criterion. That is, a false similar impression of a kind scotches any cognitive impression of that kind because what must be reliable is the kind of criterion, and not merely the particular criterion. The Academics attribute to the Stoics a reliability analysis of cognitive impressions. Though this analysis does not identify a cognitive impression with a merely reliable criterion, it nevertheless differs only verbally from Plato's account of knowledge, as I earlier interpreted him – the verbal difference being that the Stoics individuate criteria as narrowly as possible, restricting them to exactly similar impressions, while Plato allows criteria to cover somewhat dissimilar impressions. Equivalently we may say that the Academics assume that a cognitive impression must be, not merely reliable, but reliable with probability one. The Academics seek an actual false impression because they wish to establish, not the mere *possibility* that any given criterion is unreliable, but the non-zero *probability* that it is. The fact that there is an actual similar false impression renders all impressions doubtful because a cognitive impression is a criterion of truth only if it is reliable with probability one.[12]

Attributing to the Stoics the requirement that cognitive impressions belong to a reliable kind explains the intractability and longevity of the dispute between Stoics and Academics – facts not explained by attributing the requirements of reliability or of a guarantee of reliability. The Academics may reasonably raise objections to cognitive impressions. For they may cite actual false impressions of the same kind (or actual similar false impressions – e.g., dream impressions). At the same time, the Stoics have a plausible response. They may deny that such false impressions belong to the same kind or are sufficiently similar. It is plausible to reply to the Academic dream and madness challenges by saying that the external conditions of dreaming and madness are so different from normal perception that false impressions produced by dreaming and madness are irrelevant to the existence of cognitive impressions in waking. (I admit, however, that I can find no evidence that the Stoics did reply in this fashion.) And it is equally plausible to respond to the Academic challenge that there are similar false impressions in cases of twins or eggs by claiming that these cases are irrelevant to other cases in which there are no similar false impressions. The wise man will simply suspend judgment as to whether this is Castor rather than Polydeuces until he has attended well enough to discriminate Castor from Polydeuces (*LS* I 245; *M* VII 410). It is true that there may be cases in which this much attention does not suffice and one ends with a false belief. But such cases are not relevant to the optimal cases in which sufficient care is taken to discriminate the objects. The Stoics do in fact make this response. These responses would enable the Stoics to maintain that there are cognitive impressions of a reliable kind even in the face of the dream and madness challenges and similar false impressions. Of course these responses assume that the external conditions of dreaming and madness, and the dissimilarity of cases in which there are twins, are factors that individuate kinds of impressions. That is, the responses assume an externalist account of the individuation of kinds of impressions.

The Academic skeptical challenge, I would argue, differs from Descartes' dream challenge in the same way as Plato's does. In a provocative paper on the relation of Cartesian skepticism to classical skepticism, Michael Williams (1986) proposes that the Academics never raise Cartesian dream skepticism. In his view, the Academics are prevented from doing so by their acceptance of the Stoic premise that dissimilar impressions arise from dissimilar objects, which rules out dreaming impressions similar to waking impressions, since their objects are dissimilar. In Williams's view, the Academics employ dream skepticism only to question whether waking impressions are more striking than dreaming impressions. Here Williams extends Burnyeat's suggestion that the Greeks do not conceive of experience like our actual experience without the subject's body. He speculates that the Academics are unable to pose the Cartesian dream challenge because they do not sharply distinguish mental states from bodily and environmental states, as Descartes does.

I do agree with Burnyeat and Williams that Descartes raises a new kind of skepticism in the dream and demon challenges. I agree that the Greeks lack the inclination, or perhaps even the conceptual resources, to raise the demon challenge. And, as I proposed earlier, Plato fails, in the *Theaetetus* at any rate, to make the numerical distinction in reason between experience and its bodily and environmental correlates needed to raise Cartesian dream skepticism, the prima facie possibility that our experience is dreaming experience. But I do not agree with Williams that the Academics fail to make such a distinction. They do not in fact raise Cartesian dream skepticism, but the reason is not that they lack the inclination or resources to make the relevant metaphysical distinction, to distinguish experience from its bodily and environmental correlates. On the contrary, they in fact make such a distinction. It is rather that they are engaged in a very different kind of *epistemological* project from the one in which Descartes is engaged. They promote a different kind of skepticism, for which purpose they in fact deploy the very metaphysical distinction at issue.

Williams is mistaken in claiming that the Academics accept the Stoic premise that dissimilar impressions arise from dissimilar objects. This is evident from a report of Cicero's we have already quoted (*LS* I 245–6; *Acad.* II 83–5). The Academics are content to observe that there are similar impressions even if objects are always dissimilar. Thus, the Academics do not tie impressions to their objects as closely as the Stoics do. Indeed Cicero reports them as allowing similar impressions, one of which has no object at all: "The Academics say 'This is a sign, or proof, of that, and I therefore follow it, but it could be that what it signifies is either false or nothing at all'" (*LS* I 261; *Acad.* II 30). Thus, the Academics pose a dream challenge parallel to their challenge from similar false impressions, and they have the resources to raise at least a limited version of dream skepticism. Williams is mistaken in saying that the Academics employ dream skepticism only to question whether waking impressions are more striking than dreaming impressions. It is true that they observe that dreaming impressions are equally striking, but they do so only because similar impressions must be equally striking:

> For impressions arise from what is not as well as from what is. The fact that they are found to be equally self-evident and striking is an indication of their indiscernibility, and an indication of their being equally self-evident and striking is the

27

fact that the consequential actions are linked to [both kinds of impressions]. Just as in waking states a thirsty man gets pleasure from drinking and someone who flees from a wild beast or any other terror shouts and screams, so too in dreams people satisfy their thirst and think they are drinking from a spring, and it is just the same with the fear of those who have nightmares.

(*LS* I 244; *M* VII 401–10)

Clearly, Sextus is trying here to describe dreaming states that are not merely as striking as but indiscernible from actual (or likely) waking states, and, though he says that their being equally striking indicates indiscernibility, he surely means that their being equally striking is a necessary condition of indiscernibility. The Academics pose the dream challenge to show that there are false impressions of a relevant kind, so that all impressions belong to an unreliable kind. There is thus no novelty in Descartes' use of dreaming to describe impressions like waking impressions that are false in virtue of having no corresponding object.

In my view the real difference between the Academics and Descartes does not lie in the fact that the Cartesian dream challenge describes false impressions of the same kind as waking impressions. Rather it lies in the modality of the descriptions of the false impressions – or in other words, in whether the challenge rests on externalism or internalism. Descartes, at least as standardly interpreted, raises the prima facie possibility that my actual experiences are dreaming experiences, while the Academics claim instead that our actual waking impressions are of the same kind as dreaming impressions. Descartes' challenge does not assume, as the Academics' does, that our actual waking impressions are like our actual dreaming impressions, rather that it is prima facie possible for them to be dreaming impressions. The Academic challenge rests on observations of the actual falsity of dreaming impressions, or at least on observations of the inconsistency of waking and dreaming impressions, so that one must be false and hence both belong to an unreliable kind, since they belong to the same kind. If the Academics intend the former challenge, they are comparing the contents of impressions with features of the external world and thus committing themselves to claims about the external world. If instead they intend the latter challenge, they relinquish the ability to doubt that the external world has neither of the features represented in dreaming and waking impressions. In neither case are they in a position to doubt the existence of the external world. To doubt its existence, one must raise a prima facie possibility, and that is an internalist challenge. Descartes' challenge rests, as the Academics' does not, on the internalist requirement that our criteria not be prima facie possibly unreliable. Thus the difference between the Academic and Cartesian challenges lies, not in the metaphysical resources they employ, but in the epistemological conditions they assume. Here, as elsewhere, epistemological differences in skeptical challenges turn on epistemological, not metaphysical, assumptions.

3 Pyrrhonian skepticism

An internalist basis for skepticism comes into play in Greek epistemology only when we turn from Platonic and Academic skepticism to Pyrrhonian skepticism. Pyrrhonian skepticism does not arise from an observation of the unreliability of criteria. It depends rather on what Williams calls epistemological skepticism. In claiming such a dependence I contradict Williams's claim that Pyrrhonian skepticism differs dramatically from Cartesian skepticism in the variety of its doubts, epistemological doubt being only one among them. In Williams's view, Pyrrhonian doubts are specific: they infect only particular kinds of propositions. There is no attempt to raise a *general* doubt as in Descartes. But I believe that all Pyrrhonian doubt rests on a general epistemological doubt.

There is much evidence for Williams's claim that Pyrrhonian doubt is eclectic and specific. Sextus' own definition of skepticism in the *Outlines of Pyrrhonism* suggests an eclectic method for raising doubt, ranging over many kinds of doubt:

> Skepticism is an ability to place in antithesis, in any manner whatever, appearances and judgments, and thus – because of the equality of force (*isostheneian*) in the objects and arguments opposed – to come first of all to a suspension of judgment (*epochen*) and then to mental tranquility (*ataraxian*).
>
> (*Et.* 32–3; *PH* I 8)

This definition suggests that skepticism about an issue will arise when the appearances equally favor contrary propositions. Skepticism for Sextus might seem to amount to underdetermination of

contrary propositions by the available appearances. The contents
of these appearances are specific to contrary propositions on given
topics. Nor does Sextus offer any general argument that there will
always be equal force on both sides of any issue. Indeed, he
disclaims the completeness of his list of oppositional arguments.
The possibility of further oppositions is left open, and the search for
oppositions never officially terminates. Sextus even characterizes
the skeptic as one who "keeps on searching," a description
close to the original meaning of "skeptic" – "inquirer." The
definition of skepticism thus suggests an open-ended, piecemeal,
pluralistic doubt. One might take this to be confirmed by the
motley assortment of skeptical modes listed by Sextus – the ten
oppositional modes attributed to Aenesidemus (*PH* I 36–163),
the five modes attributed to Agrippa (*PH* 164–77), and the final
two modes of circularity and regress (*PH* 178–9). All this might
seem to support Williams's view of the contrast between Pyrrhonian
and Cartesian skepticism.

Yet a closer look at the Pyrrhonian modes reveals that the
appearance of eclecticism is due more to the disorganization and
incompleteness of Sextus' presentation of the modes than to any
variety in the modes themselves. When properly elaborated, the
modes share a common structure and content, and this content
is epistemological. Moreover, the epistemological skepticism on
which the modes rest is supportable only if there is a comprehensive
doubt, as in Descartes' demon challenge.

To elucidate the argumentative structure of the Pyrrhonian
modes, we may begin by cautioning against assimilating Pyrrhonian
skepticism, as some do, to underdetermination of contrary propositions by appearances. I would not deny that the oppositional
modes involve underdetermination. But Sextus' argument that
appearances equally favor contrary propositions does not entail
underdetermination as now understood. In modern treatments
of underdetermination, like those in Galileo's *Two Chief World
Systems* (1967) and Descartes' *Principles of Philosophy* (*CSM* I;
AT VIIIA), the justification of competing propositions by the
appearances is measured and claimed (or denied) to be equal.
Sometimes, as in the case of the Copernican and Ptolemaic
theories of planetary motion, the appearances are themselves
objective phenomena (e.g., the observed planetary positions, or
the telescopically observed sunspots or mountains on the moon).

There are intersubjective standards for assigning weight to such appearances, or at least (as in the case of Galileo's telescopic observations) it is agreed that we can and ought to settle on such standards. Sometimes the appearances are *subjective* phenomena, as in the case of Descartes' demon challenge. The subjective appearances are weighed against one another. These subjective appearances, however, are always appearances that appear to a *single* subject. The Pyrrhonian oppositional modes differ markedly from modern underdetermination in mixing objective and subjective appearances, and refusing to weigh objective appearances against subjective appearances, or subjective appearances against one another. The first four oppositional modes pertain to the subject judging, the seventh and tenth to the object judged, and the fifth, sixth, eighth, and ninth to the combination of subjective and objective appearances. The modes differ most strikingly from modern underdetermination in comparing the subjective states of different subjects, and refusing to claim the equal justification of the opposing appearances.

The modes do not compare the degree of justification supplied by the appearances or even suggest that the appearances equally justify contrary propositions. It is true that the modes are intended to show that the appearances equally favor contrary propositions. But they are not supposed to show this because these appearances provide equal justification. Rather, they are supposed to show it because we cannot say that the appearances provide *any* degree of justification. Since the modes do not depend on weighing the appearances favoring contrary propositions, we cannot interpret them in the manner of modern underdetermination, as making the reliabilist argument that criteria that favor a proposition in the presence of appearances favoring a contrary proposition are unreliable.

Each of the modes begins with the claim that there are antithetical criteria for given contrary propositions on specified topics (i.e., there are criteria that sanction the contrary propositions). Since the propositions these criteria sanction are contraries, one of the criteria must be less than perfectly reliable (indeed, if the criteria cover a range of such propositions, one of them must be very unreliable, or several of them rather unreliable). For example, in the second oppositional mode "from the differences between men," Sextus lists bodily differences that bear on impressions:

As for the body, we have different figures and constitutional peculiarities. And according as different humours predominate in men, their sense-impressions also are different . . . . But if it is because of the difference between men that the same objects affect us differently, then this would be another good reason for bringing suspension of judgement. We are, perhaps, able to say what each external object appears to be from our several different points of view, but we are unable to give an account of its true essence.

(*Et.* 54–6; *PH* I 79–87)

In his presentation of some oppositional modes, Sextus offers no further argument for skepticism. Yet it is obvious that further argument is needed to reach a skeptical conclusion. For the modes show only that at least one criterion must be unreliable. Thus they leave open the possibility that the other criterion is reliable. And on a reliabilist account of justified belief, the subject who employs the reliable criterion is justified. The skeptical challenge of the oppositional modes is quite unlike that involved in Platonic or Academic skepticism, where no criterion is reliable because the same criterion yields all beliefs, at least one of which is false. Nor can the Pyrrhonian criteria be aggregated so as to form a kind that covers all the contrary propositions in a given case, and thus be deemed unreliable: the appearances involved in the various criteria are not at all similar to one another, and there is no natural aggregate criterion. The oppositional modes must therefore leave open the reliability of some criteria. They must rely on a stronger condition than reliability (*LS* I 476–7; *PH* I 79–91).

Sextus introduces the required further argument for skepticism in a continuation of the above passage:

For we shall have to believe either all men or some of them; to believe all would be an impossible undertaking, as we should have to accept contradictory accounts, while if we are to believe some, let them tell us who it is we are supposed to agree with. The Platonist will say Plato, the Epicurean Epicurus, and so on with the others.

(*Et.* 56; *PH* I 88)

Why should we not, however, follow our *own* appearances? Why, indeed, are we not *committed* to doing so? Sextus answers that we ourselves are party to the disagreement, and it would therefore beg the question to follow our own appearances. Here Sextus appeals to an epistemological doubt: we do not have a guarantee that our criterion is reliable while other contrary criteria are unreliable. Similarly in the fourth oppositional mode from "dispositions," Sextus opposes appearances in waking and sleeping, drunkenness and sobriety, sickness and health: "And the same honey that appears sweet to me appears bitter to those suffering from jaundice" (*Et*. 59; *PH* I 101). But ". . . whoever attempts to resolve this discrepancy will find himself either in one or the other of the aforesaid states or else in no state at all . . . the fact of his being in some state or other while attempting to pass judgement will make him a party to the controversy" (*Et*. 61–2; *PH* I 112–13).

When Sextus says that anyone who attempts to resolve the discrepancy will be a party to the controversy, he means to demand proof (*apodeixis*) that our criterion is reliable.[13] In the course of presenting the oppositional modes, he offers two arguments that no proof can be given: a *regress* and a *circularity argument*. These arguments are, in my view, effectively equivalent, and it will suffice to examine the former. The regress argument appears in the fifth oppositional mode "depending on positions, distances and locations" and again in the second mode of Agrippa:

> anyone who wishes to give any of these impressions the prefer-
> ence over the others will be undertaking an impossible task.
> For . . . if he says that proof is true, he will be asked for a
> proof of its truth, and another proof for that one, and so on
> *ad infinitum*. But it is impossible to prevent an infinite series of
> proofs; therefore he will not be able, even by the use of proofs,
> to prefer one impression to another.
>
> <div align="right">(<i>Et</i>. 64; <i>PH</i> I 121–3)</div>

This formulation suggests an appeal to what it is *humanly feasible* to prove: any justification necessarily requires a proof of the reliability of the criterion, and any proof necessarily in turn requires justification, so that any justification necessarily requires an infinity of proofs; but it is not humanly feasible to present an infinity of proofs. But I doubt whether Sextus really intends to make the implausible claim that justification necessarily requires an infinity of proofs. I suspect he means to leave open the logical possibility of proof coming to an end when the right kind of proof is reached. Conversely, it would appear from his formulation of the second mode of Agrippa that he would not regard an infinity of proofs as necessarily satisfying his demand – it matters what *kind* of proofs they are:

> The mode based on the extension to infinity is the one in which we say that the proof offered for the verification of a proposed matter requires a further verification; and this one another, and so on to infinity, so that since we lack a point of departure for our reasoning, the consequence is suspension of judgment.
>
> (*Et.* 73; *PH* I 166–7)

This formulation suggests that even an infinite regress of proofs would not necessarily satisfy Sextus' demand. And so his skepticism does not merely rest on the claim that an infinite regress of proofs is impossible.

What is missing from these formulations of the regress argument is an argument that it will not do merely to stop with a proof that meets a reliable criterion. On reliabilism, such a proof would suffice. Sextus assumes, then, an internalist condition that requires more than the reliability of the criterion. The condition must require that we have the *right kind* of proof of reliability. This is the requirement that touches off a regress that we cannot terminate. The oppositional modes thus depend on epistemological skepticism.

Unfortunately Sextus does not tell us just what the right kind of proof is. It is natural, however, to say that the right kind of proof requires a criterion the reliability of which is not called into question in the given case. This requirement would allow for the logical possibility of terminating the regress, but at the same time make it difficult to terminate the regress. And it would entail, in keeping with what is suggested by the second mode of Agrippa, that even an infinite regress of proofs is not necessarily sufficient for justification. (Of course there remains the question, which we will tackle in the next chapter, why we should think that knowledge imposes such a requirement.)

Though this development of Sextus' regress argument is natural, and seems the only way to make his oppositional modes yield a skeptical conclusion, it must be admitted that Sextus shows little awareness of what is entailed by such an argument. The skepticism to which such an argument gives rise is no longer piecemeal. Indeed it threatens to escalate in the end into Cartesian skepticism. For the regress leads clearly to a skeptical conclusion only if every criterion that might be employed in the regress of proof can be brought into question at once. Only in that case will it clearly follow that there are no independent criteria by which we may tell that our initial criterion is reliable. In other words, this natural way of developing the regress argument clearly yields a skeptical conclusion only if doubt is relatively comprehensive, questioning large classes of criteria at once. It requires doubt of the sort Williams believes to be original with Descartes. Sextus shows no inclination to raise such a doubt, but he must raise it if he is to use the oppositional modes to reach a skeptical conclusion.

At the same time, such a doubt threatens to make the oppositional modes superfluous. It is unclear what the oppositional modes can add to a comprehensive doubt. If there is a comprehensive doubt about criteria belonging to a certain class, that would seem to be enough to yield a skeptical conclusion, in the presence of the requirement of an independent proof, since such a doubt makes it impossible to terminate the regress of proof. If the comprehensive doubt applies to the initial criterion we employ in judgment, then no opposition of specific appearances and judgments is needed. The oppositional modes are needed, then, only if the comprehensive doubt does *not* apply to the initial criterion. Sextus can maintain the need for oppositional modes only by distinguishing the sort of doubt that applies to the initial criterion (and thus first-order justification) from the sort of doubt that applies to subsequent criteria (and thus second- and higher-order proof). As we will see this distinction is common in recent internalism, which requires that we have a sort of justification for epistemic beliefs – justification by reflection alone – that we need not have for nonepistemic beliefs (these may be justified by sensation). Internalists give arguments for requiring the reflective justification of epistemic beliefs. We will examine some of these arguments in chapter IV. But I do not see that these arguments, even if they work, either entail the applicability of comprehensive doubt to subsequent criteria or exempt the initial criterion from such doubt. Nor does Sextus show any inclination to distinguish initial from subsequent criteria. Without this distinction, however, the oppositional modes have no work to do.

Perhaps the oppositional modes could continue to function as a *basis* for comprehensive doubt. We could perhaps generalize a comprehensive doubt by induction from the opposition of specific appearances and judgments. Much of what Sextus says suggests such an inductive generalization, though officially he presents his examples of opposition as paradigms for instruction in the technique of raising future oppositional doubts, rather than as premises for an induction to a comprehensive doubt. On the other hand, one might seek a comprehensive doubt directly, as in Cartesian skepticism.[14]

I have argued, against Williams, that Pyrrhonian skepticism depends on the epistemological skepticism assumed by the regress and circularity arguments. Such skepticism in turn requires a comprehensive doubt, rendering the oppositional modes unnecessary, useful at most for generalizing doubt, and suggesting a turn to Cartesian comprehensive doubt. Nevertheless, it is important to note that as long as the oppositional modes are retained – and there is nothing that forces their abandonment – Pyrrhonian skepticism will remain significantly different from Cartesian skepticism. Most importantly, Pyrrhonian skepticism remains to a large extent externalist. For it rests on the point that not all the criteria that people actually employ – indeed, very few such criteria – can be reliable, since the propositions sanctioned by these criteria are contrary. The ground on which criteria are rejected is that not all can be reliable. And this is very different from Cartesian dream and demon skepticism, which do not claim that any criteria are actually unreliable, only that any criterion is prima facie possibly unreliable. Greek skepticism, even in its farthest reaches, remains largely externalist.

In my view, Descartes' originality consists precisely in raising a doubt that does not depend merely on externalism. It is Descartes' flight from the actually unreliable to the prima facie possibly unreliable, and not the comprehensiveness of his doubt or his ability to question the existence of his own body, that most strikingly marks his departure from ancient skepticism. For this reason, I would venture that Hume, whose skepticism, I will argue, depends solely on externalism, is the true heir of classical skepticism.

CHAPTER II

Descartes' Skepticism

Cartesian skepticism shifts from the Greek focus on whether sense is reliable – on consequent skepticism – to a focus on antecedent skepticism. Here I describe Descartes' version of the antecedent skeptical challenge in the *Meditations*, together with his reply. In focusing on Descartes' antecedent skepticism, I do not mean to deny that he also grapples with consequent skepticism. I believe he addresses consequent skeptical worries throughout the *Meditations*, though his treatment is submerged below the surface of the text. But that is a story for another day (Schmitt 1988). Here I offer an orthodox interpretation of Descartes, or a variant of one, in order to highlight the commitments and pitfalls of the antecedent skeptical project. I also offer orthodox criticisms of that project.[1]

Antecedent skepticism is a philosophical chimaera whose nature was, I believe, more accurately understood by Descartes' successors than by the philosopher himself. As Hume observes, it brooks no response but fails to undermine our confidence in the external world (*EU* 149–50). On the one hand, the combination of views about justification that give rise to antecedent skepticism – reliabilism and accessibility internalism (or a near variant) – make antecedent skepticism seem inevitable. Once accepted, these views leave little room for response to skepticism. Thus, Descartes' own heroic struggle with skepticism has seemed to many doomed from the start. In this regard, antecedent skepticism differs strikingly from consequent skepticism, which does not clearly follow from the reliabilism on which it rests. On the other hand, the combination of reliabilism and accessibility internalism is surely more difficult to motivate than reliabilism alone, and so antecedent skepticism has always seemed undermotivated. The tension between the inevitability of antecedent skepticism, given the principles that lead to it, and its lack of motivation explains its "now you see it, now you don't" character and its elusive hold on our conviction.

1 The antecedent skeptical challenge

As an introduction to his antecedent skeptical project, Descartes does propose a consequent skepticism about sense similar to Platonic and Academic skepticism.[2] He rejects beliefs when they fall under an unreliable principle.[3] The relevant principles are, as Margaret Wilson (1978: 38–42) has subtly argued, belief-forming processes. In this regard, Descartes differs from the Greeks, whose criteria are not processes.[4] Thus Descartes rejects indiscriminate sensory beliefs by observing that indiscriminate sense is unreliable: "the senses occasionally deceive us with respect to objects which are very small or in the distance" (*CSM* II 12; *AT* VII 18). I am unjustified in my belief that the tower is round because upon approaching the tower sense corrects that belief and leads to the judgment that the tower is square. The two beliefs cannot both be true, so indiscriminate sense yields a false belief and is thus unjustifying. Though Descartes points here to occasional false beliefs, I do not think that he relies merely on the Stoic requirement that a criterion of truth be perfectly reliable.[5] For he immediately observes that *discriminate* sense – sense under favorable external conditions – avoids the objection of unreliability – this despite the fact that discriminate sense is obviously not *perfectly* reliable. Descartes' objection to indiscriminate sense is, therefore, that it is rather unreliable and not merely less than perfectly reliable. (This is not to say that he does not demand perfect reliability on some topics – in particular, on the topic of the *foundations* of knowledge, of the beliefs used to select the principles by which we make judgments. A single error in these foundational beliefs can lead to the choice of an unreliable process and thus ultimately cause extensive error.[6])

Though Descartes clearly rejects indiscriminate sense on consequent skeptical grounds, his subsequent rejection of discriminate sense is less easily attributed to consequent skepticism.[7] He challenges discriminate sense by appeal to madness and dreaming. These challenges, like Plato's madness and dream skepticism, may be interpreted as consequent skeptical challenges, objecting to the actual reliability of discriminate sense. Or they may be interpreted as antecedent skeptical challenges rejecting discriminate sense because it is prima facie *possible* that it is unreliable.

The consequent skeptical interpretation is most plausible for the madness challenge. On such an interpretation, sane and mad sense are regarded as a single process, so that the unreliability of mad sense infects sane sense and entails its unreliability. In favor of this interpretation is the fact that Descartes immediately rejects the madness challenge with this explanation: "But such people are insane, and I would be thought equally mad if I took anything from them as a model for myself" (*CSM* II 13; *AT* VII 19). It is natural to read Descartes as abandoning the madness challenge because the mad sensory process differs so much from the sane sensory process that it cannot count as the same process, so that the unreliability of mad sense does not infect discriminate sense.

The madness challenge might, however, be interpreted as an antecedent skeptical challenge, raising the prima facie possibility that sane sense is unreliable.[8] Raising the prima facie possibility of unreliable sane sense amounts to a skeptical challenge if the subject must not only exercise a reliable process but be able to guarantee its reliability against this prima facie possibility. Descartes may offer a skeptical challenge by raising the prima facie possible unreliability of sane sense if he assumes what we may call *independent accessibility internalism*, a variant of accessibility internalism: a subject must be able to tell that the process is reliable in a manner independent of exercising any doubted process – i.e., independent of exercising any process the prima facie possibility of which has been posed. The subject must be able to guarantee the reliability of the process against doubts that raise the prima facie possibility of unreliability. The prima facie possibility of unreliable sane sense thus poses a skeptical challenge because it requires us to be able to tell that sane sense is reliable without employing any process against which the prima facie possibility of unreliability has been raised – including of course the process of sane sense, but perhaps including other processes as well, depending on just how the prima facie possibility of unreliability has been raised (if by a scenario that ensnares only sane sense, then no other process). The point of adverting to the prima facie possibility of madness, on this interpretation, is to restrict the class of processes by which the subject can tell that the target process is reliable. But how does the prima facie possibility of madness warrant this restriction? The answer must be that the possibility indicates which processes are so similar to the target process that they cannot be used to tell that the process is reliable. We will return to this matter in section 3 below.

The antecedent interpretation of the madness challenge does face an obstacle that did not need to be surmounted by the consequent interpretation: explaining why Descartes so quickly abandons the madness challenge. The only explanation that seems available here is that mad sense is not sufficiently similar to sane sense, or sufficiently probable for a person like the meditator, to raise the prima facie possibility that the sensory process employed by the meditator is unreliable. One way to develop this explanation is unsatisfactory: supposing that the prima facie possibilities that must be ruled out are limited to those meeting certain *external* constraints – notably, the *similarity* of the mad circumstances to the sane circumstances, or the *probability* of the mad circumstances. There is nothing philosophically wrong with limiting the prima facie possibilities in this way, though it would seem to be warranted only by an externalist and not an internalist rationale. The trouble is a textual one: this way of limiting the prima facie possibilities is not consistently respected by Descartes. Consider, for example, the prima facie possibility of deception by a demon. The circumstances of deception by a demon are neither similar to normal sense nor probable. A more satisfactory way to develop the present explanation of Descartes' rejection of the madness challenge on the antecedent interpretation is to say that Descartes regards the mad sensory process as *intrinsically* unlike the sane sensory process, and thus as a different process. Processes are individuated in part by the intrinsic similarity of their exercises (a suggestion we will develop in chapter VI). The subject need rule out only prima facie possibilities in which the very process which forms the subject's belief is exercised. Thus the subject need not rule out the prima facie possibility of madness. The madness challenge can, then, be interpreted as an antecedent skeptical challenge.

The dream challenge presents the same interpretive options. But here the text clearly favors the antecedent skeptical interpretation. The dream possibility is intended to raise the prima facie possibility of the unreliability of sense.[9] For Descartes answers the dream possibility in *Meditation* VI, not by showing the irrelevance of actual vivid dreams to sense, as required by the consequent skeptical interpretation, but by arguing that our means of distinguishing dreams from waking experience is in general reliable – precisely the answer required by the antecedent skeptical interpretation.[10]

Moving now to the demon challenge, we observe first that, unlike the madness and dream challenges, it *cannot* be understood as a consequent challenge, but only as an antecedent challenge, for the reason mentioned in chapter I. Though some people are mad and everyone dreams, no one is in fact deceived by a demon; so the appeal to demons cannot show the actual unreliability of sense. Descartes' demon hypothesis must be understood as moving to a different logical level and criticizing discriminate sense on the ground that it is prima facie possibly unreliable.[11] Again Descartes assumes independent accessibility internalism: we must be able to tell that discriminate sense is reliable without exercising a doubted process. The demon challenge is directed against sense in *Meditation* I, but in *Meditation* III Descartes extends the challenge to reason – that is, to clear and distinct perception. The demon challenge appears to establish a global skepticism. It casts doubt on all processes at once: the demon might deceive us about any process. We are left without any process we might exercise to tell that any process is reliable. Our predicament is not, however, quite as hopeless as it might seem – at least not *logically* hopeless.

2 The validation of reason

At the opening of *Meditation* III, Descartes sets out to answer the demon challenge by validating reason. He must find a way of telling that reason is reliable without exercising any doubted processes. He must, in other words, supply an argument for the reliability of reason from premises that are admissible in the face of the demon challenge. On one popular reading, well supported by the text, the premises of his validation of reason are admissible because they are *clearly and distinctly perceived*: "The longer and more carefully I examine all these points, the more clearly and distinctly I recognize their truth" (*CSM* II 29; *AT* VII 42). But this reading is inconsistent with my interpretation of the dream and demon challenges. For on my interpretation, the point of the challenges is precisely to prevent responding by exercising a doubted process. And clear and distinct perception is a doubted process. We may therefore test the plausibility of my interpretation by considering

41

whether this popular interpretation is inevitable, or whether there is some alternative to it.

I reject the interpretation because I see the demon challenge as a challenge to all clear and distinct perception. The demon challenge is designed precisely to prevent the use of clear and distinct perception in the validation. On my interpretation of the demon challenge, appeal to clear and distinct perception in the validation is expressly forbidden – the charge of circularity is precisely what the demon challenge would entail. Nevertheless, the textual evidence for the clear and distinct perception interpretation is substantial. Descartes worries repeatedly about the charge of circularity and tries to meet it. Let me begin my response to the clear and distinct perception interpretation by introducing the alternative interpretation of the validation that fits my interpretation of the skeptical challenge.

On the interpretation of the validation I favor, we are able to tell that reason is reliable without employing reason because we can deduce the reliability of reason from *indubitable* premises – premises that may be assumed even in the face of the prima facie possibility of unreliability. In the cogito passage of *Meditation* II, Descartes locates the first indubitable premise, "I exist":

> If I convinced myself of something then I certainly existed. But there is a deceiver of supreme power and cunning who is deliberately and constantly deceiving me. In that case I too undoubtedly exist, if he is deceiving me; and let him deceive me as much as he can, he will never bring it about that I am nothing so long as I think that I am something.
>
> (*CSM* II 17; *AT* VII 25)

Descartes argues here that "I exist" is indubitable – i.e., may be assumed in the face of the prima facie possibility of the unreliability of sense and reason – because it is in some way given by the skeptical challenge itself – by the description of the possibility of deception by a demon.

There are, however, two possible accounts of indubitability. On one account, propositions are indubitable just when they are true in any situation in which I entertain the demon challenge. Thus, "I exist" is patently indubitable. This account has two disadvantages. It has a serious textual disadvantage. For it entails that some mental state propositions – like "I will" and "I sense" – are dubitable, since they are not true in all situations in which I entertain the demon challenge. Yet at *Principles* I.9 (*CSM* I 195; *AT* VIII 7), Descartes allows *any* first-person mental state proposition to be a premise for the cogito. And in *Meditation* II, all first-person mental state propositions are deemed indubitable on the ground that they "cannot be false" (*CSM* II 19; *AT* VII 28) – meaning, it seems, that they are true even in the demon situation. More importantly, this account of indubitability has a philosophical disadvantage. It entails that all the premises of the validation of reason must be true in any situation in which I entertain the demon challenge. But it seems clear that this is not so. "I doubt" may well be true in any such situation, but the premises of the validation of reason include a number of mental state propositions that are not true in all such situations. On the alternative account of indubitability I wish to endorse, propositions are indubitable just when they are true in *the demon situation itself*.[12] Here too, "I exist" is obviously indubitable. But this account is more liberal than the preceding in admitting *all* mental state propositions as indubitable. It is thus textually preferable. And at the same time it entails that the mental state propositions that are premises of the validation are indubitable, so it is philosophically preferable as well.

It may be helpful here to recall the details of the validation of reason. The reliability of clear and distinct perception is supposed to follow from the existence of a nondeceiving God. In addition to the premise "I exist," Descartes employs the premise "I have the idea of a perfect being," which is plausibly indubitable because true in the demon situation. Another premise he employs is the causal principle that "there must be at least as much reality in the efficient and total cause as in the effect of that cause," which holds "not only in the case of effects which possess actual or formal reality, but also in the case of ideas, where one is considering only objective reality" (*CSM* II 28; *AT* VII 41). This causal principle might also be thought true in the demon situation. From these premises Descartes deduces the existence of a nondeceiving God. He then argues that all clearly and distinctly perceived propositions are true: ". . . since God does not wish to deceive me, he surely did not give me the kind of faculty which would ever enable me to go wrong while using it correctly" (*CSM* II 37–8; *CSM* VII 54). Descartes continues: "If however, I simply refrain from making a judgment in such cases where I do perceive the truth with sufficient clarity and distinctness, then it is clear that I am behaving correctly and avoiding error" (*CSM* II 41; *AT* VII 59). Yet ". . . my nature is such that so long as I perceive something very clearly and distinctly I cannot but believe it to be true" (*CSM* II 48; *AT* VII 69). So I cannot refrain from believing what I clearly and distinctly perceive. I behave correctly, therefore, when I believe what I clearly and distinctly perceive. It follows that clearly and distinctly perceived propositions are true.

Having sketched my interpretation of the validation and the demon challenge, we may return to the plausibility of the popular interpretation of the validation on which its premises are admissible because they are clearly and distinctly perceived, rather than indubitable. The clear and distinct perception interpretation gives rise to the charge that the validation is circular. We must consider, then, whether there is a satisfactory response to the charge of circularity. A successful response would render the clear and distinct perception interpretation philosophically more palatable and to this extent undermine my interpretation of the demon challenge.

There are two ways to respond to the charge of circularity. One is to maintain that the circularity is harmless because the aim of the validation is to see whether clear and distinct perception validates itself. This is Harry Frankfurt's (1970) response. This response disagrees with my interpretation of the demon challenge in denying that the demon challenge forbids employing clear and distinct perception in the validation. It disagrees with my interpretation of the validation in denying that the premises of the validation must be indubitable. Frankfurt's interpretation is supposed to gain plausibility from an interpretation of the skeptical challenges on which sense and reason raise doubts about themselves. On this interpretation, Descartes' first doubt about sense (translating freely from Frankfurt's idiom into our own) is that indiscriminate sense yields inconsistent beliefs and thus a belief in its own unreliability. Descartes' other doubts about sense are that discriminate sense yields a belief in its own *possible* unreliability. In other words, sense undermines itself. The point of the validation of reason is to show that reason does not suffer the same fate. In my view, however, the point of the skeptical challenges to sense and reason is not to show that sense and reason raise doubts about themselves. Indeed, the skeptical challenges to sense do not arise from sense alone, but require at least customary logical beliefs of the sort reason yields to recognize that inconsistencies are false, as well as imagination to generate the prima facie possibility of unreliability. Nor is it obvious that the skeptical challenge to reason derives from reason alone; it may employ imagination (though I can find no textual evidence to rule out the possibility that Descartes postpones the fully general demon challenge until *Meditation* III because he wishes the protagonist to employ only conception and not imagination in raising the doubt). Let it also be noted that there is no textual evidence that Descartes offers a self-validation of reason. Nor is it easy to see the philosophical point of self-validation, even if self-validation is not trivially guaranteed (Wilson 1978: 135). As Frankfurt admits, showing that reason validates itself does not answer the worry that reason undermines itself, since it leaves open the possibility that reason inconsistently both validates and undermines itself.

An alternative response to the charge of circularity is to deny that the demon challenge applies to all clearly and distinctly perceived propositions. Clearly and distinctly perceived propositions are exempt from the demon challenge – are admissible as premises of the validation. On this response, not all clear and distinct perception is called into question; enough of it is left untouched by doubt to exempt the premises of the validation. This is Descartes' official response to the circle. Concerning the premises of the validation, he says: "I know I am not deceived with regard to them, since I am actually paying attention to them. And as long as I do pay attention to them, I am certain that I am not being deceived and I am compelled to give my assent to them" (*CB* 6; *AT* V 148). Descartes' point is that the premises of the validation are what we might call *evident* propositions: we must accept them whenever we attend to them. In this case, we cannot entertain the demon doubt about them without accepting them, and thus they are not subject to the demon doubt when we attend to them. This response contradicts my interpretation of the demon challenge by denying that the challenge applies to all clearly and distinctly perceived propositions. And it contradicts my interpretation of the validation by denying that the premises of the validation must be indubitable.

There are, however, textual and philosophical objections to this response. The textual objection is that Descartes subjects all beliefs to the demon challenge, and he accordingly treats all knowledge by clear and distinct perception as dependent on the validation of reason: "Thus I see plainly that the certainty and truth of all knowledge (*scientiae*) depends uniquely on my knowledge (*cognitione*) of the true God, to such an extent that I was incapable of perfect knowledge about anything else until I knew him" (*CSM* II 49; *AT* VII 71). In *Meditation* III, paragraph 4, Descartes raises the demon challenge even for those propositions that are evident. It is true that in raising the doubt, he refers to the psychological power of such propositions:

> Yet when I turn to the things themselves which I think I perceive very clearly, I am so convinced by them that I spontaneously declare: let whoever can do so deceive me, he will never . . . bring it about that two and three added together are more or less than five, or anything of this kind in which I see a manifest contradiction. . . .
>
> (*CSM* II 25; *AT* VII 36)

But in the next sentence, he raises the demon challenge against these very propositions, and there is no suggestion that the challenge is raised against these only when we are not perceiving them. Moreover, the premises of the validation are clearly not evident in the required sense. Not even the premise "I exist" is a proposition I must accept whenever I entertain it – at least not in the sense that I am psychologically compelled to believe it whenever I entertain it. Still less are the other premises of the validation evident. On my interpretation, Descartes has misspoken at *CB* 6 and what he should have said is not that I am compelled to assent to these propositions whenever I entertain them, but that these premises must be true whenever I assent to them, even in the demon situation (as he says in the cogito passage that "I exist" is necessarily true whenever I conceive it). The philosophical trouble with exempting evident propositions from the demon challenge is that there is no reason to treat our evident clear and distinct perception as escaping the challenge, however subjectively convincing it may be. The fact that we cannot psychologically doubt a proposition while we entertain it does not show that there is no *reason* to doubt it. As Margaret Wilson has put it, "The crucial issue is whether we can *know* certain propositions prior to proving God; the observation that there are certain moments when we cannot for the moment doubt is epistemically irrelevant" (Wilson 1978: 133). And, as Harry Frankfurt (1970) has shown, Descartes does recognize the distinction between psychological inability to doubt and there being no reason for doubt. It seems that all clearly and distinctly perceived propositions must be submitted to doubt.

We should, then, reject both of these ways of responding to the charge of circularity and thus the idea that the premises of the validation are admissible in virtue of being clearly and distinctly perceived. Rejecting this idea of course entails attributing to Descartes a rather elementary confusion about his own answer to skepticism, since he does prominently defend himself from the charge of circularity. But if the point of the demon challenge is to bar reliance on doubted processes in the validation, then there is no choice but to reject the clear and distinct perception interpretation. Let us, then, return to the interpretation that the premises are admissible in virtue of being indubitable.

It must be admitted, however, that even on this interpretation, the validation of reason has no prospect of success. But this is simply because the premises of the validation are not all indubitable. The causal principles in the arguments for the existence of God are unlikely candidates for indubitability. For example, the principle that there is as much reality in the cause as in the effect is not plausibly true in the demon situation. This principle certainly does not follow logically from the assumption that I am deceived by a demon. Nor will it help to claim that the principle is necessarily true, hence true in the demon world. Such a claim would establish that the principle holds in the demon world if that world is genuinely possible, since any necessary truth must be true in a genuinely possible world. But in fact appeal to the demon situation in the skeptical challenge is only an appeal to a prima facie possible world, and what is necessary need not be prima facie necessary – it need not be true in all prima facie possible worlds, and thus need not be true in the demon world. It is true that in raising the demon challenge in *Meditation* I, Descartes assumes a principle similar to the present principle: "since deception and error seem to be imperfections, the less powerful they make my original cause, the more likely it is that I am so imperfect as to be deceived all the time" (*CSM* II 14; *AT* VII 21). And it might be urged that this principle therefore describes the demon situation. But this principle is not the same as the present principle; it is merely a principle about my probable cause, whereas the present principle says that my cause *is* as perfect as I am and not merely likely to be so. To raise the prima facie possibility that sense or reason is unreliable, Descartes need not assume that my cause is as perfect as I am – only that it is *likely* to be so. But to *establish* the reliability of reason Descartes must assume that my cause *is* as perfect as I am. The present principle, to repeat, is not indubitable. The premises of the validation are not in general indubitable.

The failure of Descartes' validation would have little import for epistemology if it did not suggest the conclusion that we have no prospect of answering antecedent skepticism. Descartes' failure highlights the fact that there are very few indubitable premises beyond the proposition "I exist" and other first-person mental state propositions. Once we have rejected phenomenalism as an analysis of physical object propositions and idealism about physical objects, it seems clear that there are too few indubitable premises to establish the reliability of any processes capable of generating many beliefs about the world. Descartes' difficulty here does not derive from the fact that he seeks a validation of the *perfect* reliability of clear and distinct perception. I have argued elsewhere (1986) that he also attempts a validation of the less than perfect reliability of hypothetico-deduction. But there are not enough indubitable premises to establish this conclusion either.

None of this is news. I believe it was all well appreciated before the middle of the eighteenth century. After Berkeley it was understood that antecedent skepticism is unanswerable without idealism – so well understood that Hume could assume that his audience would reject the project of answering antecedent skepticism without his repeating the reasons for doing so. Berkeley's idealism enabled him to retain the aim of answering antecedent skepticism, but those who were unable to follow his lead had to abandon this aim. Some philosophers – providential naturalists like Kames and Reid – did retain the validation of our faculties, but without pretending to answer antecedent skepticism. According to these philosophers, we must presuppose the justifying power of our faculties in order to provide a divine guarantee of their reliability. There are various ways to interpret what the providential naturalists attempt. One may see them as subscribing to reliabilism and using the divine guarantee to establish that our faculties are justifying, or one may see them as subscribing to the view that justified belief is natural belief, and merely using the divine guarantee to add to the patent justification of our beliefs the claim that they are reliable. On either interpretation, however, we are left with the question of the point of a divine guarantee, as we were in the case of Frankfurt's interpretation of Descartes. I will argue in the next chapter that Hume, too, offers arguments for the reliability of our processes (though not theological arguments), but his arguments are given point by the kind of skepticism he raises. What is common after Berkeley, in any event, is agreement that antecedent skepticism is unanswerable and determination to replace the project of answering antecedent skepticism with other epistemological projects – not least the efforts of Reid and Kant to explain and resist the powerful temptation of Cartesian skepticism.

This has not prevented the revival of the antecedent project in recent years. It is natural to attempt an answer to the antecedent skeptical challenge by turning from a deductive validation to a *probabilistic* validation, the aim of which is not to deduce but merely to probabilify the conclusion that a specified process is reliable, given indubitable premises. Laurence BonJour's (1985) metajustificatory argument that coherent beliefs are likely to be true may be an attempt along these lines. If so, it is fair to object to it on the same ground on which we have already objected to Descartes' validation: there are still too few indubitable premises to probabilify the reliability of any powerful process. On the other hand, BonJour may intend a different answer to antecedent skepticism by a probabilistic argument that relies on *dubitable* premises. But even granting that the argument probabilifies its conclusion, we must ask what sort of skepticism admits dubitable premises and, since not all dubitable premises can be admitted, on pain of reducing antecedent skepticism to consequent skepticism, why some dubitable premises are admitted and others excluded. I see no plausible answer to these questions. Finally, there are efforts by coherentists that are motivated by the desire to answer some sort of skepticism (Lehrer 1974). Reflective equilibrium accounts of justification sometimes seem designed to do this. But again, I can locate no significant form of skepticism between antecedent and consequent skepticism to which such efforts might be an answer.

3 Does justified belief require an answer to antecedent skepticism?

If we are unable to answer the antecedent skeptical challenge, we may infer skepticism, or we may follow post-Cartesian epistemology in rejecting the combination of principles that lead to the challenge. To decide between these alternatives we must know the merits of the principles that lead to the challenge: reliabilism, independent accessibility internalism, and the prima facie possibility of deception by a demon. Opponents of Cartesian skepticism have typically attacked the prima facie possibility of deception by a demon. In chapter I I mentioned a tradition that traces antecedent skepticism to Cartesian mind–body metaphysics. Reid (*EI* II.xii) and Kant (*C* A368ff) both respond to antecedent skepticism by denying that we can have experiences just like our actual experiences (or experiences which have the same representational content as actual experiences) in the absence of an external world. These writers trace antecedent skepticism to Descartes' alleged indirect theory of perception. Reid differs from Kant most basically in assuming that indirect realism may be rejected without significant alteration of the rest of Cartesian metaphysics – i.e., without distinguishing empirical from transcendental realism. But even allowing the questionable supposition that Descartes subscribes to indirect realism (O'Neil 1974), it is doubtful that the prima facie possibility of deception by a demon rests on indirect perception. The prima facie possibility of such deception does not even entail its metaphysical possibility, and so does not entail any metaphysical claim. And in any case, even if antecedent skepticism did rest on indirect realism, there would remain a far less strenuous response to the Cartesian claim that knowledge requires an answer to the demon challenge: simply observe that there is no reason to accept independent accessibility internalism.

The most common argument for independent accessibility internalism is that telling by exercising a doubted process – dependent telling – is in an important way circular, and the circularity is objectionable.[13] Of course dependent telling is not a circular *inference*. When we dependently tell that clear and distinct perception is reliable, we do not infer the belief that clear and distinct perception is reliable from beliefs that include, or can only be justified on the basis of, this belief. Rather dependent telling is supposed to be circular in a manner *analogous to* circular inference.

Before we ask what the analogous circularity is supposed to be or why it is supposed to be objectionable, we must first consider why circular *inference* is objectionable. Circular inference is objectionable because it fails to fulfill what is arguably the key epistemic function of inference – to *increase the stock of justified beliefs* without further sensory perception. In the simplest case of circular inference, the concluding belief is identical with some member of the basis from which it is inferred, while in more complicated cases, it is inferred from other beliefs that are justified by inference from it. Either way, the inference justifies the concluding belief only if the concluding belief is already justified. Thus, circular inference is deficient in failing to fulfill its key epistemic function: increasing the stock of justified beliefs.

How might dependent telling be analogously circular, and is there anything objectionable about this analogous circularity? Dependent telling does seem to be analogously circular in one way: it selects for exercise the very process exercised in telling. When we dependently tell whether clear and distinct perception is reliable, we employ the very process in question, clear and distinct perception, to tell whether this process is reliable.

Unfortunately, there is no obvious case that this kind of circularity is objectionable in a manner analogous to that in which the circularity in circular inference is objectionable. To establish an analogous circularity, it would have to be shown that the circularity in dependent telling prevents it from fulfilling the key epistemic functions of telling that processes are reliable ("telling", for short). We must specify, then, the key epistemic functions of such telling and ask whether the circularity in dependent telling prevents these functions from being fulfilled.

A key epistemic function of telling would seem to be that of selecting reliable processes for exercise. To select such processes, we must arrive at true beliefs about the reliability of available processes. The trouble is that nothing prevents dependent telling from yielding such beliefs. On the contrary, it is guaranteed to yield a high percentage of true beliefs, since it employs a reliable process.

There is, to be sure, one epistemic function of telling that dependent telling cannot fulfill. It cannot fulfill the epistemic function of selecting processes for exercise in such a way as to expand the repertoire of processes. For it involves exercising a process in order to tell the reliability of that process. But

51

nothing in dependent telling prevents other kinds of telling that do expand the repertoire of processes. For example, we can expand the repertoire by telling in virtue of exercising the very same processes one exercises in dependent telling, by recognizing the reliability of new processes.

Let it be noted as well that there are other epistemic functions of telling that do not rule out dependent telling. Telling has the more general function of selecting processes for exercise, and there is nothing about dependent telling that disqualifies it for such a general function. It is true that we will select reliable processes by relying on some process we already exercise only if that process is reliable. But what matters is the reliability of the process, not whether it is the same as or different from any of the processes selected. It is also true that it takes luck to be endowed with reliable processes. No doubt it is the point of the antecedent skeptical challenge to ask us to transcend luck. But the proponent of the circularity objection has given us no reason to think that knowledge or justified belief requires more than the luck of exercising reliable processes. We might consider instead the stronger claim that telling has the epistemic function, not merely of selecting reliable processes to exercise, but of selecting such processes under a constraint – in particular, under a constraint that prohibits exercising any process whose reliability is called into question by the demon challenge. But why should we suppose that telling has such a function, or that knowledge requires our ability to tell in a way that fulfills this function? To make these suppositions is to beg the question in favor of independent accessibility internalism. One can recognize the function of telling in selecting reliable processes, without having to take antecedent skepticism at all seriously. With no obvious prospect for the circularity objection in sight, it would seem that the proponent of the antecedent skeptical challenge is left with no recourse but falling back on the intuition that knowledge and justified belief do require us to transcend luck. But an appeal to intuition here can have no more force than our willingness to accept a skeptical outcome. And most of us find that too high a price for honoring this intuition.

CHAPTER III

Hume's Skepticism

Hume turns from the Cartesian focus on antecedent skepticism to a focus on consequent skepticism.[1] According to the traditional interpretation, Hume embraces consequent skepticism, demonstrating that rationalism, with its emphasis on reason, and empiricism, with its emphasis on sense, both lead to skepticism (Fogelin 1985). There is, however, a naturalistic, antiskeptical countertradition of interpretation (Kemp-Smith 1941). Countertraditional interpreters also see Hume as arguing that rationalism and empiricism lead to skepticism, but they regard this as a reductio intended to make way for a novel positive epistemology. I believe the traditional interpretation makes too much of Hume's skepticism and the countertraditional too little. Hume has a positive epistemology, but it is of a piece with his consequent skeptical critique of rationalism and empiricism. My ultimate aim in interpreting Hume is to explore the principles that underlie Hume's treatment of consequent skepticism.

The skepticism at issue here is *epistemological*, not *conceptual* skepticism. Hume does subscribe to conceptual skepticism: he denies the very existence of basic metaphysical ideas or concepts – of body (as philosophically understood), causal powers, substance, and the like. And one might suppose that conceptual skepticism forestalls epistemological skepticism, since for Hume beliefs are ideas, and thus conceptual skepticism implies that we have no beliefs, a fortiori no justified beliefs, about bodies, etc. But we ought not to rest much weight on his identification of beliefs with ideas. For he clearly holds that we have beliefs about bodies and causal powers despite our lack of ideas about such things. Indeed, he goes so far as to assert the existence of bodies, "a point which we must take for granted in all our reasonings" (*T* 187), and he assumes the existence of causal powers (*T* vi). He calls belief

53

in bodies and other basic metaphysical entities "suppositions" or "hypotheses."[2]

Hume thus assimilates the question of the justification of our belief in body and in causal powers to the Cartesian question of the justification of our belief in hypotheses such as atoms. He inherits from Descartes, Malebranche, and Locke the question of the psychological nature and epistemic status of the operations that lead to hypotheses and suppositions. On the Cartesian view, hypotheses are justified by hypothetico-deduction (which, in turn, is validated in much the way clear and distinct perception is). Locke, on the other hand, avoids explicit endorsement of hypothetico-deduction in favor of analogical inference (i.e., argument from like effects to like causes). Locke regards such inference as useful and reliable (*E* IV.xvi.12), but he has no theoretical ground for this view comparable to Descartes' validation of hypothetico-deduction. He seems to have little sense of a skeptical problem.

One of Hume's most impressive contributions to epistemology is his resolute refusal to accept orthodox thinking about hypotheses. He systematically rethinks skeptical challenges on the basis of a more sophisticated psychology of hypothesis. He does not accept the assumption that there must be a universal source of hypothesis, whether it be hypothetico-deduction or analogical inference.[3] Rather, he undertakes a detailed survey of the psychological operations that actually yield our hypotheses and discovers that they stem from imagination. This is a discovery that raises troubling grounds for skepticism about supposition. These grounds, however, threaten different degrees of skepticism about different suppositions. Hume is, for example, more skeptical about substance than about body or causal powers. His survey of the psychological sources of suppositions defies easy summary. I will have to focus here on his treatment of a single supposition – that of body – and leave for another day his treatments of causal powers, induction, and reason, which all differ from one another substantially.

1 Hume's reliabilism

Perhaps the boldest claim I will make here is that Hume subscribes to reliabilism. It is his adherence to reliabilism that unifies his negative and positive epistemology. Attributing reliabilism to Hume is not as odd as it might at first sound. I interpret his negative epistemology as a cluster of consequent skeptical worries assuming reliabilism in much the way that Academic skepticism assumes that knowledge requires a criterion of truth. This claim will need sustained defense.

Hume's consequent skeptical challenges to sense and reason and his consequent skeptical worry about imagination are all based on reliabilism. Challenges of the former sort take this form: sense and reason do not yield our basic metaphysical beliefs, since they would be unreliable if they did. Challenges of the latter sort are based on the commonplace that imagination is evidently unreliable. Reliabilism is the engine that drives Hume's consequent skeptical challenges. While he does reject rationalism and empiricism on skeptical grounds, he ultimately averts an unqualified skeptical conclusion about imagination.

There is textual evidence that Hume subscribes to reliabilism – evidence apart from his discussions of skepticism. Reliabilism is assumed in his "official" positive epistemology in the early sections of Part III of Book I of the *Treatise* – a neglected stretch of his key epistemological work. In these sections of the *Treatise* he undertakes to define knowledge, proof, and probability. It is little noted that his discussion is marked by a tone of cautious optimism about knowledge. In the course of this discussion he makes a vast number of claims to knowledge, proof, and probability. Nor is there any sign that he intends these only provisionally, or that his claims await future revision.

Hume's definitions of knowledge, proof, and probability are linked by the assumption that beliefs deserve epistemic epithets in virtue of bearing various degrees of what he terms "evidence," though it is not clear that he means by this just what twentieth-century internalists mean by the same term. He assumes that these various degrees are attributable to the various operations which give rise to the beliefs.[4] He also assumes that there is a single scale of "degrees of evidence" – that evidence is a single epistemic property varying only in degree. When there is sufficiently much evidence a belief is said to be *justified* (*T* 113, 218). Beliefs are justified in virtue of resulting from *just* operations (*T* 74, 75, 88, 135, 186, 262).[5] I will continue speaking of such operations as *justifying*.[6]

55

When is a belief justified, or an operation justifying? Hume's practice rests on the assumption that an operation is justifying when it is reliable. A systematic review of Book I shows that Hume is persistently concerned to judge the reliability of our operations. Here are a few examples: methods in geometry are fallible (*T* 71);[7] the observations and inferences concerning the three philosophical relations which can vary without a change in ideas are fallible (*T* 73); "When the imagination from any extraordinary ferment of the blood and spirit, acquires such a vivacity as disorders all its powers and faculties, there is no means of distinguishing betwixt truth and falshood" (*T* 123); "our confidence in the veracity of that faculty [memory] is the greatest imaginable and equals in many respects the assurance of a demonstration" (*T* 158); "Our reason must be consider'd a kind of cause, of which truth is the natural effect" (*T* 180); introspection leading to the belief that a given state is a perception is infallible (*T* 190); and "whatever ideas place the mind in the same disposition or in similar ones, are apt to be confounded" (*T* 203). These and many similar passages make it difficult to avoid the conclusion that Hume's central concern in epistemology is the assessment of the reliability of operations. Since his central concern is also the assessment of justification, it is plausible to see him as defining justifying operations as reliable ones.[8] The attribution of reliabilism is confirmed by the correlation in the text between talk of justified belief (perceptions) or justifying operations and talk of true belief (perceptions): "We may draw inferences from the coherence of our perceptions, whether they be true or false; whether they represent nature justly, or be mere illusions of the senses" (*T* 84); "What, then, can we look for from this confusion of groundless and extraordinary opinions but error and falshood? And how can we justify to ourselves any belief we repose in them?" (*T* 218).[9]

2 Skepticism with regard to the senses – or rather, imagination

A chief locus of the skepticism traditionally credited to Hume is his discussion of skepticism about body in *Treatise* I.IV.II, "Of Scepticism With Regard to the Senses." Reid (*EI* II.xii) and Kant (*C* A368ff) regard Hume as a skeptic about body and attribute his skepticism to his endorsement of an indirect theory of perception. A commitment to such a theory is supposed to give rise to skepticism about body in this way: we perceive bodies only indirectly; thus we cannot compare the features of bodies represented in our perceptions with the features bodies actually have; indeed we cannot even check whether bodies exist; so we can never be justified in believing that bodies exist as we perceive them. I agree that Hume holds an indirect theory of perception. Moreover, I agree that he employs his indirect theory to show that sense cannot justify the philosophical belief in body. But I do not think that his indirect theory gives rise to *his* skepticism about body, since for him the belief in body does not arise from sense, and thus the question whether it is justified does not turn solely on whether sense enables us to improve the features of bodies represented in our perceptions with the features bodies actually have, or on whether it enables us to check whether bodies exist.[10]

To begin with, as John Wright has urged in his pioneering study, *The Sceptical Realism of David Hume* (1983), Hume's argument for indirect perception assumes that bodies actually have some of the features we attribute to them on the basis of perception. Hume establishes indirect perception by his double-image experiment: when I produce a double-image of a body by pressing on one eye, there are two impressions neither of which is plausibly identical with the body; thus impressions are distinct from bodies (*T* 211). This argument assumes that the body in question has some of the features we attribute to it on the basis of perception – most importantly, it has the feature that its qualities do not vary with my action; that it does not split in two when I press my eye. We cannot, consistently with the premises of this argument, withhold our belief that the qualities of body do not vary with my action.

Now, this fact does not yet show that we could not, consistently with the premises of the argument, deny that our belief in body is *justified*, and so it does not yet entail that Hume cannot consistently accept skepticism about body while accepting the premises of his argument for indirect perception. But an inconsistency between skepticism about body and the premises of his argument does arise if he subscribes to reliabilism. For, on reliabilism, the premises of the argument about body support the reliability of the operations that yield our beliefs about body – or so I will eventually argue. The premises of the argument for indirect perception support the claim that our beliefs about body are *justified* as well as true.

I wish to propose an alternative to Reid and Kant's explanation of Hume's skeptical worries about body, an explanation that traces his very evident tendency to skepticism about body to his psychology, in the presence of his reliabilism, without going so far as to make him a skeptic. To develop the explanation, we will need to review his discussion of body closely and in all its complexity.[11]

Hume's discussion begins with an examination of the psychological source of our belief in body. He asks "whether it be the *senses*, *reason*, or the *imagination*, that produces the opinion of a *continu'd* or of a *distinct* existence" of body (*T* 185). And he observes right off that neither reason nor sense produces the *vulgar* belief in body – the belief in body as a collection of perceptions.[12] For the *senses* "give us no notion of continu'd existence, because they cannot operate beyond the extent, in which they really operate" (*T* 191). And

> we can attribute a distinct continu'd existence to objects without even consulting REASON, or weighing our opinions by any philosophical principle . . . 'tis obvious these arguments are known but to very few, that 'tis not by them, that children, peasants, and the greatest part of mankind are induc'd to attribute objects to some impressions, and deny them to others.
> (*T* 193)

The vulgar belief in body is not produced by sense or reason. It is produced rather by *imagination*. We suppose our impressions continued (and thus distinct) because of the constancy of impressions across interruptions. Reason and sense cannot yield a supposition; only the imagination can do so. For the imagination alone continues in a train of thinking "even when its object fails it, and like a galley put in motion by the oars, carries on its course without any new impulse" (*T* 198). Thus the vulgar belief in body is produced by the "galley" of imagination.

Hume argues next that there is an operation leading to the conclusion that the vulgar belief in body is *false*. This is the operation of *causal inference*, an operation that he has already established belongs to imagination (*T* 130–42). Here Hume speaks of this operation as belonging to "reason" or "reflection," but by this he means only that the operation would be ascribed to reason by conventional rationalist or empiricist psychology, not that the operation actually belongs to reason. Reason in the rationalist sense does *not* deny the vulgar belief in body. For "there is no absurdity in separating any particular perception from the mind" (*T* 207), and thus "the supposition of the continu'd existence of sensible objects or perceptions involves no contradiction" (*T* 208). It is causal inference, not reason, that denies the vulgar belief in body. For if vulgar body continues to exist unperceived, then the perceptions of which it is composed must have not only a continued but a *distinct* existence. Yet we know by causal inference based on experiment (namely, the double image experiment we have already mentioned) that perceptions do not have an existence distinct from the mind. Thus, causal inference leads us to reject the vulgar belief as false.

According to Hume, then, the "galley" of imagination produces the vulgar belief in body, while causal inference (also an imaginative operation) leads to its denial – an inconsistency between these operations. Since the outputs of these operations are quite extensive – covering all vulgar beliefs in body – this inconsistency entails the extensive false output of at least one of the two operations.

Hume may proceed in either of two ways. He may argue that at least one of the two operations is unreliable, prefer one of these operations to the other on grounds of reliability, and thus reject the output of one in favor of that of the other. The difficulty with this line of argument is that it requires him to infer the unreliability of one of the operations from the fact that it has extensive false output concerning vulgar body. Such an inference would require him to judge the extent of, and frequency of truths in, the output of this operation beyond its output concerning vulgar body – a judgment he finds it difficult to make, since, as we will see, he lacks a principled individuation of operations. Alternatively, Hume may proceed by correcting the exercise of one operation by the other, and embracing the resulting output. The difficulty with this way of proceeding is that it requires him to ascertain which operation is to be corrected – a judgment that must apparently be made on grounds of reliability, either of the original operations or of the vectorial operation that would result from correcting in one way or the other. Again, such a judgment would require him to judge the extent of, and frequency of truths in, the output of the two operations. Either way of proceeding encumbers Hume with the need to judge the extent of the output of these operations. He does not explicitly endorse either way of proceeding, since he does not argue in favor of one operation over the other, but simply employs one of the two operations. It seems, however, that the first way of proceeding is implicit in what he says, though shortly afterward he considers a correction to the imaginative galley. Despite the fact that he is loath to judge the extent of the output of causal inference and the imaginative galley, he does favor the former over the latter, for reasons that will eventually emerge. Thus he accepts the output of causal inference over that of the imaginative galley and concludes that the vulgar belief in body is false. This conclusion assumes the reliability of causal inference.

So far, there is no hint of skepticism in Hume's discussion. He endorses the conclusion that the vulgar belief in body is false. He does not yet argue that there are no justified beliefs about body. The imagination, however, not only yields the conclusion that the vulgar belief in body is false. It seeks to replace the vulgar belief with another belief in body. The result is the *philosophical* belief in body:

> The imagination tells us, that our resembling perceptions have a continu'd and uninterrupted existence, and are not annihilated by their absence. Reflection tells us, that even our resembling perceptions are interrupted in their existence, and different from each other. The contradiction betwixt these opinions we elude by a new fiction, which is conformable to the hypothesis both of reflection and fancy, by ascribing these contrary qualities to different existences; the *interruption* to perceptions, and the *continuance* to objects.

(*T* 215)

The imaginative galley insists on a belief in continued existence even when the falsity of the vulgar belief is exposed by causal inference. It evades an inconsistency with causal inference by forming the philosophical belief in body – the belief in the continued and distinct existence of something other than a collection of perceptions. The philosophical belief differs from the vulgar belief in body in not entailing that perceptions continue to exist unperceived. It is thus consistent with the conclusion that perceptions do not continue to exist unperceived. In other words, the philosophical belief in body satisfies the demands of causal inference. At the same time, it satisfies the impulse of the imaginative galley because it claims that body has continued and distinct existence. In this way, the imaginative galley is corrected by or combined with causal inference so as to avoid an inconsistency with it.

But Hume sees the philosophical belief as "only a palliative remedy." For it "has no primary recommendation to the *imagination*": "that faculty wou'd never, of itself, and by its original tendency, have fallen upon such a principle," since the "abstractness and difficulty" make it "an improper subject for the fancy to work upon" (*T* 212–13). Hume even goes so far as to complain that the philosophical belief "contains all the difficulties of the vulgar system, with some others, that are peculiar to itself" (*T* 211).

I believe that Hume intends here an argument that the philosophical belief in body is unjust. But we must be clear what the argument is. One might suppose that Hume's skepticism lies in his observation that the philosophical belief has no primary recommendation to the imagination. I believe that this observation plays a role in his skeptical worry, as I will explain shortly. But on my interpretation what matters is not whether the imaginative galley would of its own accord yield the philosophical belief in body, but whether the corrected imaginative galley is reliable. One might suppose that Hume introduces his skepticism in claiming that the philosophical belief in body has all the difficulties of the vulgar belief. But that claim is in fact false, and there is no doubt that Hume is aware of its falsity. The point of his earlier argument was precisely that the philosophical belief averts the chief difficulty of the vulgar belief – the inconsistency between the causal inference and the imaginative galley. Thus the philosophical belief is superior to the vulgar belief in being consistent with causal inference. Though causal inference leads us to deny the vulgar belief in body, it does *not* lead us to deny the *philosophical* belief. For it provides a reason only for denying that *impressions* have a continued and distinct existence, and once we have given up identifying bodies with collections of impressions, we cease to be committed to the opinion that impressions are distinct. Hume's earlier argument, then, precisely shows that the philosophical belief in body does *not* have all the difficulties of the vulgar belief. He is entitled at most to complain that causal inference fails to provide any reason for believing that bodies are distinct or continue to exist. The imaginative galley, however, does supply a basis for belief in the continued and distinct existence of body.

I believe that Hume introduces his skeptical worry when he refers to the difficulties peculiar to the philosophical belief. He does not say immediately just what those difficulties are. We must speculate. I believe the best account of Hume's skeptical worry is that he doubts the reliability of the imaginative galley, even when corrected by, or combined with, causal inference. His chief complaint about the philosophical belief in body is that philosophers "arbitrarily invent a new set of perceptions [i.e., body], to which they attribute these qualities" (*T* 216).

One objection lurking here is that qualities resembling *perceptions* are ascribed without justification to body. Indeed, causal inference leads to the belief that philosophical body is composed of corpuscles, a hypothesis inconsistent with ascribing resembling qualities. Certainly this is an objection to a particular philosophical practice – ascribing qualities resembling perceptions to bodies. But the philosophical belief in body hardly entails this practice, so the erroneousness of these ascriptions does not immediately impugn the philosophical belief. Perhaps Hume's worry is rather that the very imaginative galley that leads us to the philosophical belief in body also leads to the ascription of qualities resembling perceptions to bodies. So the imaginative galley must be rejected as unreliable. It is not entirely clear that the imaginative galley does lead us to these ascriptions, or at any rate that it imparts the same degree of force to our conviction in them. It is much easier to resist the tendency to ascribe qualities resembling perceptions to bodies than to resist belief in the existence of distinct bodies, and the belief in resembling qualities can be at least momentarily corrected by pertinent counterevidence, such as that bodies are corpuscular. Nevertheless, the erroneousness of these ascriptions does raise a significant worry about the reliability of the imaginative galley. What is more, the imagination may need perpetual correction in this regard, since it may incline perpetually to color philosophical bodies with resembling qualities. This worry would explain the skeptical force of Hume's observation that the philosophical belief is "an improper subject for the fancy to work upon." The imagination cannot form the philosophical belief in body without a corresponding tendency to imbue body with the sorts of qualities that render it a more suitable subject for the fancy. Such a tendency entails an increased risk of erroneous beliefs about bodies and the costly need to suppress this tendency.

But I believe Hume has in mind an additional, broader skeptical worry about the philosophical belief in body, one that extends beyond his worry about the imaginative galley. He is bothered by the *arbitrariness* of the imaginative galley in inventing the supposition of body. Arbitrary imagination is rampantly unreliable elsewhere. Hume's problem is to distinguish the imaginative galley from the usual run of wild imagination or "bright fancy," which contradicts sense or causal inference, or indeed, to distinguish it from the imaginative galley that yields the vulgar belief in body. He indicates at *T* 266 that his skepticism emerges from the worry that the widespread unreliability of operations of the imagination tends to impugn the reliability of all its operations: "This contradiction would be more excusable, were it compensated by any degree of solidity and satisfaction in the other parts of our reasoning." Hume's worry is more explicit in later work, especially his treatment of the argument from design. Particularly revealing is this remark in a letter to Gilbert Eliot of Minto of March 1751:

> I cou'd wish that Cleanthes' Argument be so analys'd, as to be render'd quite formal & regular. The Propensity of the Mind towards it, unless that Propensity were as strong & universal as that to believe in our Senses & Experience, will still, I am afraid, be esteem'd a suspicious Foundation. Tis here I wish for your Assistance. We must endeavour to prove that this Propensity is somewhat different from our Inclination to find our own figures in the Clouds, our Face in the Moon, our Passions & Sentiments even in inanimate Matter. Such an inclination may, & ought to be controul'd & can never be a legitimate Ground of Assent.
>
> (*L* I: 155)

Hume refers here to Cleanthes' argument from design for the existence of God stated in the *Dialogues Concerning Natural Religion* (1970/1751), and he raises the skeptical problem of distinguishing this inference from operations of wild imagination. At the same time, he raises the more general problem of distinguishing any inference that is not as strong and universal as sense from bright fancy. I will not rule here on whether Hume wishes to defend the argument from design, or whether he accepts a minimal version of the argument. But the passage does reveal the character of his skeptical worry about the argument and about causal inference in general.

I believe, then, that Hume's skepticism arises from the theoretical worry that operations of the imagination are to be individuated so that the imaginative galley cannot be distinguished from bright fancy, and thus the unreliability of bright fancy impugns the justifying power of the imaginative galley.[13] So understood, Hume's skepticism has much the same source as Academic skepticism, as he himself insisted.[14]

The case for skepticism gains force from the proposal that operations are individuated in such a way as to group together stretches of belief with the same frequency of truths – a proposal we considered in connection with Platonic dream skepticism and one to which we will return in our full-scale discussion of individuation in chapter VI. The operations of a faculty ipso facto employ common mechanisms. Yet mechanisms, in conjunction with environment, are responsible for the frequency of truths among the beliefs they produce. The frequency of truths in a stretch of belief of a faculty will thus tend to be the same as that of other stretches of the same faculty, other things equal. Thus, on the present proposal for individuation, these stretches will be grouped together as outputs of the same operation. As we noted in chapter I, this proposal tends to undermine Platonic dream or madness skepticism, since it distinguishes the operation that gives rise to dreaming and mad beliefs from that which gives rise to waking and sane beliefs. But the proposal tends to have the opposite effect on skepticism about the imaginative galley that leads to the philosophical belief in body, since it groups that operation with other, unreliable operations of the imagination. This is because mechanisms, in conjunction with environment, are responsible for the frequency of truths in the beliefs to which they give rise. And these operations are underwritten by the same mechanism, according to Humean psychology. For Hume is committed to a psychophysical theory of operations – namely, Cartesian psychophysiology, and in particular, a brain trace theory of imaginative operations (Wright 1983) – on which the imaginative galley is underwritten by the same neural mechanisms as bright fancy. Both operations result from the impulse of animal spirits beyond the traces to which they are conveyed by sense. Of course this point of psychophysiology is not authoritative, physiology being in Hume's day a speculative science, and the hypothesis of psychophysical correlations even more speculative. Moreover, the proposal that operations be individuated in such a way as to group together stretches of belief with the same frequency of truths needs important qualification. As we will see in chapter VI, there are many factors relevant to individuation besides the frequency of truths in stretches of belief, and these factors may weigh against grouping bright fancy with the imaginative galley that leads to the philosophical belief in body. Nevertheless, Hume's worry, unlike the Platonic and Academic skeptical worries, is given notable force by such theoretical considerations about individuation as readily come to mind.

Yet, I claim, these worries do not lead Hume to an unmitigated skeptical conclusion. For without a principled individuation of operations, and a firm psychophysiology of imagination on which to rely in applying this individuation to imaginative operations, the upshot of the problem of individuation is uncertain. These worries do not establish the inconsistency or unreliability of imagination. Rather they show that we have as yet no theoretical ground for distinguishing the imaginative galley from bright fancy.

Our lack of a principled individuation of operations leaves us with unresolved doubts. In a dark moment Hume verges on skeptical despair: "I am confounded with all these questions, and begin to fancy myself in the most deplorable condition imaginable, inviron'd with the deepest darkness, and utterly depriv'd of the use of every member and faculty" (*T* 269). But here, we must notice, Hume plants a clue that may reassure us. For the doubt that arises from the problem of individuation, when carried to the verge of despair, is itself the product of "fancy." Hume intimates that skepticism deriving from an inability to provide a principled individuation is not a product of reason but of bright fancy and can therefore have no more epistemic claim on us than that operation.

Thus Hume's subsequent observation that nature returns even the most cloistered theorist from skeptical despair to the positive epistemological attitude associated with a practical frame of mind (*T* 269) is not the refuge of the ostrich, an acquiescence in mere psychological comfort, as it is usually taken to be. On the contrary, it is an important epistemological point. Hume teaches us that in suppressing bright fancy nature restores the theorist to the right attitude. Our inability to provide a theoretical individuation of operations does not entail that we are unjustified in our belief in body. This point is characteristically Humean, of a piece with his frequent complaints about reflection (e.g., *T* 177). He emphatically rejects *iterativism*, that being justified in our belief in body requires being justified in believing that we are justified. There are, as we will see, countervailing reasons for thinking that the imaginative galley that yields the belief in body (or the corrected philosophical belief in body) is reliable. (And there is more to Hume's retreat to nature than the point that skepticism is unwarranted by theoretical inadequacy. Behind it lies the assumption that nature makes the right choices, even if it cannot theorize for us.)

To summarize my interpretation till now, I have proposed that Hume does not conclude skepticism with regard to imagination. He is reduced, not to skepticism, but to a theoretical suspicion about certain operations of the imagination. The point of his skeptical arguments is not the destructive one of establishing that our operations are unjustifying, but rather the positive theoretical purpose of making a tentative and incomplete (though perhaps terminal) step in the business of sorting operations of the imagination into the reliable and unreliable.

If this were all that Hume had to say about the reliability of imagination, it would leave him without any reason for thinking that the imaginative galley is reliable. The result would be *meta-skepticism* – that we do not know whether consequent skepticism is true. Alternatively, as naturalistic interpreters would have it, the result might be a radical turn away from reliabilism to an entirely different account of justified belief on which justified belief is merely natural belief, not reliable belief, so that we are unproblematically justified.

I reject both of these options. Hume avoids metaskepticism by offering an account of justified belief on which our belief in body is justified (though I admit that he does eventually subscribe to a limited metaskepticism). He also avoids the naturalistic view that justified belief is merely natural belief. Hume supports the reliability of imagination in the Conclusion of Book I. We will consider the support he offers shortly. To appreciate his position it will be useful to consider for a moment the naturalistic interpretation of his epistemology.

3 Hume's positive epistemology: strength, naturalness, and adaptiveness

On the naturalistic interpretation, as on the traditional skeptical interpretation, Hume's skeptical arguments are designed to show that rationalism and empiricism lead to skepticism. The naturalistic interpretation differs from the traditional skeptical interpretation, however, in declining to attribute skepticism to Hume (Kemp-Smith 1941; Lenz 1964; Loeb 1990). On this interpretation, the skeptical arguments are designed to reveal the inadequacy of rationalism and empiricism in restricting the sources of justification to sense and reason. Imagination is also a source of justification, despite its unreliability. On the naturalistic interpretation, Hume escapes scepticism by rejecting reliabilism and other orthodox epistemological theories in favor of a novel naturalistic account of justified belief, on which justified belief is strong, natural, or adaptive belief. Hume's most impressive contribution to epistemology, according to this interpretation, is his unprecedented naturalism about justified belief.

In support of this interpretation is Hume's express turn, in the face of cumulative skeptical worries, from a reliabilist account of justification to a naturalistic account. Having rejected the philosophers' tendency to ascribe resembling qualities to bodies, Hume asks: "What then can we look for from this confusion of groundless and extraordinary opinions but error and falsehood? And how can we justify to ourselves any belief we repose in them?" (*T* 218). Here Hume clearly associates justification and truth, plausibly in the manner ascribed by the reliability interpretation. But shortly thereafter he seems to abandon this account of justification in favor of a radically different account, on which some of the beliefs rejected as unjustified on the traditional skeptical interpretation are restored to justification.

Hume signals what appears to be a new account of justified belief in an astounding passage, for which he supplies little preparation, at the opening of the section "Of the Modern Philosophy" at

Treatise I.IV.IV. In this passage he explains why, in his view, causal inferences are justifying, while the operation that yields belief in the ancient doctrine of substance is unjustifying:

> In order to justify myself, I must distinguish in the imagination betwixt the principles which are permanent, irresistible, and universal; such as the customary transition from causes to effects, and from effects to causes: And the principles, which are changeable, weak, and irregular; such as those I have just now taken notice of. The former are the foundation of all our thoughts and actions, so that upon their removal human nature must immediately perish and go to ruin. The latter are neither unavoidable to mankind, nor necessary, or so much as useful in the conduct of life; but on the contrary are observ'd only to take place in weak minds, and being opposite to the other principles of custom and reasoning, may easily be subverted by a due contrast and opposition.
>
> (*T* 225)

In this key passage, Hume seems to break radically with previous accounts of justified belief. He seems to identify justified belief, at least in the case of imaginative belief, with belief that results from a strong or natural operation. Causal inference is justifying because it is strong, while the operation that yields belief in the ancient doctrine of substance is unjustifying because it is weak.[15] On this interpretation, Hume seems to propose what we may call *strength psychologism*: a belief is justified just in case it results from an operation that is sufficiently strong.[16]

Such a radical break with previous accounts of justified belief would afford a significant advantage over those accounts: an easy avoidance of skepticism: imaginative operations are quite obviously strong even if unreliable. However, it would purchase this advantage at the risk of changing the subject to gain a false appearance of averting skepticism. The charge of changing the subject is a difficult one to answer because there is nothing intuitive in the idea that justified belief is belief that results from a strong operation. It is far from clear what is gained by claiming skepticism is averted on such an account.

It must also be noted that the attribution of strength psychologism has little basis in Hume's text. His distinction between strong and weak operations is, it turns out, only introductory.

The key passage above continues and shifts focus, turning to the distinction between natural and unnatural operations:

> One who concludes somebody to be near him, when he hears an articulate voice in the dark, reasons justly and naturally; tho' that conclusion be deriv'd from nothing but custom, which infixes and inlivens the idea of a human creature, on account of his constant conjunction with the present impression. But one, who is tormented he knows not why, with the apprehension of spectres in the dark, may, perhaps, be said to reason, and to reason naturally too: But then it must be in the same sense, that a malady is said to be natural; as arising from natural causes, tho' it be contrary to health, the most agreeable and most natural situation of man.
>
> (*T* 226)

Here Hume distinguishes two senses of "natural" (or perhaps two degrees of naturalness). One characterizes the psychologically proper functioning of the mind. The other admits both proper and improper functioning. Justified beliefs are those formed by natural operations in the first, narrower sense. Hume's point is that the distinction between strong and weak operations provides an incomplete account of justified belief. The improper operation which yields belief in specters in the dark is not justifying, even though it is just as strong as a proper operation. So strength is not sufficient for justified belief. Hume's concern with strong operations, then, turns out on further inspection to derive from a concern with natural operations. This brings us to a second naturalistic interpretation of his account of justified belief: a belief is justified just in case it results from a *natural* (i.e. proper) operation.

Before we can judge the philosophical merits of such an account of justified belief, we must add to it an account of natural psychological functioning. I believe Hume assumes that natural operations are those that are *adaptive* in the sense of being conducive to human self-maintenance. Speaking of the irresistibility of belief in body, he proclaims: "Nature has not left this to chance and has doubtless esteem'd it an affair of too great importance to be trusted to our uncertain reasoning and speculations" (*T* 187). And elsewhere he speaks of our great fortune that nature has provided strong operations of imagination which yield beliefs about bodies. His view seems to be that the natural operations are those without which we would "immediately perish and go to ruin" (*T* 225; cf. *EU* 55) – or, more liberally, those conducive to survival in a style to which we have become accustomed, complete with refined amusements (*T* 269).

The adaptiveness account of justified belief is a considerable philosophical and textual improvement over the strength account. Nevertheless, I believe that Hume himself attempts an objection to it in the section "Of Unphilosophical Probability," where his purpose is to exhibit unjustifying operations. He poses a stunning example of an *unjustifying* adaptive operation:

> consider the case of a man, who being hung from a high tower in a cage of iron cannot forbear trembling, when he surveys the precipice below him, tho' he knows himself to be perfectly secure from falling, by his experience of the solidity of the iron, which supports him . . . . The circumstances of depth and descent strike so strongly upon him, that their influence cannot be destroy'd by the contrary circumstances of support and solidity, which ought to give him a perfect security.
>
> (*T* 148)

Hume goes on to argue that the man has a lively idea of his own danger – hence a belief. The operation of the imagination by which we are impressed with danger is adaptive – at least if great adaptiveness of some outputs is allowed to affect the adaptiveness of the operation itself, as it will if the adaptiveness of the operation is the average adaptiveness of its outputs. Yet the belief in this particular case is not justified. It seems that operations can be adaptive but not justifying.

One might respond to Hume's objection by proposing that the relevant operation to assess is not that of being impressed with danger, but the broader operation of causal inference that ignores information, and this operation is not adaptive. In response, I would urge that it is far from obvious that this broader operation of causal inference is not adaptive. On the contrary, it would appear that attention to all pertinent evidence in causal inference would often use cognitive resources better spent on matters of survival. By the same token it is doubtful that the counterexample can be handled by arguing that the opposing operation of causal inference, which moves from support and solidity to security, is more adaptive. The strategy of the timid squirrel, attending to danger signals whenever they occur, even to the exclusion of all other information, is highly adaptive in an environment in which food is often enough available in the absence of such signals. There is an adaptive advantage to exaggerating dangers. And the strategy of inferring security from support is likely less, not more, adaptive than that of exaggerating danger. Thus, while I am not entirely confident that Hume has proposed a decisive objection to the adaptiveness account, I believe his example presents enough of a problem that it is reasonable to look elsewhere for an account of justification. What seems wrong with the belief in danger in the tower case is that it derives from an operation (believing in danger when presented with a danger signal?) that is unreliable.

It must be admitted that the adaptiveness account of justified belief frequently yields intuitively plausible evaluations in particular cases. But that may be due to the fact that adaptive operations are frequently reliable (at least in natural circumstances, the circumstances in which they are arise). It is plausible to suppose that beliefs are frequently adaptive in virtue of the true information they carry and counteradaptive in virtue of their false information. Even a belief like "Apples are delicious" is adaptive because deliciousness is correlated with nutritiousness, while a false belief like "Wolves are vicious" is adaptive because it enables us to reason to the true conclusion that wolves are dangerous. And beliefs with more false information will tend to be less adaptive, since they will yield more opportunities for inferences with false counteradaptive conclusions. Of course, beliefs can be adaptive for reasons having nothing to do with their true information; perhaps religious beliefs are adaptive because they make people co-operative. But we can recognize such exceptions and avoid inferring reliability from adaptiveness in these cases. These exceptions aside, it is plausible to suppose that adaptive operations will frequently produce beliefs with more true and less false information. Thus, adaptive operations will tend to count as reliable, at least if we define reliability as a high ratio of true to total information in the output. Nevertheless, not all adaptive operations are reliable, as Hume's tower case shows: the operation in that case is adaptive because of the true information in those of its outputs that are adaptive. But few of its outputs are true – they are beliefs in danger when there is no danger. An operation can be adaptive on average even though unreliable. This is because average adaptiveness can result from very high adaptiveness of a few outputs.

I have argued that Hume rejects adaptiveness as an account of justified belief. I do not see him as offering a radically new account of justified belief at *T* 225 in answer to the question intimated at *T* 218. It remains, however, to ask why he accords such epistemological weight to adaptiveness at *T* 225. The only answer that seems plausible is that he assumes adaptiveness and reliability broadly coincide. Adaptiveness is an indicator of reliability. It will thus figure centrally in a general assessment of reliability in answer to consequent skepticism. With qualification, the same may be said of strength. Strength and reliability are correlated, though less broadly and less tightly than adaptiveness and reliability. Strength too will figure importantly in a general assessment of reliability. It goes without saying that Hume does not propose that adaptive or strong operations are reliable in all their possible stretches of output. We expect adaptive or strong operations to be reliable only in those circumstances in which the operation came to be employed because of its adaptiveness (what Hume terms "natural" or "original" circumstances). Hume never tires of cautioning philosophers against using adaptive operations outside their original circumstances, and his reason is evidently that we cannot infer their reliability elsewhere from their adaptiveness in original circumstances.

I have suggested that the philosophical and certainly the textual liabilities of an adaptiveness interpretation should lead us to reject it. It is best to see the key passage at *T* 225, not as proposing an adaptiveness account of justified belief, but as contributing a probabilistic argument for the reliability of certain operations of the imagination within their output in original circumstances.

4 Hume's answer to consequent skepticism

These reflections return us to Hume's treatment of consequent skepticism. I have already proposed that his tendency to skepticism derives from the apparent unreliability of imagination. We cannot readily distinguish the imaginative galley that yields our (philosophical) belief in body from bright fancy or other unreliable operations of imagination. Considerations of strength and adaptiveness may supply a counter to the case for the unreliability of the imaginative galley.

Hume's worry about consequent skepticism should not be confused with the worry that science undermines its own credibility by entailing a belief in the unreliability of its own operations – the sort of worry that Harry Frankfurt (1970) ascribes to Descartes. This worry cannot be answered by relying on science to establish the reliability of its operations, since showing that science entails the reliability of its operations does not show that these operations are not unreliable (unless the operations of science are methodologically consistent in the sense that they cannot both yield a belief in the reliability of science and a belief in its unreliability – but we have no way to establish such methodological consistency). Yet Hume relies on science to establish the reliability of its operations. Nor is the worry that if the operations of science yield a belief in their unreliability, they must be unreliable. On the contrary, mere inconsistency of this sort does not entail unreliability. Hume's worry is rather that our operations might actually *be* unreliable. The consequent skeptical challenge is an effort to raise the doubt that imaginative operations are unreliable, not merely the doubt that science entails that they are unreliable or that these operations yield a belief in their own unreliability. And the answer to the consequent skeptical challenge is to argue that imaginative operations are reliable, despite the challenge.

It is important to realize that Hume's answer to consequent skepticism is not a *local* antiskeptical project, if that is construed as an attempt to establish the reliability of imaginative operations by relying on the products of sense and reason. He does not assess the reliability of imagination from the vantage of sense and reason. On the contrary, his objection to rationalism and empiricism is precisely that sense and reason tell us nothing about the truth-values of suppositions about body. Thus he cannot engage in a local antiskeptical project. He cannot use sense and reason to argue that imaginative operations are reliable (say, because they have a property correlated with reliability, such as adaptiveness). For extending the correlation from sense to imagination would require an *inductive* inference – and that is an imaginative operation. Moreover, one can argue for the adaptiveness of imaginative operations only by assuming general beliefs about body – something we can only know through imagination. Hume can assess the reliability of imaginative operations only from a standpoint that includes imaginative belief. But most importantly, to suppose that he is engaged in a local antiskeptical (or skeptical) project is to misunderstand his whole way of thinking, which is to question the credentials of sense and reason in the realm of basic metaphysical and inductive beliefs. His great originality lies precisely in refusing to treat either sense or reason as privileged in judging the reliability of operations.

Hume is engaged, then, in an empirical assessment of the reliability of our operations, an assessment based on science. He never attempts a thorough or systematic review of the considerations for and against the reliability of imagination, and such a review would be needed to reach firm conclusions about its reliability. He does, however, review the reliability of imaginative operations in a freewheeling, uninhibited way in the dazzling, baffling Conclusion of Book I of the *Treatise*. Hume's review employs the Pyrrhonian method of opposition of appearances and judgments. He takes up a variety of intellectual stances and considers what is to be said from each stance on the question whether our basic metaphysical and inductive beliefs are justified. Though he swings wildly from dogmatism to extreme skepticism, he ends with what he clearly regards as Academic skepticism, a modesty in claims to knowledge and justification. In my view Hume is correct in seeing the outcome of his review as Academic skepticism.

I will not undertake here the formidable task of interpreting or reconstructing Hume's review. I will instead highlight some considerations that should go into any such review. There are powerful objections to the very idea of answering consequent skepticism with such a review, objections that must be met if the idea is to be taken seriously.

Let us begin with the bearing of strength and adaptiveness on reliability. How do these enter an assessment of reliability? I believe they enter in two ways. First, strength enters our assessment in virtue of the fact that in a thorough review of the evidence for and against reliability, we rely on what we already believe about the truth-values of the outputs of the relevant operations, and what we believe is the product of strong operations. Second, as I suggested in the preceding section, strength and adaptiveness enter in virtue of being correlated with reliability within their original circumstances. Let me explain the first point and return to the second after considering some objections to Hume's approach.

Hume wishes to assess the reliability of imaginative operations. To assess a given operation, we must rely on our present beliefs on the topics of the operation's outputs (call such beliefs "topic beliefs") and on our beliefs about whether the operation has properties correlated with reliability (call these "correlation beliefs"). So, for example, bright fancy is rejected as unreliable because its outputs conflict with our topic beliefs (which are the product of sense and causal inference) (*T* 267). Similarly, hasty generalization is judged unreliable because its outputs systematically conflict with counterexamples to its generalizations (these counterexamples having been established by sense and causal inference) (*T* 150). The operations which yield our topic beliefs are in both cases strong operations. Thus strength affects our assessments of reliability. We will return momentarily to consider how correlation beliefs enter the assessment of reliability.

At this point we have seen enough of Hume's answer to consequent skepticism to be able to consider some fundamental charges that might be brought against it. It might be criticized from several perspectives. Let us consider first the perspective of those who, accustomed to viewing epistemology as an attempt to answer antecedent skepticism, doubt that reliance on science in answering skepticism can establish the reliability of imaginative operations. Such a reliance will perhaps be allowed in answering any doubts that science raises about the reliability of its operations, since such doubts are themselves based on science – though, as I have noted, reliance on science can never suffice to answer a global doubt about science. But it will be denied that such a reliance is permissible in establishing the reliability of our operations beyond a mere reply to such doubts. Such a reliance can offer no positive reason for thinking that our operations are reliable.

There are two possible sources of the objection that the answer to consequent skepticism can offer no positive reason for thinking that our operations are reliable. One is that any consequent epistemology simply relies on our beliefs and operations to validate our operations, and that is bound to lead to a mere *rubberstamping* of the reliability of our operations: we will simply evaluate as reliable the operations that yield our actual beliefs, and so we will judge our actual beliefs to be justified. Our metaoperation answering consequent skepticism ensures, not merely that we may be able to answer consequent skepticism, but that we could not fail to answer it. Concluding that our operations are reliable on such a basis has all the force of an empty boast. (Of course, if our metaoperation really does rubberstamp our operations, then there never was a genuine danger of consequent skepticism.)

The charge of rubberstamping assumes that rubberstamping is objectionable and that our metaoperation entails rubberstamping. Neither of these assumptions is obviously true. Why is rubberstamping supposed to be objectionable? The most obvious objection is that it leads to the approval of our processes quite independently of whether they are actually reliable. That is true. But is it objectionable? In answering consequent skepticism, we seek to arrive at correct judgments of the reliability of processes. But, as in any other endeavor to discover the truth, we do so by attempting to arrive at justified belief. On reliabilism, that means attempting to employ reliable processes. We will have done as much as we may hope if the metaoperation we employ in judging the reliability of our operations is itself reliable. But rubberstamping does not interfere with the reliability of our metaoperation. Even if we conceive of the metaoperation as taking any given system of beliefs (plus operations) as inputs and yielding assessments of the reliability of operations as outputs, and even if in every exercise the operations approved by the metaoperation are those that yield the input beliefs, as rubberstamping presumably implies, it still does not follow that the metaoperation is unreliable. For it may still be that on average the operations approved are in fact reliable. Moreover, this way of conceiving of the metaoperation may not be correct. The metaoperation may have a much broader output – it may indeed be nothing other than an instance of induction and thus be reliable. (Nor does rubberstamping even entail that when we judge the reliability of our metaoperation we are bound to deem *it* reliable independently of whether it actually is.)

We may also question whether the metaoperation does in fact rubberstamp all, or even any, of our processes. Clearly it does not rubberstamp *all* of them, on any plausible version of reliabilism. To be sure, it would rubberstamp all of them if the following conditions obtained:

(a) the reliability of an operation is identical with the frequency of true beliefs among its *actual* outputs;

(b) our current topic beliefs mostly coincide with the actual outputs of our operations; and

(c) we assess the reliability of the operation solely on the basis of our topic beliefs.

But (a) fails to hold on any plausible version of reliabilism, since the reliability of an operation is a matter, not just of the frequency of true beliefs in its actual output, but of true beliefs in some counterfactual output. And (c) fails to hold because our *correlation* beliefs also enter into our judgment of reliability. These beliefs can preempt the assessment we might otherwise make on the basis of our topic beliefs alone. More importantly, Hume's struggle with skepticism shows that it is possible to judge *all* of our operations unreliable, if operations are individuated broadly enough. For if the operations that yield our belief in body are not distinguished from bright fancy, we will end with a global skepticism (from which only the operations of reason and sensory operations escape, on the narrow understanding Hume gives them). Rubberstamping, in short, is not obviously a pitfall of the metaoperation.

However, even barring the charge of rubberstamping, there remains the dogged charge of circularity against the idea that the answer to consequent skepticism establishes the reliability of our operations beyond a mere reply to self-doubts. Even if our beliefs do not necessarily sanction our operations, our operations sanction our beliefs, and judgments of the reliability of our operations are justified on the basis of topic and correlation beliefs that are themselves justified only in virtue of being sanctioned by the operations judged reliable.

The metaoperation is *not* one of reflective equilibrium, in which judgments of reliability are justified solely in virtue of being in reflective equilibrium with the topic and correlation beliefs, so that their justification does not depend on the operations that yield these topic and correlation beliefs. The trouble with reflective equilibrium is that there is no reason to suppose, on reliabilism, that it is itself a justifying operation yielding judgments of reliability. And what we want from our procedure is such a justifying operation. Reflective equilibrium is either yet another attempt, this time in coherentism's clothing, to achieve a validation of our operations that is in some way independent of those operations, or else another attempt akin to Descartes' validation of reason, as Frankfurt interprets it, in some way to vindicate our operations in the face of a skeptical challenge. The reasons why reflective equilibrium cannot succeed in either of these attempts are somewhat different from the reasons why Descartes' validation fails, and we will be unable to deal with these reasons here. It will suffice to observe that we want more from our procedure than reflective equilibrium can offer: we want a justifying procedure, as reliabilism understands justification. And that means that the metaoperation must rest on the justification of the topic and correlation beliefs – ensuring a circularity that reflective equilibrium avoids.

But it would seem appropriate to respond to the charge of circularity here just as we did in the case of dependent telling in the preceding chapter (despite the fact that we are not speaking here of whether circularity is ruled out by justification, but only of whether it is ruled out by an attempt to assess reliability that goes beyond a mere reply to self-doubts). There is no reason to insist that relying on beliefs that result from a particular operation to judge that operation reliable must enable us to expand the repertoire of operations. And as in the earlier case, our procedure has the capacity to recognize the reliability of operations we do not exercise and deny the reliability of operations we do exercise.

We have so far replied to objections to the claim that the project of answering consequent skepticism can aspire to more than an answer to self-doubts. But this is not an end to the objections that beset the project. One might object that the project has no point. The project of answering *antecedent* skepticism gives point to the very enterprise of epistemology. For independent accessibility internalism entails that being justified requires that we be able to answer the antecedent skeptical challenge. That is, we can only be justified if we can succeed in the enterprise of epistemology, conceived in the Cartesian fashion as the business of answering the antecedent skeptical challenge. It matters for our justification itself that we be able to answer the antecedent skeptical challenge. But there is no comparable urgency to epistemology conceived in the Humean fashion as the business of answering the consequent skeptical challenge. As Hume recognizes, life goes on as before even if epistemology fails. One point is that even if, relying on our science, we reach consequent skepticism, it does not follow that our operations are in fact unreliable. All that follows is that certain beliefs that result from our operations tell us that it is unreliable. These beliefs may be quite mistaken consistently with the reliability of these operations. More importantly, even setting this matter aside, a failure to show the reliability of our operations on the basis of our science would not have any tendency at all to show the unreliability of our operations.

Well, then, if Humean epistemology has no urgency comparable to the urgency Cartesian epistemology assigns itself, what is its point? The only answer is one bound to sound deflationary to proponents of antecedent epistemology, but it is, I think, a very respectable answer – indeed, the only permissible answer – once we have given up those pretensions. The chief aim of consequent epistemology is simply to judge justifiably whether our beliefs are justified and to do so in the only way that is possible once we have given up answering antecedent skepticism – by relying on our science. Hume's metaoperation gives very definite shape to the oft heard, though rarely developed, "naturalistic" exhortation for epistemology to take its place along side other sciences as part of the study of nature. His "scientific" account of nature does not consist in his psychology alone, but in his epistemology as well.

But Hume does not intend his epistemology to be a mere intellectual exercise with no implications for cognitive practice – i.e., for justifiably amending our beliefs. He claims that implementing his proposals would entail vast changes in philosophy. And he makes specific proposals for expelling or limiting offending operations (like hasty generalization and analogical inference). (Hume is, however, extremely cautious in recommending changes, since he believes that suppressing bad operations can have the unintended effect of suppressing good ones as well (*Es.* 338).)

One might worry, however, whether consequent skepticism *can* be used for revising these beliefs. Hume takes this worry seriously. He sees it as placing limits on how much we are allowed to revise our beliefs (*T* 267). Reason (i.e., causal inference) leads us to conclude the unreliability of imagination – e.g., of the imaginative operation that gives us difficulty with "remote views." Yet, as I mentioned earlier, this very imaginative operation is necessary for judging reason to be reliable, since if we did not have difficulty with remote views, reason would judge itself radically unreliable

(*T* 268). So if we did revise our operations and beliefs in accordance with our judgments of reliability, we would undermine the ground for that judgment. We would also undermine our ground for keeping causal inference while expelling unreliable imaginative operations. This is the meaning of Hume's famous remark that "We have, therefore, no choice left but betwixt a false reason or none at all" (*T* 268) – i.e., between retaining unreliable operations and relinquishing causal inference. Though he protests ignorance as to what ought to be done here (*T* 268), he gives a pragmatic ground for choosing "false reason": the alternative "if steadily executed, wou'd be dangerous, and attended with the most fatal consequences" (*T* 269). This advice prevents us from making a thorough use of our reliability judgments. The price is of course an incoherence in our system: we judge imaginative operations unreliable but find ourselves epistemically unable to suppress them, which means that our judgments of reliability conflict with the outputs of these operations.

We have looked at some objections from the vantage of those accustomed to answering antecedent skepticism, and we should now look at criticism from the opposite direction. The liberal epistemologist who undertakes an answer to the consequent skeptical challenge may be inclined to ask why Hume relies only on our *strongly formed* beliefs in his assessments of reliability. Should we not assess justification by relying on *everything* we believe – on all information in our possession, all propositions to which we are committed? Reliance on all beliefs may change the picture of what is justified, liberalizing in a way Hume would be loath to accept. For example, in Hume's view most religious beliefs are weakly formed and unjustified. But once we rely on all our beliefs, which might include religious beliefs, we might end up saying religious imagination is reliable and justifying. Similar questions may be raised about the output of inferences like hasty generalization. Even ghastly *philosophical* speculations like the belief in spiritual substance or occult qualities may turn out to be justified on a liberal answer to consequent skepticism.

I suspect Hume would reply by agreeing that in assessing reliability, we must rely on all of our beliefs, even weak ones, since there is no nonarbitrary way to pick a subset on which to rely. But the assessment involves a balancing act between beliefs, and where strongly and weakly formed beliefs favor opposing operations, the former may swamp the latter. They may do so simply because they are stronger, if they are inconsistent with the latter (in the presence of generalizations). Alternatively, they may do so because the metaoperation accords weight to beliefs in proportion to the quantity of information they carry, and, according to Hume, strong operations are broader (*T* 150, *T* 267) – have more output – than weak operations. Balancing the relevant beliefs, either by strength or by quantity of information, might well lead to rejecting weak religious beliefs, hasty generalization, and extravagant philosophical speculations. And once again, we believe in the reliability of strong operations but not weak ones.

There is, however, another criticism the liberal epistemologist might attempt. Whether a belief is strongly formed is a matter of its context. In the rush of everyday life, hasty generalization forms beliefs strongly, but in the calm reflection of the study, it forms them weakly if at all. Consequently, our assessment of hasty generalization depends on whether we are assessing it from the vantage of everyday life or of the study. There is no unique assessment of reliability. At first glance, this criticism seems misguided: since we assess reliability in the systematic way required by our procedure only in the study, there is a unique assessment. But this dismissal of the criticism may miss the point: that we have no *reason* to judge reliability on the basis of our beliefs in the study, rather than those in everyday life. So whether or not we assess reliability in the study, we must admit that there are various *vantages* from which it can be assessed, yielding different assessments, and we have no reason to prefer one to another.

One possible response to this criticism is to accuse it of back-sliding into the assumption that we are trying to answer antecedent skepticism. The idea of answering consequent skepticism is that we begin our epistemology with what we actually believe (or justifiably believe). If we assess reliability only in the study, then we must assess it on the basis of what we believe there. There can be no choice of vantage from which to assess it. We cannot question the reliability of calm reflection as part of an evaluation of our vantage itself (though of course we can assess it *within* our calm vantage, and modify our operations accordingly, indirectly affecting the content of calm reflection).

While this response seems to me correct as far as it goes, it does not take into account one way that this criticism may have force, even after the project of answering antecedent skepticism has been abandoned. Even if we are committed to our beliefs, and cannot take up another vantage, it is still true that among our beliefs are positive judgments of everyday beliefs and negative judgments of calm, philosophical beliefs. We think beliefs formed in everyday life are often true. And we also think that philosophy frequently leads us into error and confusion: "our mind being narrow and contracted, we cannot extend our conception to the variety and extent of nature, but imagine that she is as much bounded in her operations as we are in our speculation" (*Es.* 338). These negative beliefs about philosophy are incoherent with the other beliefs we have in our calm vantage. Hume does not think that these negative beliefs, when properly balanced with the rest of what we believe, will lead us to adopt a different unphilosophical vantage: that would be inconsistent with the project of answering consequent skepticism. Nor does he think there is any way to purge the incoherence so that we unambiguously favor everyday operations over all philosophical ones. Rather, our beliefs may lead us to decide *not* to judge the reliability of all operations in accordance with our calm beliefs (or at least not to modify our operations in conformity with our judgments). Though the project at hand forbids us from stepping into another vantage, it still leaves room for stepping *outside* our vantage by refusing to make judgments (or use them). This is one more reason why the metaoperation does not entail even a loose rubberstamping of our actual operations.

But of course Hume does not think that we need refrain from *all* judgments about operations. His reservations about relying on calm reflection amount only to a *limited* metaskepticism. We will certainly judge positively an operation like the imaginative galley that is strong in both everyday life and calm reflection. And we will judge negatively an operation like hasty generalization that is not very strong in everyday life and expunged entirely in calm reflection. But we may wish to refrain from judging many operations in between. As I have noted, Hume worries especially about the incoherence between causal inference and the trivial imaginative difficulty with remote views. Causal inference judges the latter unreliable, but a positive judgment of its reliability is essential to prevent causal inference from undoing itself. If we were to decide the issue by calm reflection, and eliminate trivial fancy, we would lose our reason for modifying and much else besides. Hume's solution is to step outside calm reflection and leave the decision to nature (*T* 268). But even this deference to nature need not be purely self-effacing; it may be based on the calm recognition that nature knows best.

To summarize my reconstruction of Hume's positive epistemology: Operations are justified when reliable. We assess reliability in calm reflection by relying on all of our beliefs (or the justified ones, anyway), including the output beliefs and correlation beliefs. This process of assessment can be tumultuous and inconclusive, but strong and adaptive operations tend to win the reliability contest because they have a lot of output and correlation beliefs on their side. Sometimes we can't resolve issues of reliability because our beliefs are too incoherent or because we distrust our own reflection. At that point, we defer to a wiser nature.

This completes our examination of the internalist and externalist principles that underlie consequent and antecedent skepticism. I have argued that consequent skepticism is a historically dominant form of skepticism underwritten by reliabilism, and that antecedent skepticism finds its clearest expression in Cartesian skepticism, underwritten by a combination of independent accessibility internalism and reliabilism. Independent accessibility internalism makes a relatively brief and unsuccessful appearance on the world epistemological stage. We have yet to encounter a pure internalism in history. There are those who regard Reid as an internalist of sorts, but there is a better case for regarding him as a naturalist or reliabilist. I believe internalism finds its first pure expression in this century, despite the claims of contemporary internalists to carry on the Cartesian tradition. Nor is the move to internalism fully warranted by our experience with Cartesian skepticism, since our inability to answer that kind of skepticism warrants at most abandoning *either* independent accessibility internalism *or* reliabilism, not both, as the internalist proposes to do. We must consider whether there is another case for internalism.

CHAPTER IV

Accessibility Internalism

Let us turn, then, to contemporary internalism and consider first *accessibility internalism*, a natural sequel to independent accessibility internalism. According to accessibility internalism, the subject's being justified in believing *p* (whether doxastically or propositionally) is accessible to her in the sense that she can tell by reflection alone (though not necessarily independently) that she is (propositionally) justified in believing *p*. If the conditions of justified belief characterize what subjects have in mind in evaluating justification, then the view entails the requirement that the subject be able to tell by reflection alone that her belief *p* satisfies the conditions of justified belief.

I wish to examine the positions and arguments of two prominent accessibility internalists. We may begin with Carl Ginet's (1974) formulation of the view:

> Every one of every set of facts about *S*'s position that minimally suffices to make *S*, at a given time, justified in being confident that *p* must be *directly recognizable* to *S* at that time. By "directly recognizable" I mean this: if a certain fact obtains, then it is directly recognizable to *S* at a given time if and only if, provided that *S* at that time has the concept of that sort of fact, *S* needs at that time only to reflect clear-headedly on the question whether or not that fact obtains in order to know that it does.
>
> (Ginet 1974: 34)

Ginet's formulation of accessibility internalism is slightly weaker than our formulation above.[1] He employs the term "know" where I have employed "tell" – knowing is presumably weaker than telling. And he qualifies the requirement of an ability to know with the condition that *S* have the concept of justified belief.[2] These differences in formulation will turn out to be significant below. For Ginet's own argument for accessibility internalism supports the requirement of an ability to *tell*, and not merely know, by reflection, and it supports this requirement *without* his qualification that *S* have the concept of justified belief.

Roderick Chisholm (1977, 1982) formulates yet a different version of accessibility internalism, one that strays a bit further from ours than Ginet's does. Like Ginet, Chisholm sees that a subject might fail to be justified in believing that she is justified in believing *p* for the trivial reason that she fails to have the concept of justified belief, but he proposes a different way to handle the problem:[3]

> it is possible that there is a person who does not yet have the concept of evidence or knowledge, but for whom, all the same, a certain proposition is known . . . .
>
> Shall we say, then, that if a proposition is evident, and if one asks oneself whether it is evident, *then* it is evident that the proposition is evident? This is less objectionable, for one cannot ask oneself such a question unless one does have the concept of a proposition being evident. But let us say more simply that, if a proposition is evident and one *considers* the proposition, then it is evident that the proposition is evident.
>
> (Chisholm 1977: 114)

If we may assume that Chisholm's "evident" is the same as our "(propositionally) justified," his requirement differs from ours and Ginet's in several respects. It requires that (under certain conditions) the subject *actually be justified* in believing that she is justified in believing *p*, not that she be *able* to *tell* or *know* that she is justified in believing *p*. And it does not require that the subject be able to tell or know (or be justified in believing) by *reflection*, but merely that she be justified in believing she is justified in believing *p* *if* she considers the proposition (or, what is more likely Chisholm's intent, considers whether she is justified in believing *p*). That requirement is consistent with the subject's not being able to tell or know or be justified in believing by reflection. We will need to return to some of these complications in Chisholm's view below.

Chisholm and Ginet decline to define justified belief in terms that are not explicitly normative. Chisholm in particular rests his characterization of the concept of justified belief on formal principles constraining the basic normative concept used to define justified belief. For example, he characterizes "evident" in terms of "more reasonable than" and observes that "more reasonable than" is transitive and asymmetric (1977: 13). He also offers a normative paraphrase of his basic epistemic notion: "p is more reasonable than q for S at t" is understood as "S is so situated at t that his intellectual requirement, his responsibility as an intellectual being is better fulfilled by p than by q" (1977: 14).

Chisholm develops a list of principles or rules that sanction certain beliefs, a list that imposes a foundationalist structure on justification. His rules are of two kinds. First, there are *basis* rules – or more accurately, there is a definition of what it is for a belief to be basically justified, together with a claim that beliefs with a certain propositional content meet that definition. Second, there are rules for *nonbasic* beliefs. The basically justified beliefs are beliefs in what Chisholm calls *self-presenting states of affairs* – i.e., beliefs that p where if p, then S is justified in believing p. For example, the belief that this object appears red to me – or in the more cautious language "Chisholmese," I am appeared to redly – is a belief in a self-presenting state of affairs (my being appeared to redly). The claim that the belief is a belief in a self-presenting state is (with a slight qualification we need not go into) equivalent to the rule "if I am appeared to redly, then I am justified in believing that I am appeared to redly." The rules for nonbasic beliefs would presumably take the form "if I am justified in believing p, then I am justified in believing q." (But strangely, the rules Chisholm actually gives take quite a different form, as William Alston (1980) has noted – e.g., "For any subject S, if S believes without ground for doubt, that he is perceiving something to be F, then it is beyond reasonable doubt for S that he perceives something to be F." Despite Chisholm's foundationalist advertising, there is no way to reconcile such rules with foundationalism.) The proposed list of rules is taken to characterize justification synthetically (though the rules are knowable a priori).[4]

It is worth noting that on such a "list" version of accessibility internalism, the subject must be able to tell by reflection, not only that her belief is justified, and not only that it satisfies the conditions of justified belief, but also that it conforms to the rules. For if the rules were exempt from the requirement of accessibility, then accessibility internalism would no longer obviously exclude a suitably revised version of reliabilism – one that does not characterize the conditions of justified belief but rather supplies rules that characterize justified belief (e.g., the rule "If *S*'s belief *p* results from the exercise of a reliable process, then *S* is justified in believing *p*"). Such a revised version of reliabilism would be consistent with accessibility internalism. Thus accessibility internalism has the power to exclude all versions of reliabilism only if it entails that conformity to the rules is accessible. In fact it is doubtful that conformity to Chisholm's rules is accessible, but I will waive this doubt for purposes of discussion.

One question before we proceed is what accessibility internalists mean by "reflection." There are inclusive and exclusive readings of "reflection." On the *inclusive* reading, a subject tells that *q* by reflection alone just in case she tells that *q* in virtue of reflecting on, in the sense of considering, whether *q*. In reflecting inclusively on whether *q*, the subject may employ whatever cognitive resources are permitted by considering whether *q* – introspective, inductive, deductive, and memorial processes. What reflecting inclusively rules out is further research – specifically, it rules out the exercise of sensory processes, observations of external conditions, physical experimentation, measurement with instruments or calculators, and the use of complex statistical methods the subject is unable to exercise without sensation or observation. Reflecting inclusively does not, however, prohibit relying on what one *already* knows about the external world as a result of sensation, observation, experimentation, measurement, and the use of complex methods. On the *exclusive* reading of reflection, reflecting prohibits not only further research but also reliance on sensory knowledge the subject *already* has. Only knowledge based on introspection, induction, or deduction is allowed.

In point of fact, it does not matter for the opposition between accessibility internalism and reliabilism whether the accessibility internalist adopts the inclusive or exclusive reading. On either reading of "reflection," accessibility internalism is at variance with reliabilism (unless strong foundationalism holds – that is, unless all knowledge is ultimately based on introspection, induction, and deduction).[5] It is true that a subject may tell by inclusive reflection whether she exercises a reliable process on many occasions. In particular, she may tell this on occasions on which telling such a thing does not require further research (which it usually will not, at least on the version of reliabilism I will develop in the final chapters of this book). But it is not possible for a subject to tell this by reflection on *every* occasion. For example, she cannot tell this by reflection on the occasion of her *first* justified beliefs, since on this occasion she lacks any prior sensory knowledge and therefore lacks any sensory knowledge by which she might tell by reflection whether her belief is justified.[6] (This argument assumes that telling q entails knowing q, and knowing q entails being justified in believing q.)

Chisholm does not attempt to say what makes the rules he proposes rules of justification. He does not seem to regard the rules as having anything in common other than characterizing justification in accordance with accessibility internalism and the formal constraints or normative paraphrase he provides. In fact, it does not seem open to proponents of a list epistemology under accessibility internalism to claim that the rules have in common such interesting properties as codifying our actual cognitive or evaluative practice, or what it is natural for us to believe. For such a claim would make it difficult to avoid admitting that what the rules have in common here *defines* justified belief – what else could explain why the rules have such a property in common? – and hence admitting that *codifying our actual practice* defines justified belief. But if the latter did define justified belief, then accessibility internalism would entail that subjects must be able to tell whether a belief conforms to rules that codify our actual practice, and it is too much to suppose that subjects will always be able to tell by reflection what it is so difficult for cognitive social psychologists and sociologists to tell even by diligent research. I would not deny that accessibility internalists who subscribe to a list epistemology may consistently claim that the rules in the list define justified belief, though most do not make such a claim. But they do seem barred from claiming that what the rules have in common is codifying our actual practice or any other interesting property. I regard this as a deep objection to the view. The choice of rules in the list must necessarily remain arbitrary and unmotivated. Such list epistemologies, and I suspect all other specific accounts of justification that conform to accessibility internalism, are congenitally unsupportable. But I will lay aside here this reservation about list epistemologies – as well as reservations about particular proposed rules – in order to discuss the general merits of accessibility internalism.

In my view the most serious objection to accessibility internalism is that it bars any account of justified belief capable of explaining the value we ascribe to justified belief. As we have just seen, it excludes even an account on which justified belief is belief that conforms to rules that codify our actual practice. And it seems for similar reasons to exclude all other candidates for an account that assign justified belief value. Admittedly, this objection could be proven only by making a complete survey of conditions of justified belief that might be taken to assign value to justified belief and showing for each that accessibility internalism excludes it. It goes without saying that we cannot undertake such a survey here. But even without it, I believe we can see that candidates for accounts that assign value to justified belief are ruled out by accessibility internalism. There does not seem to be any valuable property that is accessible.

Indeed, it is doubtful that accessibility internalism can retain the epistemic end of true belief. To be sure, Chisholm proposes this end when he offers his paraphrase of "p is more reasonable than q for S at t" as "S is so situated at t that his intellectual requirement, his responsibility as an intellectual being is better fulfilled by p than by q." For he understands S's responsibility as an intellectual being as trying to bring it about that S believes a proposition r if and only if r. This characterization of "more reasonable than" implicitly defines the epistemic end as true belief. But it is doubtful that Chisholm is allowed such a definition. Accessibility internalism requires that the subject be able to tell by reflection alone that the conditions of justified belief are satisfied, and thus that the conditions of the paraphrase are satisfied. But there is no reason to suppose that a subject will be able to tell by reflection alone that he is so situated that his trying to bring it about that he believes r if and only if r is better fulfilled by p than by q. For if Chisholm's paraphrase is to characterize a valuable condition, it cannot simply characterize justified belief in terms of trying to believe what is true. It must idealize the subject's effort by placing a qualification on the subject's "situation." And there is no reason to think that an ideal situation will be introspectible – that trying in an ideal way will be accessible (see the next chapter). Moreover, the question re-emerges whether there is any idealization that is both valuable and consistent with accessibility internalism. Chisholm cannot, for example, idealize trying to believe what is true by requiring that it conform to the rules that codify our actual practice, since conformity to such rules is not accessible. The preceding complaint about the value of conditions of justified belief under accessibility internalism now applies to the paraphrase that implicitly defines the epistemic end as true belief.

Of course none of this shows that *conforming to the rules* listed by accessibility internalists is not valuable. But it does seem that accessibility internalism excludes conditions capable of explaining the value we ascribe to justified belief. Without an account of the value of justified belief, the accessibility internalist will have to support the view by appeal to a formal conception of justified belief. It is to this appeal that we now turn.

1 The deontic argument for accessibility internalism

Ginet makes such an appeal when he attempts to derive accessibility internalism from a particular conception of justified belief – what is best called the *deontic* conception.[7] On the deontic conception, justified belief is simply epistemically *permissible* belief: S is justified in believing p just in case it is epistemically permissible for S to believe p – i.e., it is not the case that S epistemically ought not to believe p. This is an extremely attractive, perhaps inescapable, conception of justified belief, and it is thus a promising premise for an argument. Here is Ginet's formulation of the deontic argument:

> Assuming that S has the concept of justification for being confident that p, S ought always to possess or lack confidence that p according to whether or not he has such justification. At least he ought always to withhold confidence unless he has justification. This is simply what is meant by having or lacking justification. But if this is what S ought to do in any possible circumstance, then it is what S can do in any possible circumstance. That is, assuming that he has the relevant concepts, S can always tell whether or not he has justification for being confident that p. But this would not be so unless the difference between having such justification and not having it were always directly recognizable to S. And that would not be so if any fact contributing to a set that minimally constitutes S's having such justification were not either directly recognizable to S or entailed by something directly recognizable to S (so

that its absence would have to make a directly recognizable difference).

(Ginet 1974: 36)

We may schematize this argument, omitting some complications that do not bear on our purposes, in the following way:[8]

(a) *S* ought always (i.e., on any possible occasion of belief-formation) to withhold the belief *p* in case *S* is not deontically (propositionally) justified in believing *p*.
(b) If *S* ought to do something, then *S* can do it.
(c) Therefore, *S* can always withhold the belief *p* in case *S* is not justified in believing *p*.
(d) If *S* can always withhold the belief *p*, then *S* can always tell whether *S* is justified in believing *p*.
(e) *S* can always tell this only if *S* can always tell by reflection alone whether *S* is justified in believing *p*.
(f) Therefore, *S* can always tell by reflection alone whether *S* is justified in believing *p*.

Premises (a)–(d) are designed to establish that justified belief requires telling whether one is justified in believing *p*. Premise (e) is designed to establish the accessibility internalist requirement of an ability to tell *reflectively*. Ginet prefaces his formulation of the argument with the qualification "Assuming that *S* has the concept of justification for being confident that *p*," but the argument would seem to go through without this qualification, if the conception of justified belief is deontic. If, as the deontic conception entails, to say that one is justified in believing *p* is simply to say that it is not the case that one ought not to believe *p*, it follows trivially that one ought always to withhold the belief *p* in case one is not justified in believing *p* (at least, if withholding the belief *p* is simply not believing *p*). It does not immediately matter whether or not one has the concept of justification. Or another way to put it: if it matters, then this must be because not having the concept prevents it from being the case that one ought not to believe *p* – though of course Ginet would have to make a case for this independently of the deontic argument. Of course the requirement of having the concept of justified belief does follow from the requirement of being able to tell that one's belief is justified.

91

Is the deontic argument persuasive? There is much to be said for the first two premises. For the reasons I have already given, premise (a) follows immediately from the deontic conception of justified belief: if *S* is not deontically justified in believing *p*, then *S* ought to withhold the belief *p*. Premise (b) would be widely accepted as the epistemic analogue of the principle widely accepted in ethics that "ought" implies "can." Nevertheless, I regard the premise as doubtful. It is worth noting before we proceed that this premise imposes a *narrow* rather than broad sense of "able." We may define broad ability in terms of narrow ability in this way: I am broadly able to lift seventy pounds on an occasion when I would be narrowly able to do so on this occasion were I in peak form – or alternatively, I would be narrowly able to do so in my best moments suitably related to the occasion. The deontic conception entails narrow and not broad ability. For the principle that "ought" implies "can" is, as usually intended, a principle concerning the narrow "can." If I had to climb twenty stories to reach the fire hose and douse the fire, but I was too weak from fatigue to be narrowly able to do so, no proponent of the principle that "ought" implies "can" would insist that I could do so in a way relevant to whether I ought to have done so just because I am able to do so in my peak moments. The argument therefore establishes accessibility internalism on a narrow understanding of "able."

The most evident problems with the argument concern premises (c) and (d). Let us look first at premise (e). It must be admitted that this premise is hardly obvious. Why is it supposed to follow from the fact that *S* can always tell whether *S* is justified in believing *p*, that *S* can always tell this *by reflection*? Ginet offers an argument, but it has been well criticized by William Alston (1989a).[9] Nor can I find any plausible replacement for it. It will not do, for example, to fasten on the occasion of the subject's first justified beliefs and argue that she must be able to tell by reflection on this occasion if she is to tell at all, since on this occasion she does not already have sensory beliefs on the basis of which to tell that her belief is justified. This argument will not do because on this occasion, the subject does not have reflective beliefs on the basis of which to tell either. Yet if having sensory beliefs is necessary for being able to tell by sensation that one's belief is justified, then having reflective beliefs would equally be necessary for being able to tell by reflection that one's belief is justified. Either the subject can drum up enough sensory beliefs to be able to tell on this occasion, or she cannot drum up enough reflective beliefs to be able to tell. There is no asymmetry between sensation and reflection here that would force a preference for reflection as a means of telling. I see no case for premise (e). Even if Ginet's argument establishes that the subject must be able to tell whether she is justified, it does not establish that she must be able to tell by reflection.

Moreover, premise (d) is implausible. It must be qualified in a way that allows versions of externalism to survive the argument (though admittedly reliabilism is not among these versions). To see the problem, note that by the time he gets to premise (d), Ginet has dropped the qualification that appears in premise (a), "in case *S* is not (deontically) justified in believing *p*." Premises (a)–(c) show at most that the subject must be able to withhold belief on all occasions on which she might be forbidden from belief. They do not show that the subject must be able to tell whether her belief is justified when she is not forbidden from any belief. Thus premises (a)–(c) do not entail that the subject must be able to withhold belief on all possible occasions, and so do not entail that she must be able to tell whether she is justified on all possible occasions, even if being able to withhold belief on a given occasion entails being able to tell whether she is justified on that occasion. But perhaps *all* beliefs are permitted early on in the subject's cognitive development. Perhaps the subject is permitted to believe anything until such time as she acquires the ability to tell whether she is justified. After that time, she is forbidden from some beliefs and must therefore (by the remainder of Ginet's argument) be able to tell whether beliefs are justified. Premise (d) yields the conclusion Ginet desires only if there is no time before which all beliefs are permitted. If there is such a time, then perhaps the subject can acquire enough justified beliefs that she need not be able to tell to be justified to be able to tell subsequent beliefs to be justified. Once premise (d) is qualified to allow such a time, it no longer rules out conditions of justified belief, externalist or otherwise, that allow the subject sufficiently many beliefs that she need not be able to tell to be justified to be able to tell subsequent beliefs to be justified. Of course, premise (d) so qualified still contradicts reliabilism, since reliabilism entails that only some early beliefs are permitted – the reliable ones. But the premise is consistent with a qualified reliabilism on which early beliefs are all permitted and subsequent beliefs must be reliable. (Or, more cautiously, it is consistent with reliabilism to whatever extent the requirement that in maturity one be able to tell that one is justified is consistent with reliabilism.) The point remains that premise (d) cannot rule out external conditions that apply to subsequent times.

Finally, there is no basis for premise (b) of Ginet's argument. The principle that "ought" implies "can" does not hold for all "oughts." One ought to turn the handlebar to the left when the bicycle leans to the left, even if one is not sufficiently skilled at bicycling to be able to do so. One ought to drive on the designated side of the road even if one inadvertently though unavoidably swerves to the other side. One ought to abstain from eating fatty food even if one is unable to shake one's junk food habit, and in some sense of "ought," even if one has available only fatty tropical foods. No doubt the end of evaluating actions in terms of "oughts" is to get people to perform those actions. But fulfilling that end does not require applying "oughts" only to actions that the agent is able to perform. When "ought" is employed in this way it characterizes actions constitutive of an activity, as in the examples of bicycle riding and driving, or in some other way mandatory, as in the case of fatty foods. Presumably the same may be true of the epistemic "ought." Thus, the mere fact that our conception of justification is deontic does not show that it conforms to the principle that "ought" implies "can."[10]

In rejecting premise (b), I am most emphatically *not* rejecting the deontic conception of justified belief. On the contrary, I see no compelling objection to that conception. William Alston (1989a) has criticized the idea that the deontic conception applies directly to beliefs on the ground that we cannot literally be obligated to believe a proposition, since we do not directly control whether we believe it. But our most recent remarks undermine this criticism. Being obligated to believe a proposition does not entail that we directly control whether we believe it, any more than it entails that we can believe it.

Alston does allow the deontic conception to apply indirectly to beliefs. He plausibly denies that we have voluntary control over our beliefs – both what he calls direct basic voluntary control (as in basic actions like moving one's finger), direct nonbasic immediate voluntary control (as in nonbasic actions over which one has immediate control like flipping a light switch), and long-range voluntary control (as in one's control over one's weight or blood pressure). But he does admit that we have what he calls indirect voluntary influence on our beliefs. And he allows the deontic conception to apply to beliefs in virtue of this kind of influence:

> Suppose that, although I did not do anything with the intention of bringing about my cholesterol buildup, still I could have prevented it if I had done certain things I could and should have done, for instance, reduce fat intake. In that case I could still be held responsible for the condition, and it could be my fault . . . . This suggests that even if propositional attitudes are not under our effective voluntary control, we might still be held responsible for them, provided there is something we could and should have done such that if we had done it we would not have had the attitude in question.
>
> (Alston 1989a: 137)

Alston does not believe that such an indirect conception of justified belief has significant epistemological work to do. However this may be, there is no reason for rejecting a direct conception of justified belief in favor of an indirect one.

In fact Ginet concedes that the deontic conception does not strictly apply to involuntary beliefs, as he must if he is to maintain premise (b) of his argument. Accordingly, he proposes a way to extend the deontic conception to beliefs that are not voluntary: "we can interpret an ascription of unjustifiedness to a belief that the subject cannot help having as saying that if the subject were able to help it, she ought not to hold the belief" (1974: 183). However, Ginet's proposal has a serious drawback: if beliefs are involuntary, then there will be instances in which a subject is intuitively unjustified in a belief she cannot help having but nevertheless, if she were able to help having it, her system of beliefs would differ in ways that would entail that it is permissible for her to hold the belief. Suppose the subject has an involuntary but unjustified faith in her political beliefs, a faith that prevents her from acquiring evidence that would in fact support her political beliefs. Suppose, however, that if she were to help having her faith, then she would develop the capacity to acquire this evidence, so that it would be permissible for her to hold these beliefs. On Ginet's extended deontic conception, she is justified in her political

95

beliefs, contrary to intuition. I believe Ginet ought to abandon this extended deontic conception, and with it premise (b) of his argument.

Alston offers two replies to Ginet's extended deontic conception that are intended to scuttle the very attempt to apply the deontic conception to involuntary beliefs:

(1) This renders epistemic justification quite different from the justification of action, where "justified" and other deontological terms are withheld from actions the subject couldn't help performing.
(2) Insofar as we can make a judgment as to what would be permitted or forbidden were a certain range of involuntary states within our voluntary control, it will turn out that the deontological evaluation is simply a misleading way of making evaluations that could be stated more straightforwardly and candidly in other terms.

(Alston 1989a: 125n18)

Alston suggests the terms "desirable" and "worthwhile" as less misleading alternatives to "permissible." But our observation a moment ago that there are "oughts" without corresponding "cans" seems sufficient to respond to Alston's replies. Epistemic justification need not differ from other "oughts" that apply to involuntary actions. Nor is it true that "oughts" that so apply are merely misleading stand-ins for terms like "desirable" or "worthwhile." To say that one ought to turn the handlebar to the left when the bicycle leans to the left is clearly not to say merely that it is desirable or worthwhile to do so – that would be an odd way to describe the action, and itself misleading. It is to say that doing so is mandatory – in this case, in virtue of being constitutive of the activity.

Perhaps Alston will say that there is a disanalogy between the epistemic "ought" and the bicycle "ought": there are no directly basically voluntary or directly nonbasically voluntary beliefs, and there are few long-term voluntary beliefs, whereas there are many voluntary actions involved in riding a bicycle (1989a: 118n6). I will content myself with this short response: even if *all* of our bicycle-riding actions were involuntary, it would still be true that we ought to turn the handlebar to the left when the bicycle leans to the left. Perhaps we would no longer employ the term "ought" if there were *nothing* we could do to influence our behavior in a way that would eventually lead to conforming to this bicycle-riding norm. Perhaps "ought" is necessarily guiding in the sense that we apply the term only when we think talk of what we ought to do could help to bring about the specified actions. But Alston admits that there are things we can do to influence our beliefs. If, as I believe, the most that we can demand of the deontic conception of justified belief is that it employ a guiding "ought," then the involuntariness of all belief does not rule out this conception.

Thus, I am willing to go along with Ginet's claim that our conception of justified belief is deontic, despite the fact that belief is involuntary. But by the same token I deny that our deontic conception has any internalist punch. Etymologically, justified belief is belief made just – made to conform to law. And justified belief may therefore be said to be permissible belief – belief permitted by law. But such a deontic conception does not exclude externalism. This is not to say that the deontic conception excludes no substantive accounts of justified belief. It arguably excludes any account appropriate to an *aretaic* conception of justified belief. For example, it arguably excludes the view that justified belief is belief that results from the exercise of a process that is a typical manifestation of a proper combination of epistemic virtues (such as wisdom, intelligence, insight, intellectual diligence, etc.) (Sosa 1985). But I have no objection to excluding this account, since I find it implausible. Reliably formed perceptual beliefs, for example, are justified even though the perceptual processes that form them are not typical manifestations of any epistemic virtues or combination of virtues, at least in any ordinary sense of "virtue." My justified visual beliefs need not result from any process that manifests intelligence or diligence, or even visual acuity or attentiveness. Justified belief is one thing and epistemically virtuous belief is another, however closely related the two may be. Moreover, I doubt whether it will be possible to say what a *proper* combination of epistemic virtues amounts to without falling back on some feature of processes involved in their manifestation (most likely, the feature of reliability). That may well render the reference to virtues otiose. Of course if it does, the aretaic account may simply revert to an account of justified belief that conforms to the deontic conception. However this may be, I do not see that the deontic conception bars any plausible theory of justified belief.

I would like to note, finally, that Ginet's and Chisholm's versions are supported by the deontic argument only by way of overkill. For the deontic argument, if successful, shows that a subject can tell whether she is justified in believing p on all possible occasions of belief-formation (i.e., all occasions on which she might be forbidden from believing p), whether or not she possesses the concept of justified belief, and whether or not she considers the proposition. And it therefore entails that the subject can tell that she is justified whenever she is justified. Thus, the deontic argument supports Ginet's and Chisholm's versions only if it is assumed that occasions on which the subject might be forbidden from believing p do not include occasions on which she lacks the concept of justification or she considers the proposition. But I can see no argument for this assumption that does not make an ad hoc appeal to save accessibility internalism from implausible consequences. From the standpoint of Ginet's and Chisholm's versions, the deontic argument yields too strong a conclusion.

Beset by all these difficulties, Ginet's argument would seem to have little prospect of establishing accessibility internalism, or even of showing that subjects must be able to tell in any way, reflectively or otherwise, that they are justified.[11] There is no reason here to doubt that reliabilism can characterize the deontic conception of justification.

2 Against accessibility internalism

While there is no convincing argument for accessibility internalism, and the view itself lacks intuitive appeal, it is surprisingly difficult to state a compelling objection to it. Nevertheless I believe there are sufficient objections. These objections will tell, not only against accessibility internalism, but against any view on which the subject must always be able to know, or be (doxastically or propositionally) justified in believing, that she is (propositionally) justified in believing p. There are also good objections specifically against accessibility internalism, but I will have to omit them here.

One objection to accessibility internalism derives from a plausible account of the justification for believing that one is justified proposed by Alston:

in taking a belief to be justified, we are evaluating it in a certain way. And, like any evaluative property, epistemic justification is a supervenient property, the application of which is based on more fundamental properties . . . . Hence, in order for me to be justified in believing that S's belief that *p* is justified, I must be justified in certain other beliefs, viz., that S's *belief that p* possesses a certain property Q, and that Q renders its possessor justified. (Another way of formulating this last belief is: a belief that there is a valid epistemic principle to the effect that any belief that is Q is justified.)

(Alston 1989a: 24)

Alston claims here that justification is supervenient on some property Q, and thus a subject – call her "May" – is justified in believing that she is justified in believing *p* only if she is justified in believing that:

(a) her belief *p* has property Q on which justification supervenes; and
(b) beliefs that have Q are justified.

Presumably, May is justified in her epistemic belief (her belief that she is justified in believing *p*) *on the basis of* her justified beliefs (a) and (b). The objection to accessibility internalism suggested by Alston's account of the justification of our epistemic beliefs is this: May is not always able to be justified in believing (b), and thus is not always able to be justified in her epistemic belief, when she is justified in believing *p*. In particular, she does not have the cognitive resources to be justified in believing (b), or perhaps even to believe (b), on the occasion of her first or earliest justified beliefs. Since (b) is a generalization, it must be justified on the basis of other beliefs in virtue of the availability of an inductive inference from particular beliefs, or of a conceptual analysis of justified belief in terms of Q, or of some other way of supporting generalizations yet to be specified, a way that enables a synthetic generalization to be justified a priori. The trouble is that these means of justification are unavailable on the occasion of the subject's first justified beliefs – at least they are unavailable if, as accessibility internalists claim, basic beliefs like "I am appeared to redly" are justified whenever the subject is appeared to redly. The latter circumstances just do not guarantee that the subject will have the justified beliefs

99

about particulars from which they could infer the generalization by induction, or the necessary skills to analyze justified belief in terms of Q. Actually, on Alston's account of the justification of May's epistemic belief, her belief (b) cannot be inductively justified, on pain of circularity, since the particular epistemic beliefs on the basis of which her belief (b) would have to be inductively justified are themselves justified on the basis of (b). Belief (b) would presumably have to be justified by conceptual analysis. But this is a plausible view of the justification of (b). It goes without saying that even if belief (b) cannot be inductively justified, it might be that one can only be inductively justified in believing (a), that a belief has Q (reliability, for example). In this case, the subject cannot be justified in believing (a) on the occasion of her earliest justified beliefs. I would argue as well that subjects are not always justified in believing (a) whenever they they are justified in believing p, but let me postpone that argument for a moment. The point concerning (b) suffices to undermine accessibility internalism.

Chisholm would agree with Alston that justification supervenes on some property Q of beliefs – the property (or disjunction of properties) specified by the antecedents of the rules of justification (e.g., the belief's being such that I am appeared to redly). I think that Chisholm would also agree with Alston that May's epistemic belief is justified only if she is justified in believing (a). He would, however, deny that her epistemic belief is justified only if she is justified in believing (b). Nor would he allow that her epistemic belief is justified *on the basis of* her belief (a) – she need not even believe (a) to be justified in her epistemic belief. Here it will help to restrict our attention to basically justified beliefs p. A similar but more complicated story may be told for nonbasically justified beliefs. For a basically justified belief p, what justifies the belief p is simply the state of affairs that p. A basically justified belief is a belief in a self-presenting state of affairs – (with qualification) a belief p such that if p, then S is justified in believing p. For a basically justified belief p, one and the same thing justifies both May's epistemic belief and her belief (a) – namely, the same state of affairs that p that justifies her belief p. What justifies the subject's epistemic belief is simply this state of affairs. May is justified in her epistemic belief only if she is justified in (a) because one and the same thing justifies both her epistemic belief and her belief in (a).

(For an argument that Chisholm is committed to the view that, for a basic belief p, the state of affairs that p justifies both the belief p and the epistemic belief, see Alston (1980: 575–6).) Of course Chisholm's accessibility internalism consists simply in holding that for any belief p, basic or otherwise, if May is justified in believing p (and May considers whether p or whether she is justified in believing p), then she is justified in her epistemic belief. Alston's account of the justification of May's epistemic belief is consistent with there being self-presenting states, but not with Chisholm's (or any other) version of accessibility internalism. Nor is it consistent with saying as Chisholm does that one and the same thing justifies both the epistemic belief and the belief (a).

Noah Lemos (1989) has replied to the present objection to accessibility internalism by asking whether it would not be possible for May's epistemic belief to be justified on the basis of her belief in (a) alone, without her also being justified in believing (b), in a manner analogous to that in which, according to W.D. Ross, we can have ethical knowledge – knowledge that an action is right – based on our knowledge that it has a particular character, without also being justified in believing an ethical principle. As Ross puts it:

> It is only by knowing or thinking my act to have a particular character, out of the many that it in fact has, that I know or think it to be right . . . . Now it seems at first sight to follow from this that our perception of the particular duty follows from the perception of a general duty . . . . Yet it will not do to make our perception of particular duties essentially an inference from general principles . . . . Their rightness was not deduced from any general principles; rather the general principle was later recognized by intuitive induction as being already implied in the judgment already passed on particular acts.
>
> (Ross 1939: 168–70)

Lemos proposes to extend these claims to the justification of epistemic beliefs:

> If, as Ross suggests, we have some justified ethical judgments which do not depend for their warrant on our being justified in believing certain general ethical principles, it also seems possible that we might have some justified epistemic judgements which

do not depend upon our being justified in believing epistemic principles.

(Lemos 1989: 467)

On this view, May's epistemic belief is justified on the basis of her justified belief (a), even though she is not justified in believing the generalization (b). In this case, she would not need to have the cognitive resources to believe (b). The advantage of this account of the justification of her epistemic belief over Alston's account is that we can now explain her justification for believing (b) in a natural way – as deriving from the availability of an inductive inference, rather than from the availability of a conceptual analysis of justified belief in terms of Q.

The trouble with this account is that it assumes something not at all obvious – that there is an available justifying inference from the belief (a) to the epistemic belief. Alston's account has the advantage of explaining the justification of the epistemic belief in an unproblematic way: the belief follows from (a) and (b) via universal instantiation. The present account of the justification of the epistemic belief requires that we show that this belief can be justified on the basis of (a) alone – perhaps, that there is an available justifying inference from (a) to the epistemic belief. An accessibility internalist might add yet another rule sanctioning this basing relation. But without some theoretical ground for such a rule, the addition will be blatantly ad hoc. (On reliabilism, such an inference would be justifying if it were reliable and also relevant, but I see no reason for supposing that it is relevant.) Thus, we must reject the proposal that the epistemic belief is justified on the basis of (a) alone and give preference to Alston's account of the justification for the epistemic belief, since it is the only one that identifies a clearly justifying basing relation. But then the objection to accessibility internalism returns.

Not only is there a difficulty in May's always being justified in believing (b), there is also a difficulty in her always being justified in believing (a). Subjects do not always have the cognitive resources to be justified in believing that the belief p has Q. May can be justified in believing that she is appeared to redly without having the capacity to be justified in believing, or for that matter, even to believe, that her belief has the propositional content p, that her belief has Q (is such that she is appeared to redly), or indeed that she believes any proposition at all. (I have assumed for convenience that accessibility internalism requires the accessibility of doxastic justification, but as I have indicated parenthetically above, the deontic argument really only shows that it requires the accessibility of *propositional* justification. If the latter is taken to be a property, not of an actual or possible belief, but of a proposition, then we should strictly say that the difficulty is that May can be justified in believing that she is appeared to redly without being able to be justified in believing, or even to believe, that any *proposition* has a property analogous to Q, or indeed any property at all.) There is clearly a difficulty here for immature subjects, but I will argue that there is a difficulty as well even for mature subjects. Even mature subjects sometimes fail to be in a position to be justified in believing (a) when they are justified in believing p. Thus, May can be justified in believing p without being justified in believing (a), and consequently, on Alston's account of her justification for her epistemic belief, she can be justified in believing p without being justified in her epistemic belief.

There are two ways to answer this objection. One is by appeal to the conditions that qualify accessibility internalism in the versions proposed by Chisholm and Ginet. Let me turn first, however, to a proposal of Lemos which would, if successful, respond not only to this most recent objection concerning (a) but to the preceding objection concerning (b) as well. Perhaps May can be justified in her epistemic belief without being justified in either (a) or (b):

> While it seems plausible that many of our evaluative judgments are justified in virtue of our being justified in believing other things, it is not clear that all of them are. If I am justified in believing that a particular apple is a good apple, it seems reasonable to suggest that I am justified in believing this because I am justified in believing that it is sweet, juicy, worm-free, etc. Similarly, it seems reasonable to hold that if I am justified in believing that a particular action is right it is in virtue of the fact that I am justified in believing certain other things about that action, e.g., that it is an instance of promise-keeping or loyalty. But it is far from clear that all of our evaluative judgments are justified in virtue of other beliefs . . . if a man has a painful headache, it is not clear that his judgment that it is bad must depend upon his having certain justified beliefs

about his headache. One could maintain, I think, that it is the nature of his experience which justifies him in believing that it is bad . . . One might hold (i) that the nature of the experience justifies both the evaluative belief and the belief that it is painful and (ii) that the former belief does not depend for its warrant upon the latter belief.

(Lemos 1989: 467–8)

Lemos suggests here, in line with the view attributed to Chisholm by Alston, that, at least for a basic belief *p*, May's epistemic belief that her belief *p* is justified might be justified by the same state of affairs *p* that justifies her belief *p* without her being justified in believing (a) or (b).

There is, however, a problem with this way of responding to our objection. Adopting the proposed account of the justification of epistemic beliefs prevents accessibility internalism from excluding externalism. Let us note first that this way of responding can work only if it denies, not only that May's epistemic belief must be justified *on the basis of* her justified belief (a), but also that it is justified *only if* she is justified in believing (a). For our objection depends on the latter, rather than the former, assumption. Now the problem is this. If it is possible for May to be justified in her epistemic belief directly on the basis of the state of affairs that *p*, without her being justified in believing that her belief *p* has *Q*, on an account of *Q* like Chisholm's, then we must ask why it would not be possible for her to be justified in her epistemic belief in virtue of her belief *p*'s having *Q*, *regardless* of what account is given of *Q*, without her being justified in believing that her belief *p* has *Q*. And in particular, we must ask why it would not be possible for her epistemic belief to be justified in virtue of her belief *p*'s being (availably) *reliably formed* without her being justified in believing that her belief *p* is (availably) reliably formed. If the experience of being appeared to redly is enough to justify her epistemic belief, why could (available) reliable formation not be enough to justify it? But if the justification of her epistemic belief is divorced in this way from the justification of her belief that her belief *p* has *Q*, then the requirement that justification be accessible loses its force. Justification as understood on reliabilism could be accessible because the subject could be justified in believing that she is justified in believing *p*, even though she is unjustified in believing that her belief *p* is reliably formed. It would seem that the accessibility internalist must deny that May's epistemic belief can be justified in virtue of her belief *p*'s being reliably formed, despite the fact that it can be justified on the basis of her experience. But on what ground might this be denied?

Obviously the accessibility internalist cannot appeal to the claim that May's epistemic belief is not correlated with her belief *p*'s being reliably formed as it is with her experience. It will not do to say that she might still hold her epistemic belief even if her belief *p* were not reliably formed, while she would not hold her epistemic belief if she did not have the experience of being appeared to redly. Nor will it do to say, more modestly, that there is no available process that generally maps her belief *p*'s being reliably formed into her epistemic belief, whereas there is an available process that generally maps her experience of being appeared to redly into her epistemic belief. While these correlational claims are plausible, the accessibility internalist can hardly use them, since they are relevant to the justification of the epistemic belief only on an externalist account of justified belief. To be sure, these points do not show that Lemos' account of the justification of epistemic beliefs reconciles accessibility internalism with a fully general reliabilism, since for the reasons just given Lemos' account is inconsistent with a reliabilist account of the justification of epistemic beliefs. But Lemos' account does divest accessibility internalism of the power to exclude hybrid versions of externalism fused with an internalist account of the justification of epistemic beliefs. While such hybrid versions of externalism may be ad hoc, we have no reason to think accessibility internalism is any less so on the present account. Hybrid reliabilism says that the belief *p* is justified in virtue of being reliably formed, while the epistemic belief is justified in virtue of the belief *p*'s being reliably formed. The view is ad hoc because it assigns arbitrarily different conditions of justification to the belief *p* and the epistemic belief. Accessibility internalism on the present account says that the belief *p* is justified in virtue of (and on the basis of) an experience, while the epistemic belief is justified in virtue of the same experience. The proponent of accessibility internalism on Lemos' account must convince us that this view is not ad hoc in assigning arbitrarily *similar* conditions of justification to the belief *p* and to the epistemic belief. These two beliefs have, after all, very different propositional contents. In the

105

absence of an argument to the contrary, we may conclude that Lemos' account of the justification of epistemic beliefs deprives accessibility internalism of any polemical force. Thus the present account is unavailable to the polemically motivated accessibility internalist and cannot be used to defeat an objection concerning (a).

Let it also be noted that there is an objection to May's always being able to be justified in her epistemic belief parallel to our objection concerning (a), and this parallel objection is left untouched by Lemos's defense from the objection concerning (a). Even if May's epistemic belief is justified by the state of affairs that p, the fact remains that it will be so justified only if May has the cognitive resources to be justified in believing, and to believe, that her belief p has the property of being justified. And these are not resources available to her on the occasion of her first justified beliefs.

Chisholm and Ginet qualify their formulations of accessibility internalism in a way that might be thought to get around this last objection, as well as the objection concerning (a) (though not the objection concerning (b)). As we earlier noted, Ginet inserts into his formulation the conditional "provided that S at that time has the concept [of justified belief]." In other words, Ginet's accessibility internalism requires only that May be able to know that she is justified in believing p, and hence know that (a), *if* she has the concept of justified belief. We cannot, then, object that she cannot know these things on the occasion of her first justified beliefs on the ground that she lacks the concept of justified belief. Similarly, Chisholm inserts the qualification "if . . . one *considers* the proposition" (or whether the proposition is evident) and observes that "one cannot ask oneself such a question unless one does have the concept of a proposition being evident." Thus, again, we cannot object that May cannot be justified in her epistemic belief or in believing (a) on the occasion of her first justified beliefs because she lacks the concept of justified belief.

Nevertheless, Ginet's and Chisholm's qualifications do not circumvent our objections concerning (a) and concerning the requirement that May always be able to be justified in her epistemic belief. It will suffice to deal with Chisholm's qualification, since it is stronger than Ginet's and thus provides greater resources for generating justification for the epistemic belief. Despite these greater resources, Chisholm's qualification does not intuitively

seem to offer sufficient resources to guarantee justification for
the epistemic belief. It does not seem to follow intuitively from the
fact that May is appeared to redly and that she considers whether
her epistemic belief is justified, that her epistemic belief is in fact
justified. No matter how carefully she considers the matter, it seems
possible for her to miss the relevant considerations – to miss even
her being appeared to redly, but in any event to miss whatever
considerations would make her justified in believing that her belief
p has the property Q or justified in her epistemic belief. We have
all had the experience of looking for something – an umbrella, for
example – and, despite its size, distinctive shape, and loud colors,
failing to find it even though it lies right before our eyes, and this
despite the fact that we fully well know everything about it relevant
to our finding it. It would seem that in such a circumstance, despite
the plainness of the truth that the umbrella is before our eyes,
we are not justified in believing that it is there. Why would
the fact that the belief p has Q or is justified be any different?
Chisholm might claim that it differs at least in the case of beliefs in
self-presenting states, since the presence of a self-presenting state
entails that one is justified in believing it present, and this would be
enough to guarantee justification for believing that the belief in the
self-presenting state is justified. But even if this is true, it does not
handle the case of nonbasic beliefs. And I doubt whether it is true.

It is not easy to find a natural and compelling example to make
the point, but I regard the following as sufficient. Like many people
I have had the startling and unpleasant experience of imbibing what
I expect to be milk and discovering that it is actually orange juice.
My initial experience on drinking the orange juice might plausibly
be described in either of two ways. It might be said that the
beverage appears at first to taste like milk and only subsequently to
taste like orange juice. Or it might be said that it appears from the
start to taste like orange juice, though at first I believe it to be milk.
I am inclined to think that the latter description is more plausible,
but I believe we can construct an objection to Chisholm's version of
accessibility internalism no matter which description is true. Let us
consider the first description. At first I am appeared to milkly, and
I believe myself to be so appeared to, though subsequently I come
to be appeared to orange-juicely. (I assume here that "milkly"
describes a gustatory character comparable to the visual character
described by "redly," but if not, we can no doubt choose a more

suitable example.) I am inclined to say that in these circumstances I am (normally) at first justified in believing that I am appeared to milkly. At any rate, I do not wish here to challenge the claim that my being appeared to milkly is a self-presenting state. Rather I wish to suggest that in these circumstances I would not necessarily be justified in believing that I am justified in believing that I am appeared to milkly upon considering whether I am so justified.

It is difficult to know just what would happen were I to consider this matter under these conditions, but the difficulty of knowing this can hardly be a comfort to Chisholm, since his version of accessibility internalism entails that there is a definite answer to the question, and the application of his version to real life situations requires that we be able to know what would happen in cases like this. Assuming there is some definite answer, it is fair to ask what would happen if, as seems quite possible, my considering whether I am so justified were to cause my experience to change in such a way that I would come to be appeared to orange-juicely rather than milkly. Chisholm would surely have to allow that in these counterfactual circumstances I would no longer be justified in believing that I am appeared to milkly. And then I would no longer be justified in believing my epistemic belief. So it is not true in the actual circumstances that if I consider whether I am justified in believing that I am appeared to milkly, my epistemic belief is also justified. And this is so despite the fact that it is true that if I am appeared to milkly, I am justified in believing that I am so appeared to. (I have interpreted the conditional in Chisholm's formulation of accessibility internalism as a counterfactual conditional, even though it is written as a material conditional, since the material conditional is surely not what he intends.)

Suppose, on the other hand, as I think more plausible, that from the start I am appeared to orange-juicely, though at first I believe the beverage to taste like milk. Here again I will not dispute that I may be justified in believing that I am appeared to orange-juicely, despite the fact that I believe that I am appeared to milkly. One might think that my justification for believing that I am appeared to orange-juicely is undermined by my belief that I am appeared to milkly. And of course a cautious version of foundationalism will allow the undermining of the justification provided by self-presenting states (this will require that the rule associated with self-presenting states, "if p then I am justified in believing *p*," be qualified by the phrase "prima facie" and a rule for undermining be introduced). But surely my belief that I am appeared to milkly will not undermine my justification for *p* unless it is a *justified* belief, which it need not be. So we may assume that my belief that I am appeared to orange-juicely is justified. What I wish to question, again, is the claim that on considering whether I am justified in believing that I am appeared to orange-juicely, I must be justified in believing that I am so justified. Suppose I consider this matter. I might well recognize that I believe that I am appeared to milkly, and even if this belief is unjustified, the fact that I hold it may be enough to deprive me of justification for my epistemic belief. I might ask myself whether I would hold such a belief if I did not have a reason for it, conclude that I do have a reason, and then – justifiably, it seems – judge that I am not justified in believing that I am appeared to orange-juicely. When I consider this matter, I might judge that I am unjustified in my epistemic belief as a result of reflecting that any justification for *p* I might have is undermined by my justification for believing that I am appeared to milkly. But my justification for my epistemic belief is not *itself* undermined by my justification for believing that I am appeared to milkly, since I am not justified in the latter belief. This is not, then, an instance in which I fail to be justified in my epistemic belief because it is undermined by my justification for some other belief. That point is essential for my objection, since a suitably cautious version of accessibility internalism could admit some undermining of epistemic beliefs in a manner analogous to the manner in which a cautious foundationalism will take into account the undermining of justification provided by self-presenting states. Of course it might be that on reflection I would cease to hold the belief that I am appeared to milkly, since I would recognize that I am really appeared to orange-juicely. But first, this need not be so. I might reflect and fail to recognize the true appearances. Or I might come to believe that it *seems* that I am appeared to orange-juicely, but maintain, at least for a moment, my prior conviction that I am actually appeared to milkly. Second, even if I do recognize that I am appeared to orange-juicely, I might still be worried enough by my prior conviction that I might judge my epistemic belief at least temporarily unjustified. I claim, then, that we have an example in which, for a basic belief *p*, I can consider whether I am justified in my epistemic belief and still not be justified in it, despite its appearing to me that *p*. This is enough to show that Chisholm's qualification does not avert our objections to accessibility internalism.

I have focused here on the objections concerning (a), (b), and the epistemic belief for basically justified beliefs understood as beliefs in self-presenting states. There are, however, similar difficulties for nonbasically justified beliefs, as well as difficulties of other kinds (Alston 1980). In light of these objections to accessibility internalism, we ought to reject the view.[12]

3 The fairly direct accessibility of reasons

Before quitting accessibility internalism, we should perhaps note that there are constraints on justified belief weaker than accessibility internalism that have been advertised as versions of internalism. The most attractive of these is the constraint that the (actual or available) *justifiers* of a belief (i.e., the reasons for or processes that lead to the belief) be accessible to the subject (Audi 1989) or, weaker still, that they generally be "fairly directly accessible" to the subject (Alston 1989a). These constraints are of course not intended to capture the internalist idea that subjects have access to the *conditions* of justified belief, but only to the justifying reasons.[13]

On the former constraint, subjects must always be able to tell or know by reflection that such and such a reason obtains (where, in the case of reasons with propositional content, for example, they must tell or know that a reason with propositional content *p* obtains). I find this requirement unattractive because I find it quite intuitive to say that I am justified in believing that Abraham Lincoln was born in 1809, despite the fact that I cannot recall any (actual or available) reason for believing this, perhaps no longer even possess a reason. Nor is it adequate to respond that I must at least have the reason that this is a belief of a type that is reliably formed, and I must be able to tell by reflection that I have such a reason. I think we would allow that I would be justified in my belief that Lincoln was born in 1809, and even know it to be true, if on a quiz show I correctly answered the question "When was Abraham Lincoln born?" despite my protest that I do not know and am not justified in the answer. One might respond that even if I disavowed being justified in my answer, I would still have to have a reason for thinking the belief is (availably) reliably formed, and my having this reason would still have to be accessible to me, if I were to count as justified in the belief. But I do not see why this would have to be so. We are able to assign justification to my belief on the basis of the correctness of my answer without knowing further that I have a reason for thinking the belief is (availably) reliably formed. Indeed, it seems we would maintain our assignment of justification whether or not it turned out that I did have a reason for thinking this, and even if I had this reason, my disavowal of justification might derive from an inability to tell that I had the reason. Admittedly these intuitions are controversial, but I regard them as firm enough to force a retreat to the second, weaker constraint, on which subjects must generally be able to tell or know without extensive further research that such and such a reason obtains.

Alston does not argue for this second constraint, but seeks to explain it by appeal to its role in the practice of justifying beliefs:

> I suggest that the concept was developed, and got its hold on us, because of the practice of critical reflection on our beliefs, of challenging their credentials and responding to such challenges – in short the practice of attempting to *justify* beliefs. Suppose there were no such practice; suppose that no one ever challenges the credentials of anyone's beliefs; suppose that no one ever critically reflects on the grounds or basis of one's own beliefs. In that case would we be interested in determining whether one or another belief is justified? I think not . . . . I want further to suggest that this social practice has strongly influenced the development of the *concept* of being justified. What has emerged from this development is the concept of *what would have to be specified to carry out a successful justification of the belief.* Our conception of what a belief needs in the way of a basis in order to *be justified* is the conception of that the specification of which in answer to a challenge would suffice to answer that challenge. For only what the subject can ascertain can be cited by that subject in response to a challenge.
>
> (Alston 1989a: 236)

Alston attempts here to explain why justifying reasons (i.e., reasons on the basis of which the belief is justified) must generally, though not always, be "fairly readily available to the subject through some mode of access much quicker than lengthy research, observation, or experimentation" (1989a: 238).

His explanation would appear to be this. Our concept of justified belief emerges from the practice of justifying beliefs. What is required for this practice is the concept of successfully justifying beliefs, and what is required in turn for this concept is the further concept of what would have to be specified to carry out a successful justifying of the belief. But the latter concept is the concept of justified belief (nearly enough). Now our practice of justifying beliefs requires that we often successfully justify beliefs, and this happens only if subjects are generally able to reveal their reasons to challengers, and hence only if their reasons are generally fairly readily accessible to them. Thus, the concept of justified belief conforms to the constraint that subjects' reasons are generally fairly readily accessible.

I doubt whether Alston is right that we have the concept of justified belief only because we engage in the practice of justifying beliefs and thus have the concept of what would have to be specified in order to carry out a successful justification of the belief. This seems to put too much weight on dialogue and challenge. Even if people did not challenge others' beliefs or justify beliefs to one another, there might still be an important role for the concept of justified belief: judging how much justified belief people have by observing what they say and do outside of dialogue. But I confess I have no idea how to adjudicate this question of conceptual prehistory. For the sake of argument I am willing to grant Alston's claim here. What I do not see is that this dialogical origin would explain (at least in the sense of showing that our practice mandates or would be better serviced by) the constraint of general fairly direct accessibility of reasons.

Let me list some of my reservations about Alston's explanation.

(1) Even if subjects must be able generally to reveal their reasons, it does not follow that their reasons must generally be fairly readily accessible. Of course Alston admits that there are many cases in which justified beliefs are not fairly directly accessible. If Josephine is asked her reason for judging *Rules of the Game* a better film than *Grand Illusion*, we would surely allow her to consult her diary to recall her reason. We would allow that the reason she gives

after consultation, assuming it is a good one, already justified her judgment before consultation. This is especially clear if her diary prompted her to *remember* her reason, but I think it is also true even if she cannot remember it at all. Josephine's justification does not preclude the need for her to consult her diary in order to know her reason. It is not clear, however, why our practice of justifying beliefs would mandate anything stronger than, or why it could not be serviced by, the constraint that subjects generally be able to tell or know what their reasons are by means that do not stop the conversation with their challengers. These could include means that require significant effort, as well as means that go well beyond reflection, e.g., dialogical means. Conversation might be quite a bit more lengthy and strenuous if people often needed to resort to such means. But there is nothing in the idea of justifying per se that excludes general reliance on these means. Alston can explain at most the constraint of "general conversationally compatible accessibility," not general fairly direct accessibility.

(2) Even if our practice of justifying requires that subjects are generally able to reveal their reasons to challengers, and even if our concept of justification derives from our practice, it does not follow that the concept of justification conforms to the constraint of general fairly direct accessibility. It might be that our practice itself employs a broader concept of justification, one which serves nondialogical purposes, for which the constraint is not needed. Indeed it is arguable that we do employ a broader concept of justified belief that recognizes regions of justified beliefs for which reasons are not generally fairly readily accessible – for example, memory beliefs and certain kinds of perceptual beliefs (as in the case of chicken sexers who know the sex of chickens by looking, but are not at all able to tell what their reasons are). One could of course reply that in these instances the subjects' reasons are their own memory experiences, feelings of confidence, evaluations of their beliefs, and the like – states that are fairly readily accessible. And it is true that these are the sorts of states to which subjects are entitled to appeal, at least in some circumstances, in answer to challenges. While I would not deny that these are states to which subjects can appeal to meet challenges, there is no ground for denying that the chicken sexers are justified in their beliefs even though such states are not fairly readily accessible to them. Nor is there any ground for regarding these states as reasons – calling

113

them such is at best an ad hoc measure to preserve the constraint of general fairly direct accessibility. The most Alston can explain here is the constraint that in cases where beliefs are justified only if subjects are able to justify them, subjects must generally be able to tell or know what their reason is. He cannot explain a universally applicable constraint of general fairly direct accessibility.

(3) It is not clear that the practice of justifying requires that subjects are generally able to reveal their reasons to challengers. It is a tough question what a subject must say or do to meet a challenge successfully. The following is a relatively uncontroversial necessary condition for successfully meeting a challenge: the subject must say or do something that provides the challenger with enough evidence concerning whether the belief is justified to enable the challenger to reach a *true* or a *justified* conclusion as to whether the belief is justified. This condition has two implications. (i) Successfully meeting a challenge requires that the challenger be able to believe truly or justifiably what the subject's reason is. But the challenger might be able to do this without the *subject* saying or doing anything that requires the subject to tell what the reason is. You might be justified in believing that your camera is in the trunk of your car without being able to recall your reason for believing this (that you saw it there). But a challenger might be able to reconstruct your reason from what you say in virtue of remembering that you had opened the trunk of your car, even though you cannot remember this. What you say and do here might intuitively count as meeting the challenge even though you cannot tell what your reason is.

(ii) Successfully meeting a challenge requires at most that the subject say or do something that enables the challenger to believe truly or justifiably *that the subject has a justifying reason*. But it does not require that she say or do something that enables the challenger to believe truly or justifiably *what that reason is*. Perhaps challengers must often judge what the particular reason is to judge whether it is justifying, but, as Alston notes, they do not always need to judge this, and it is not obvious that they would have to judge it most of the time. I can accurately judge that you are justified in your belief that the sunset is crimson by checking your sensory reason (perhaps by looking at the sunset myself in roughly the circumstances in which you view it) – in which case I judge what your reason is. But I can also judge that you are justified by hearing you say that the sunset is crimson and employing my background knowledge of your reliability in such matters, and this does not require me to judge what your reason is. To be sure, there may be advantages to judging the particular reason. In addition, it might plausibly be said that I cannot judge whether you are justified without judging that you exercise one of a certain range of reliable processes, and I cannot judge that without relying on prior judgments of which sorts of reasons lead to true beliefs – and the latter judgments require still prior judgments of particular reasons. But this supports at most the requirement that challengers found their judgments that the subject has a justifying reason on judgments of particular reasons. It does not support the requirement that challengers must generally judge particular reasons. And so again Alston does not explain the constraint of generally fairly directly accessible reasons.

These points seem enough to cast doubt on Alston's explanation. This is not to deny that there is any epistemic constraint on reasons. I will propose one in chapter VI. But we have no reason to accept so strong a constraint as Alston's.

In this chapter I have rejected the primary argument for accessibility internalism, and I have offered an objection to the view. I have also expressed doubts about the requirement that reasons generally be fairly directly accessible. There is, however, a great deal more to be said about internalism. I turn in the next chapter to perspectival and mental internalism.

CHAPTER V

Perspectival Internalism, Mental Internalism, and Epistemically Responsible Belief

Perspectival internalism is the view that justified belief is belief sanctioned by the subject's epistemic perspective, her epistemic principles and her views about justified belief. On the most straightforward reading, the belief *p* is sanctioned by the subject's epistemic perspective just when there is a belief (or proposition) belonging to the subject's perspective (call this a perspectival belief) according to which the belief (or proposition) *p* is justified or reliable. On this reading, perspectival beliefs are limited to (possible) beliefs of the form: the belief *p* is justified, or of the form: the belief *p* is reliable. Versions of perspectival internalism differ in their further limitations on perspectival beliefs.

Here are some important versions of the view:

(a) *Reliabilist iterativism.* S is justified in believing *p* just in case S is justified in believing that the belief *p* is reliable.

(a) is, with qualification, Laurence BonJour's (1985) view.[1] For convenience I use the term "reliable" where BonJour uses "likely to be true." (a) obviously entails an infinite hierarchical regress of justification, but we may take some of the sting out of it by interpreting justification propositionally rather than doxastically (see BonJour (1985) Introduction, note 8). BonJour takes further steps to avert the regress, but we need not consider them here.

(b) *Counterfactual reflective perspectival internalism.* S is justified in believing *p* just in case S would on reflection believe that *p* is reliable.

Richard Foley (1987) proposes this view, with minor complications.[2] Here I say that a proposition is "reliable" where Foley says that it is the conclusion of an argument likely to be truth preserving, with premises of which there is no reason to be suspicious. On (a),

116

the subject's perspective is limited to what the subject is justified in believing, while on (b), it is limited to what the subject would on reflection believe reliable. A third view is also plausibly regarded as a version of perspectival internalism, though it does not identify the subject's perspective with beliefs (or propositions):

(c) *Guidance psychologism. S* is justified in believing *p* just in case the belief *p* conforms to a cognitive norm that actually guides the subject in forming the belief (Pollock 1986).

Guidance psychologism is a version of perspectival internalism if the subject's perspective is taken to be the set of guiding norms, and sanctioning by the perspective is taken to be conformity to a norm. For simplicity of exposition, I will focus on (a), but virtually all the points I will make carry over immediately to (b), and some of them carry over to (c).

Perspectival internalism differs substantially from accessibility internalism and has considerable advantages over it. Versions of perspectival internalism do not in general satisfy accessibility internalism. On none of the versions of perspectival internalism listed above can a subject always tell by reflection that her belief is sanctioned by her perspective. A subject is not always able to tell that she is justified in believing that her belief is reliable, as required by (a), or that she would on reflection believe that a proposition she believes is reliable, as on (b). Nor, finally, is she always able to tell that her belief conforms to the norm that guides her, as on (c). Thus versions of perspectival internalism may avoid objections to accessibility internalism.[3] Nor does accessibility internalism entail perspectival internalism: what is accessible need not be the belief's being sanctioned by the subject's epistemic perspective.

We must ask whether perspectival internalism ascribes value to justified belief. That depends on whether it can characterize a status that contributes to true belief – a question equivalent to whether the view can be derived from an *advisory* conception of justified belief (Foley 1989) or a conception of justified belief as *epistemically responsible belief* (BonJour 1985). I will focus on the latter conception.[4] The attempt to derive perspectival internalism from this conception gives way rather quickly to a case for a weaker internalism.

117

Knowledge and Belief

1 The responsibility argument for perspectival and mental internalism

BonJour appeals to epistemically responsible belief to support his own perspectival internalism in the course of an objection to D.M. Armstrong's (1973) externalism:

> according to the externalist view, a person may be highly irrational and irresponsible in accepting a belief, when judged in light of his own subjective conception of the situation, and may still turn out to be epistemically justified according to Armstrong's criterion. His belief may in fact be reliable, even though he has no reason for thinking it is reliable – or even has good reason to think it is not reliable. But such a person seems nonetheless to be thoroughly irresponsible from an epistemic standpoint in accepting such a belief and hence not in fact justified.
>
> (BonJour 1985: 38)

In this passage, BonJour argues that I am justified in believing *p* *only if* I am justified in believing that the belief *p* is reliable, since it would be *epistemically irresponsible* for me to "accept" a belief that I did not believe to be reliable.[5] BonJour subsequently adds to this argument another to show that I am justified in believing *p* *if* I am justified in believing that the belief *p* is reliable, since it would surely be epistemically responsible for me to have a belief that I believe to be reliable. Here BonJour assumes that justified belief is epistemically responsible belief and claims that being justified in believing that my belief is reliable is necessary and sufficient for epistemically responsible belief. Thus, a belief is justified just in case the subject justifiably believes that it is reliable. That is, a belief is justified just in case it is sanctioned by the subject's epistemic perspective in the sense that the subject is justified in believing that it is reliable. This is supposed to establish BonJour's own perspectival internalism.

I do not know whether there is such a status as epistemically responsible belief, but I will grant it for the sake of argument. Let us ask whether the claim that justified belief is epistemically responsible belief really entails perspectival internalism. Suppose for the moment that BonJour is right in identifying justified belief with epistemically responsible belief. We might still question his

118

claim that it would be epistemically irresponsible for me to form a belief that I am not justified in believing to be reliable. Why couldn't there be conditions that make it epistemically responsible for me to believe *p* even though I am not justified in believing that my belief *p* is reliable? For example, why couldn't my *experiences* concerning *p* or my other *beliefs* concerning *p* enter here in such a way as to make the belief *p* responsible?

Unfortunately BonJour gives us no clue as to why he identifies epistemically responsible belief with justified belief as to whether the belief *p* is reliable. Nor is it easy to locate plausible grounds for this identification. BonJour does appeal to intuitions about examples to establish that this condition characterizes justified belief, but, as I will argue in chapter VII, his appeal is ineffectual. Now in arguing against foundationalism BonJour does offer a ground for restricting justifying reasons to propositional attitudes, thus excluding experiences: a nonpropositional mental state or condition does not determine any particular proposition to believe. But in offering this ground BonJour assumes a crude account of justifying reasons. It is true that a nonpropositional mental state does not by itself justify a belief, since it does not determine any particular proposition. But once we remember that mental states, even propositional attitudes like belief, do not by themselves justify beliefs but do so only in virtue of playing the role of input to a process, the obstacle to nonpropositional reasons evaporates. It is the *process* that justifies a belief, and it may do so in virtue of mapping a nonpropositional mental state to a belief in a unique proposition. It must also be noted that even if BonJour were successful in showing that justifying reasons must be beliefs, it would remain for him to show that the belief that matters is the justified belief that the belief *p* is reliable.

Not only is there no argument for perspectival internalism from a conception of justified belief as epistemically responsible belief, there are also grounds for thinking that epistemically responsible belief and belief sanctioned by the subject's perspective diverge. We will look shortly at an example of a belief that is *not* epistemically responsible though sanctioned by the subject's epistemic perspective. Here I observe that there are examples of beliefs that are condemned by the subject's perspective but are not epistemically irresponsible. Suppose I have good reason to believe that my religious beliefs are unreliable: I have never found a convincing argument for them, but believe them simply as a consequence of indoctrination.[6] Then they are condemned by my perspective. Suppose, however, that it turns out that they are irresistible. Then it would seem that they are also *not* irresponsible (though perhaps not responsible either). For plausibly, if a belief is epistemically irresponsible, then the subject can resist it. So epistemically irresponsible belief is not belief condemned by my perspective.[7] This seems enough to show that epistemic responsibility and sanction by a perspective diverge.

There is no argument for perspectival internalism from a conception of justified belief as epistemically responsible belief. We must, however, consider whether the internalist might retreat to a weaker form of internalism – *mental internalism*, on which justified belief is belief meeting a condition supervenient on the subject's mentality. According to mental internalism, if subject S in world w has the same mental states as subject S' in world w', then S and S' are justified in believing the same propositions in their respective worlds. It might be thought that epistemically responsible belief at least supervenes on mentality. Factors external to the subject's mentality, such as reliability, are then irrelevant to justified belief.

Mental internalism would seem to be the weakest constraint that might qualify as a form of internalism. For it would seem to be the weakest constraint expressing the idea that the subject possesses the conditions of justified belief. Here possession is understood as supervenience on the subject's mentality. Notice that the forms of internalism we have examined entail mental internalism. Accessibility internalism entails it: the only conditions the subject can or does always tell to obtain by reflection are introspectible conditions, or conditions that can be inductively or deductively inferred from what is introspectible, and such conditions are plausibly either mental conditions or supervenient on mentality. And perspectival internalism, in its proposed versions, entails mental internalism because the subject's epistemic perspective is understood as a set of actual or counterfactual mental states (and counterfactual mental states plausibly supervene on actual ones when the counterfactual conditions are those of disinterested reflection), and sanctioning is understood as a relation supervenient on mental states. On the other hand, mental internalism is weak enough to be *consistent* with some versions of externalism (see note 14 below).

Internalism and Epistemically Responsible Belief

It is worth asking whether an appeal to the conception of justified belief as epistemically responsible belief might support mental internalism, since such an argument would appear to be our last, best hope for a theoretical argument for any form of internalism, and because examining the argument reveals something about epistemically responsible belief, which has great interest in its own right, quite apart from its relation to internalism. (In the following section we will consider a nontheoretical argument for mental internalism – from our intuitions about examples.)

To judge the prospects for deriving mental internalism from the conception of justified belief as epistemically responsible belief, we will need some working account of epistemically responsible belief. There are two accounts with which we might work:

(a) the belief *p* is epistemically responsible just when it results in an appropriate way from the subject's doing the epistemic best she can to bring it about that she believes what she is *justified* in believing as to whether *p*;

or

(b) the belief *p* is epistemically responsible just when it results in an appropriate way from the subject's doing the epistemic best she can to bring it about that she believes what results from exercising a *reliable process* in forming a belief as to whether *p*.

Of course these two accounts are equivalent if reliabilism is true. Does the claim that justified belief is epistemically responsible belief, characterized in either of these ways, support mental internalism?

It is obvious that justified belief as epistemically responsible belief, whether characterized by (a) or (b), cannot be characterized by *reliabilism*. Indeed, epistemically responsible belief cannot be characterized by reliabilism, even if it is *not* identified with justified belief. For a subject can do her epistemic best to bring it about that she believes what results from exercising a reliable process and yet fail to exercise a reliable process. For example, in cases in which the subject's best effort involves relying on her belief as to whether she exercises a reliable process, the subject may fail to exercise a reliable process because, despite her best effort to ascertain whether she exercises a reliable process, her belief that the process she exercises is reliable is erroneous. Epistemically

121

responsible belief is thus not reliably formed belief on either (a) or (b). So far, then, we seem to be headed away from reliabilism and toward mental internalism as an account of epistemically responsible belief.

But mental internalism fares little better than reliabilism as an account of epistemically responsible belief. For one thing, objections analogous to the one we have just made against reliabilism can be made against any proposed version of mental internalism as an account of epistemically responsible belief as characterized by (a). For in cases where the subject does her best by relying on her belief as to whether she is justified in believing p, she may fail to arrive at a justified belief because, despite her best effort to ascertain whether she is justified in believing p, her belief that she is justified in believing p is mistaken. On any proposed version of mental internalism (with the important exception of versions of access internalism discussed in chapter IV, note 12), a subject can mistakenly believe that she is justified in believing p, despite her best effort to ascertain whether she is justified in believing p. And it is plausible to suppose that she can do so in cases in which she does her best by relying on her belief as to whether she is justified in believing p. No mental internalist condition ever proposed (with the above-mentioned exceptions) guarantees that the subject is right. A subject can always make a mistake in judging whether her belief coheres with other beliefs or whether it fits the condition specified by rules like "if it seems to me that the object is red, then I am justified in believing that it seems to me that it is red." Consider first accessibility internalism: nothing in this constraint guarantees that the subject's judgment of whether she is justified in believing p will be correct as a result of her best effort; it guarantees only the ability to tell that she is justified in believing p. Even when the subject's best effort requires relying on her belief about whether she is justified, an ability to tell does not guarantee that a correct belief will result from her best effort. Whether a correct belief results depends on whether her effort is best spent on telling or on some other way of judging (e.g., making a guess). And no matter how easy it is to tell, we can always imagine that the subject is so burdened with other cognitive chores that her best effort would involve a short cut that does not ensure a correct belief as to whether she is justified in believing p. Much the same may be said about perspectival internalism.[8]

These objections do not, however, apply to mental internalism as a characterization of epistemically responsible belief on (b), since the fact that the subject's belief as to whether her belief *p* is reliably formed can be mistaken despite her best effort does not, on (b), entail that she can fail to fulfill mental internalist conditions despite her best effort. Nevertheless, the claim that mental internalism characterizes epistemically responsible belief on (b) seems unpromising, for two reasons. (1) There is no reason to think that it is true. There is no reason to think that coherence, or conformity to rules belonging to a list, or conformity to a norm that guides us, or any other proposed mental internalist condition characterizes belief that results from doing one's best to exercise a reliable process. Why should we think that the beliefs that result from doing one's best to exercise a reliable process will necessarily cohere? To be sure some sort of coherence may necessarily result from a best effort. If one does one's best to exercise reliable processes, then plausibly one will sometimes rely on one's beliefs about which processes are reliable, and the beliefs that result from one's best effort will sometimes result from the processes one deems reliable. That is a sort of coherence, but it is not guaranteed to obtain universally, and in any case it is only one sort of coherence that must be balanced against others (such as explanatory and probabilistic coherence – i.e., the conditional probabilification of beliefs given other beliefs). Whether a belief will cohere all things considered, given the subject's best effort depends on such factors as the subject's resources for making beliefs cohere and the demands of other cognitive tasks at hand. Coherentism is prima facie an implausible characterization of epistemically responsible belief on (b). And I think it is fair to say that the other proposed versions of mental internalism provide even less plausible characterizations than coherentism.

(2) Defining epistemically responsible belief according to (b) concedes a great deal to reliabilism. Proponents of mental internalism like BonJour and Foley do employ the notion of reliable belief in their characterizations of justified belief. They do not seem to realize, however, that they cannot do so with impunity. We can see this by remembering that (a) is the obvious way to define epistemically responsible belief: it is, intuitively, belief that results from doing one's best to believe what one is *justified* in believing. But if (a) is the intuitive characterization of epistemically

responsible belief, why should anyone endorse (b)? Why should we switch to talk of doing one's best to believe what results from exercising a *reliable process*? The only plausible answer is that justified belief *is* reliably formed belief. But of course such an answer is not open to proponents of perspectival internalism. Thus, proponents of perspectival internalism who endorse (b) must not only concede that reliably formed belief is a significant epistemic status, a concession already implicit in their formulation of perspectival internalism. They must also offer a less plausible characterization of epistemically responsible belief than the sort that naturally supplements reliabilism, since the reliabilist can endorse the intuitive account (a) (it is simply equivalent to (b) on reliabilism).

These reflections highlight two important points. One is that once reliably formed belief is recognized as an aim of cognition and thus granted a significant epistemic status, as in (b), we ought to develop an account of epistemically responsible belief that suitably ties it to this status. Such an account will supplement the account that reliabilism gives of the status with an account of epistemically responsible belief on (b). The second, related point is that there is no reason to think that doing one's best to exercise a reliable process supervenes on mentality – that is, no reason to think that mental internalism characterizes epistemically responsible belief on (b). Let me develop these points in turn.

If, as on (b), epistemically responsible belief is belief that results from doing one's best to believe what results from exercising a reliable process, then it is natural – perhaps inescapable – to see the system of epistemic evaluation as involving two tiers. The function of the first tier is to value reliably formed belief by praising such belief. That will not only express our appreciation for the contribution of reliable processes to the epistemic end of true belief; it will also encourage subjects to aim at exercising reliable processes and to develop belief-forming dispositions, habits, and traits that lead to the exercise of reliable processes. At the same time, we recognize that it is desirable for subjects in forming beliefs to rely on their beliefs about which processes are reliable, and we also recognize that subjects are bound to make mistakes about these matters. A system of evaluation that recognized only the value of reliably formed belief would provide no dispensation for a subject who relies on her belief about which process is reliable and as a result exercises an unreliable process because this belief happens to be false despite her best efforts. And without such a dispensation, subjects would be discouraged from relying on their beliefs about reliability. A system of evaluation that recognizes the value of reliably formed belief must recognize separately the value of belief that results from doing one's best to believe what results from exercising a reliable process.

There may of course be costs in adding a second tier of evaluation. There may be some tension in simultaneously approving and disapproving the same beliefs – a tension that may send subjects conflicting signals, simultaneously encouraging and discouraging them. Adding a second tier may also cause confusion in our assignments of the statuses and in our intuitions about which beliefs have which status. Beliefs that are not reliably formed will be simultaneously disapproved by the first tier and approved by the second, though the subject nevertheless best-effort believes them to be reliably formed. And beliefs that are reliably formed will (sometimes) be disapproved by the second tier if the subject forms them despite her best-effort belief that the processes are unreliable.

It would not, however, be correct to say that in such cases the two tiers send the subject conflicting belief-forming instructions: the first tier instructs the subject to form a reliable belief, while the second instructs her to form a belief that she best-effort believes to result from a reliable process. It is true that both tiers give instructions for belief, if instructions are descriptions of what the subject should aim at (or imperatives to aim at a certain end). For both describe what the subject should aim at. But there is no conflict in their instructions so understood. The first tier supplies the aim of reliably formed belief. The second supplies an aim instrumental to that aim – forming beliefs best-effort believed to result from the exercise of reliable processes. The second tier clearly does not demand that the subject aim at forming such beliefs apart from the instrumental value of such an aim. We do not want the subject to form beliefs best-effort believed to result from a reliable process apart from the contribution forming such beliefs makes to exercising a *reliable* process, any more than we want the subject to form beliefs by exercising a reliable process apart from the contribution forming such beliefs makes to forming *true* beliefs. There is no more conflict in the instructions offered by the first and second tiers than in the instructions offered by the first tier and the imperative to aim at true belief. (Similar remarks apply if instructions are taken to be descriptions, not of what subjects should aim at, but of what they ought to do. Both tiers describe what the subject ought to do, but the modalities are different. There is no more conflict between these instructions than there is between saying that one ought to form beliefs by exercising a reliable process and saying that one ought to believe what is true.)

Best-effort beliefs are understood in such a way that the benefits of relying on them outweigh the costs, where benefits and costs are defined in terms of facilitating the exercise of reliable belief-forming processes (i.e., the number and proportion of exercises of reliable processes). On this approach, there will be two large factors that determine which beliefs about reliability we count as amounting to best-effort beliefs. One factor is which beliefs about reliability are true. Beliefs about reliability will generally facilitate the exercise of reliable processes only when true. The second factor is how many exercises of reliable processes must be forgone to form and rely on beliefs about reliability. We will discuss the former matter in some detail in chapter VIII, when we consider again the role of evaluation in forming justified beliefs. Here it will suffice to observe that we would expect best-effort beliefs about reliability to coincide generally with reliably formed beliefs about reliability. I argued in the Introduction that reliable processes are an indispensable means to true belief. We will form true beliefs in large numbers and high proportion only if we exercise reliable processes. That is, however, a general conclusion and does not imply that for any particular kind of belief, believing truths of that kind inevitably requires reliable processes. At least, this does not follow unless the kind of belief in question is coextensive with the output of some particular process (as processes are individuated on reliabilism). Nevertheless, it seems a good bet that best-effort beliefs will generally be reliably formed. It is in part an empirical question which beliefs about reliability are best-effort beliefs. We cannot rule out a priori the possibility of best-effort beliefs about reliability that are not themselves reliably formed but rather, as we may put it, reliably formed "at one remove" – i.e., result from a process reliably but falsely believed to be reliable – or reliably formed "at two removes" – i.e., result from a process falsely believed to be reliable, where the latter belief results from a process reliably but falsely believed to be reliable – and so on. It should be noted that we may have good Cartesian reasons to hold best-effort beliefs about reliability to higher standards of reliability (or of reliability at one, two, or many removes) than we do other beliefs: these beliefs have a greater impact on the reliability of the processes we exercise (see chapter II, note 6). Perhaps in the end it is most natural to say that best-effort beliefs about reliability must themselves be epistemically responsible. Of course, saying this will touch off a regress of epistemically responsible belief if every epistemically responsible belief, and hence every best-effort belief about reliability, must rely on best-effort beliefs about reliability. But the regress is avoided if we allow epistemically responsible beliefs about reliability to result from something other than best-effort beliefs – in particular, to result from a reliable process (thereby precluding, of course, any argument for perspectival internalism from a conception of justified belief as epistemically responsible belief). I will not attempt to judge here whether there are any reliable processes that yield beliefs about reliability. If there are, I would expect them to be rough approximations of the Humean procedure of judging reliability sketched in chapter III. But this is a topic beyond the scope of this book.

To return to our discussion of mental internalism as a characterization of epistemically responsible belief, the point that emerges here is that there is no reason to believe that the status assigned by the second tier will be supervenient on mentality, any more than reliably formed belief is supervenient on mentality. The function of the second tier is to encourage subjects to rely on their best-effort beliefs about reliability, but the ultimate point of such encouragement is to facilitate the exercise of reliable processes. So the status assigned by the second tier will be shaped by considerations of when and how reliance on best-effort beliefs about reliability facilitates exercising reliable processes – and these are not considerations that supervene on mentality.

One point is that what it is to be a best-effort belief about reliability will depend on considerations of how reliance on beliefs about reliability facilitates exercising reliable processes. Thus, to adapt an example of Hilary Kornblith's (1983), whether a scientist's belief that the process by which she arrives at her theory is reliable is a best-effort belief depends on whether reliance on such a belief facilitates exercising a reliable process. Of course we do not want to say that such a belief facilitates exercising a reliable process just when it is true, since that would make epistemically responsible belief equivalent to reliably formed belief, depriving second-tier evaluation of its function of encouraging reliance on best-effort beliefs. To preserve its function, we must characterize best-effort belief about reliability only in ways that entail that it is easier to rely on such beliefs than it is simply to exercise reliable processes. Reliance on such beliefs will be limited in such a way that a subject is (broadly) able to rely on these beliefs to arrive generally at exercising reliable processes, or would at some point in her education have been in a position to become (broadly) able to do so. Suppose the scientist arrives at her belief about reliability without attending to her colleagues' criticisms of her theory. Then her belief does not count as a best-effort belief and her theory is not intuitively epistemically responsible. That is so, even if her belief about reliability accords with everything she believes (and even if her belief is true). In other words, we have an example of a sort I promised above: a belief that is not epistemically responsible but is sanctioned by the subject's perspective. The reason that her belief does not count as a best-effort belief is that reliance on such a belief is not conducive to exercising reliable processes. Whether a belief about reliability is a best-effort belief will thus turn on considerations of whether beliefs of this sort facilitate exercising a reliable process.

A more radical point than all this is that whether the subject is to rely on a best-effort belief (reliably formed at any remove) about reliability may depend on considerations about when such beliefs facilitate exercising reliable processes. Perhaps there are circumstances in which epistemically responsible belief requires ignoring one's beliefs about reliability. Such a radical point would, however, entail abandoning both (a) and (b) as accounts of epistemically responsible belief, and it might be best to leave this can of worms unopened.

The upshot of all this is that we have as yet no reason to suppose that mental internalism characterizes epistemically responsible belief. On the contrary, once epistemically responsible belief is said to be belief that results from doing one's best to believe what results from the exercise of a reliable process, there is reason to doubt that epistemically responsible belief will be characterized by mental internalism. So we have no reason to think mental

128

internalism will characterize epistemically responsible belief on either (a) or (b).

A final question remains: is justified belief the epistemic status assigned by the first tier or the second tier? One might be inclined at this point to dismiss the question as merely terminological. But terminological questions cannot be so sharply distinguished from substantive questions. We cannot assign import to various possible epistemic statuses independently of supposing them to be statuses onto which we can in some fairly direct way map the terms of ordinary epistemic evaluation. The very idea of a specifically epistemic, as opposed to moral or prudential, status is already irretrievably indebted to our ordinary concepts of knowledge and justified belief. But however this may be, the answer to the question just posed is: the *first* tier – *if*, as seems intuitively right, epistemically responsible belief is belief that results from doing one's best to believe what one is justified in believing. Justified belief is reliably formed belief.

We have rejected the responsibility argument for perspectival and mental internalism. Before we turn to the intuitive case for mental internalism, it is worth noting that there are plausible counterexamples to perspectival internalism. It seems possible for a subject to believe justifiably that the belief *p* is reliable even though the belief *p* is unjustified. On the face of it, subjects can be just as mistaken in their justified epistemic beliefs as in any other justified beliefs they have. To adapt an example of Alston's:

> consider a college student who just doesn't have what it takes to follow abstract philosophical reasoning, or exposition for that matter. Having read Bk. IV of Locke's *Essay*, he believes that it is Locke's view that everything is a matter of opinion, that one person's opinion is as good as another's, and that what is true for me may not be true for you. And it's not just that he didn't work hard enough on this particular point, or on the general abilities involved. There is nothing that he could and should have done such that had he done so, he would have gotten this straight. He is simply incapable of appreciating the distinction between "One's knowledge is restricted to one's own ideas" and "Everything is a matter of opinion." No doubt teachers of philosophy tend to assume too quickly that this description applies to some of their students, but surely there can be such

cases; cases in which either no amount of time and effort would enable the student to get straight on the matter, or it would be unreasonable to expect the person to expend that amount of time or effort. And yet we would hardly wish to say that the student is justified in believing what he does about Locke.

(Alston 1989a: 68)

Alston's point is that it is possible to be blameless in one's belief, with respect to fulfilling one's intellectual obligations and yet fail to be justified in that belief.[9] In my view his example does show that epistemically responsible belief is not sufficient for justified belief.[10] However, my point here is that the example also shows something else: that a subject can be (doxastically or propositionally) justified in believing that his belief *p* is reliable and yet fail to be (doxastically) justified in believing *p*. The student is not (doxastically) justified in his belief that Locke is a relativist. Nevertheless, it is plausible to suppose that he could be (doxastically or propositionally) justified in believing that his belief *p* is reliable. He could reflect on the steps that he has taken to ensure that he has understood Locke aright, note that he has been diligent and careful, and infer with justification (though mistakenly) that he has done as much as needed for his interpretive belief to be reliable. It is true that the student would have arrived at another conclusion about the reliability of his interpretive belief had he checked his interpretation with an authority, but it does not follow that he is unjustified in his conclusion. What if he has no reason to suspect that his efforts are likely to lead to an incorrect interpretation of Locke? His observation of his own diligence will suffice, in light of his justified belief that diligence suffices for reliability here. Thus, not everything that (doxastically) justifies his belief that his interpretive belief is reliable must also justify the interpretive belief itself. We do not change our view that his interpretive belief is unjustified when we hear that he has observed his own diligence. The proponent of perspectival internalism might insist that the student is not sufficiently justified in believing that his interpretive belief is reliable if he has no reason to believe that an authority would concur, yet having such a reason would entail that his interpretive belief is justified. But I believe this runs counter to our intuition. Moreover, we may ask on what basis the perpectival internalist could insist that having reason to believe that an authority would concur is necessary for being justified in believing the interpretive belief is reliable. Certainly not on perspectival grounds alone, since there is nothing about the idea that justified beliefs are those sanctioned by the subject's perspective that would show that more is needed for this belief to be justified than a belief in one's diligence (assuming of course the presence as well of the justified belief that diligence here entails reliability). The perspectival internalist can insist on more only by bringing in something other than purely perspectival considerations, either at the second order, or at some higher order of justification. The claim that the student is justified in his interpretive belief if he is justified in believing that his belief is reliable can be made out in the present case only by importing nonperspectival considerations at some order.

The perspectival internalist might respond instead that even if being doxastically or propositionally justified in believing that the belief p is reliable does not entail being *doxastically* justified in believing p, it does entail being *propositionally* justified in believing it. For if the subject is doxastically or propositionally justified in believing that the belief p is reliable, he can always make the following inference: the process that forms the belief p is reliable. So p belongs to a reference class of propositions most of which are true. Therefore, probably p. I am willing to grant for the sake of argument that this inference would be justifying if its premise were justified, the output of the process sufficiently broad, and the process believed to be sufficiently reliable – conditions that obtain in the case of the student. But propositional justification requires something further: that the inference be not merely justifying but available for exercise, and nothing here guarantees its availability. We therefore have a counterexample to perspectival internalism.

2 The vat argument for mental internalism

It is popular to argue for mental internalism by appeal to our intuitions about the demon example, now posed as a *metaphysical* possibility in which we are bound to have justified belief, rather than as a prima facie possibility that must be ruled out if we are to have justified belief. The same example is said to tell against reliabilism (Luper-Foy 1985; Foley 1987). We are asked to consider a subject who is mentally just like an actual human subject on earth – experiences and believes what that subject does – but who is systematically deceived by a demon, or who is a brain in a vat systematically deceived by a computer. I will focus here on the vat example, since it avoids the controversial assumption that disembodied existence is possible. The claim is that intuitively the vat (or demon) subject is justified in believing exactly the propositions his earthly mental twin is justified in believing, despite the extreme dissimilarity of their external circumstances. Thus any two mentally similar subjects are justified in believing the same propositions, no matter how different their surroundings may be. That is, justification supervenes on mentality, as mental internalism claims, and reliabilism is mistaken in its judgment that the vat subject is unjustified.[11]

There are two good reasons to dismiss this argument out of hand.[12] One is that the vat example is ruled metaphysically impossible by an attractive view of mental representation, an *externalist* view, on which beliefs have propositional content in virtue of their relations (paradigmatically, causal relations) to objects in their environment. Externalism about mental representation entails that it is metaphysically impossible for a subject to represent a world wholly different from the one in which he lives.[13] Thus, the vat example is metaphysically impossible. It should be noted that my point here against using the vat example to support mental internalism or oppose reliabilism does not depend on accepting externalism about mental representation. It merely depends on the methodological principle that an argument for mental internalism or a counterexample to reliabilism ought not to turn on denying an attractive view of mental representation, especially not one to which reliabilists are apt to subscribe.

The second reason for dismissing the vat argument is that it is doubtful that we ought to have the intuition that the vat subject is justified. There are two grounds for rejecting our intuition. (1) As opponents of coherentism are fond of pointing out, we do not think that the subject who spins a coherent fantasy so convincingly that he ultimately deceives himself into experiencing and believing just what I do would be justified in his beliefs if they were completely out of line with the way things actually are (assuming, as we are now doing, that this is even possible). (This is not to deny that the coherent fantasy would be justified if the world were roughly like our own and the subject's beliefs were largely true and the processes were reliable.) Why, then, should we think that the brain-in-a-vat whose beliefs are completely out of line with the way things are is justified merely because he experiences and believes what I do?

One possible answer would be that the fantasist *induces* the experiences and beliefs in himself, while the vat subject does not do so. But why would this difference matter? A second answer is that the fantasist is engaged in self-deception and thus has contradictory beliefs, and these undermine his justification for his beliefs. But notice that the fantasist need not have contradictory beliefs at any particular time. Suppose that he deceives himself in this way: he constructs a computer that, when activated, will erase his current beliefs and memories and induce in him experiences and beliefs like the ones I have at a certain time. He then willingly activates the computer. Here there are no contradictory beliefs at any particular time. Yet we retain the intuition that he is unjustified in his beliefs. The proponent of the vat counterexample might instead maintain that the fantasist is bound to have contradictory beliefs across time, and these undermine his justification. (Such a response does, however, entail a historical view of justification contrary to the ahistorical mental internalism of most proponents of the vat counterexample (Foley 1987).) But certainly it is not *generally* true that beliefs a subject held in the past undermine his current justification merely in virtue of contradicting his current beliefs. So why should these particular contradictions across time undermine the fantasist's justification? The proponent of the vat example might, finally, claim that the fantasist's motive – self-deception rather than truth-seeking – undermines his justification. But actual motives in forming beliefs do not *generally* undermine justification. One is justified in one's reliably formed perceptual beliefs even if one fails to form them as the result of truth-seeking or indeed forms them as the result of aiming to deceive oneself. None of these ways of distinguishing the fantasist from the brain-in-a-vat is obviously successful. In the end, the best explanation of our intuition that the fantasist is unjustified would seem to be that his beliefs are so far out of line with the way things are that his processes are unreliable. But if this is the explanation of our intuition about the fantasist, our intuitions must carry over to the brain-in-a-vat. (Needless to say, this claim tells not only against the vat argument but against mental internalism as well.)

(2) An additional reason to doubt that we ought to have the intuition that the vat subject is justified is that this intuition makes it impossible for Descartes to raise a skeptical challenge to justified belief by citing the possibility of deception by a demon. If it were intuitive that we are justified even when deceived by a demon (or no less justified than we are in the circumstances we take to be actual), then Descartes could not raise the question whether we are justified by observing that it is prima facie possible that we are deceived by a demon. The demon challenge requires at least that it not be obvious that we are justified when deceived by a demon (or that it be less obvious that we are justified in such a case than in the circumstances we take to be actual). If we wish to maintain that the demon possibility raises a skeptical challenge, the only way to save the claim that the vat subject is intuitively justified is to insist that the demon possibility challenges, not justified belief, but knowledge – and thus that it challenges our satisfying the condition that consists of the difference between knowledge and justified true belief, i.e., the fourth condition of knowledge of Gettier fame. But it is surely implausible that Descartes intends to raise such a challenge, or that he has any conception of knowledge beyond what we call justified true belief (see chapter II, note 7).

Might the proponent of the vat argument and mental internalism respond by interpreting the demon challenge in another way? On this alternative interpretation, the demon challenge is this: if we are justified in our beliefs in the actual world, then we must be justified in them in the demon world; but we are not justified in them in the demon world; so we are not justified in them in the actual world. The validity of this challenge is not merely consistent with mental internalism; it *assumes* it. But on what ground could it be claimed that we are unjustified in the demon world other than the ground of unreliability in that world? Clearly the mental internalist is prohibited by his own view from appealing to unreliability to establish that the vat subject is unjustified, and so cannot support the premise of this alternative demon challenge.

I believe, then, that we have sufficient reason to reject the vat argument without further consideration.[14] We are left, however, with a significant question: why we have the intuition that the vat subject is justified in his beliefs (or if we do not have that intuition, why epistemologists erroneously judge us to have it). If we evaluate justified belief in accordance with reliabilism, we ought to say that the vat subject is unjustified in his belief. What would explain our erroneous intuition about the vat subject (or our erroneous theoretical judgment that we have that intuition)?[15]

It is tempting for the reliabilist to deny that we have this intuition, and to claim that the appearance of having it derives from a theoretical confusion – a confusion of our intuition about justified belief with our intuition about epistemically responsible belief. This response would allow that we have the (correct) intuition that the vat subject's belief is epistemically responsible, but deny that we have the quite different intuition that his belief is justified.

I believe we should resist this tempting response. For one thing, it trades one question for another: now we must say why epistemologists confuse our intuition about epistemically responsible belief with our intuition about justified belief. Another problem is that the account of epistemically responsible belief that goes naturally with reliabilism – the account suggested in section 1 – does not obviously allow the vat subject's belief to be epistemically responsible. This account keys doing the best one can to external circumstances and thus need not judge the vat subject's belief epistemically responsible. There is no reason to suppose that the vat subject's beliefs about reliability are reliably formed. On the contrary, the reliability of the process that leads to our beliefs about the reliability of perceptual processes must be low, since, as I assumed in discussing the Humean procedure for judging reliability, it depends on the reliability of these processes themselves. But if the vat subject's beliefs about reliability are not reliably formed (or reliably formed at some remove), then they will not count as best-effort beliefs, and so the vat subject's other beliefs will not be epistemically responsible on the present account of epistemically responsible belief. In short a reliabilist has theoretical reason to deny that the vat subject's beliefs are epistemically responsible.

Equally importantly, it is doubtful that we do have the intuition that the vat subject's beliefs are epistemically responsible. At the very least, there is reason to admit that we have this intuition only on mental internalism about justified belief. For consider an analogous issue: could a quadriplegic ever be said to do the best he can to play basketball? Suppose his only physical ability is to lift his head slightly above his pillow. What would doing the best he can consist in here – lifting his head and thinking

135

such thoughts as "I wish I could get on the basketball court, get possession of the ball, dribble the ball, block, etc." or, bizarrely, "I must try to get to the court, etc."? Even if he were under the illusion that he could get to the basketball court and play basketball, it is very doubtful that lifting his head and thinking such thoughts would constitute doing the best he could to play basketball (or would even constitute *trying* to play basketball). The subject would seem to be in the same position I would be in were I to undertake to fly unaided to the moon. There would not seem to be any actions I could take that would constitute doing my best to fly unaided to the moon (or would even constitute trying to do so). And this would be so, even if I were under the illusion that I could succeed in flying unaided to the moon. This is not to say that when the quadriplegic lifts his head and has his thoughts he is doing less than he could to play basketball. On the contrary, the problem is precisely that there is nothing at all he could do to bring it about that he plays basketball, or even to bring it about that he has any chance of doing so. I am suggesting that it is a necessary condition of doing the best one can to play basketball that there be something one could do that has some chance of bringing it about that one plays basketball. Whether these points carry over to epistemically responsible belief depends on whether justified belief is like playing basketball in being an externally characterized activity. If justified belief is externally characterized, then there is nothing the vat subject can do (except accidentally) that has any chance of bringing it about that he is justified. It may well be impossible for him to do his best to be justified. Thus the reliabilist ought not to admit that we have the intuition that the vat subject's beliefs are epistemically responsible. By the same token, the mental internalist is forbidden from arguing against the reliabilist account of epistemically responsible belief by appeal to the alleged intuition. Such an appeal begs the question against reliabilism. At the same time, the reliabilist must look elsewhere for an explanation of the apparent intuition that the vat subject is justified.

In my view the reliabilist should come clean and admit the plain and uncomfortable fact that we do have this intuition. While our intuition is difficult to explain, this can undermine reliabilism only if our suspicion that the intuition cannot be explained without admitting its truth overpowers our confidence in countervailing theoretical considerations. And I do not think that this is obviously so. At any rate, the most promising explanation for our intuition would seem to go something like this.

Our evaluative dispositions are forged in everyday evaluations of beliefs and therefore serve us poorly when applied to outlandish circumstances like those of the vat example. Most real life evaluation is of beliefs in the actual world (or in possible worlds rather similar to the actual world). Very little evaluation is of beliefs in remote possible worlds. People evaluate on the basis of long-standing and largely unquestioned assumptions about which processes are reliable and unreliable. The fact that most evaluation concerns beliefs in the actual world enables us to rely on a stock list of justifying processes, and evaluative efficiency encourages such reliance. Thus, in routine evaluations, we may evaluate beliefs by judging only which process is exercised, without noting whether it is reliable. The processes we evaluate retain their status from one evaluation to the next, since they remain reliable or unreliable across all examples in the actual world. The epistemically relevant processes, though numerous, belong to a few kinds – perception, induction, deduction, hasty generalization, sweeping generalization, wishful thinking, and the like – and they vary along a few manageable parameters (see chapter VI). Consequently, we do not have to assess the reliability of a new process each time we evaluate justified belief in the actual world. We make a few assessments that serve our evaluative purposes repeatedly. It is true that we must occasionally revise our assessments of reliability in light of our changing beliefs about the actual world – from time to time dropping some processes from the list of reliable processes and adding others. But belief change is slow enough that we need to revise these assessments only very occasionally. Given these facts about evaluating beliefs in the actual world, and given the fact that we must in any event identify processes by their psychological character, evaluative efficiency recommends that we evaluate on most occasions by looking only at the psychological character of the processes exercised. There is no need to consider in addition whether the processes are reliable. Thus we tend to assess beliefs as justified by considering only the psychological characteristics of the processes exercised. Our disposition to assess justified beliefs in this fashion serves us well enough when we assess beliefs in the actual world. But when we turn to the vat world, we neglect the fact that processes differ in reliability there, and we assess as justified beliefs produced by processes with the same psychological characteristics as processes that are justifying because reliable in the actual world.

It may be replied that we could be expected to notice the differences in reliability in the two cases and that we would make allowances for it if it were relevant. But this reply may underestimate the extent to which our intuitions result from long-established evaluative dispositions. It is true that evaluators must be able to revise their lists of justifying processes in accordance with their assessments of reliability. But the course of revision may itself result from certain dispositions to revise and thus be largely automatic. It is also true that it is practically desirable for evaluators to assess processes differently on the basis of differences in reliability even in worlds fairly similar to the actual world, so that evaluators must be able to bring considerations of reliability to bear in evaluating counterfactual examples. But it may be that these considerations kick in only under practical mandates, or when attention is called in a standard and useful way to the reliability of the processes evaluated – as it arguably is in the case of the unjustified coherent fantasy, where the subject's self-deception calls our attention to the reliability of the processes he employs and induces in himself. There is no comparable feature of the vat example – no unusual process exercised by the subject – that would call our attention to the reliability of the processes. In short, there is no reason to expect that in everyday evaluation we would notice the differences in reliability in the actual and vat worlds. Our evaluations of processes might well carry over in virtue of their psychological characteristics.

This explanation of our erroneous intuition about the vat example is admittedly tenuous. It depends on empirical claims that have yet to be made out. And it must be formulated more precisely than I have been able to do if we are to avoid a runaway all-purpose counterexample disarmer.[16] The present point is that some such explanation is not unpromising, and that is enough to cast doubt on the claim that reliabilism is clearly inconsistent with the correct intuition about the vat example.

To summarize: we have found the responsibility argument for perspectival and mental internalism wanting. Nor is there reason to believe that epistemically responsible belief will be characterized by mental internalism. I regard what we have said in this and the preceding chapter as undermining the general arguments for all the forms of internalism we have considered – accessibility, perspectival, and mental internalism. I believe we have also given good reason for rejecting accessibility and perspectival internalism. We have not, I admit, offered any objection to other forms of mental internalism such as coherentism. Though most versions of coherentism are supported by appeal to perspectival internalism, some are not. But we will not be able to consider these views here. Our argument suffices to motivate the long look at externalism we will now take.

CHAPTER VI

Reliability, Relevant Processes, and Metaprocesses

In the remaining chapters I will develop reliabilism and defend it from some intuitive internalist objections.[1] In this chapter I will undertake a task widely recognized to be central to the formulation of reliabilism: specifying which processes are *relevant* in evaluating justified beliefs – or equivalently, individuating processes in an epistemically relevant way. As we have already seen, it is a task that bears significantly on the case for consequent skepticism. Recall Hume's worries that imaginative operations, such as those that yield the belief in body and those involved in induction, are simply the same as those involved in wild imagination or bright fancy. I interpreted Hume as worrying that processes will be individuated so broadly that intuitively justifying imaginative processes will be dragged down by clearly unreliable ones. There are considerations that favor a broad individuation of processes, but there are also many considerations that favor a narrow individuation.

1 Relevant processes

The task before us is to specify, given a belief on an occasion, which of the processes that form the belief is relevant to judging whether the belief is justified. We must specify the process the reliability or unreliability of which determines whether or not the belief is justified. Any belief is formed by countless processes (or, if you like, by a single process describable in countless ways), and among these there will always be many reliable and unreliable processes. Thus, if reliabilism is to determine a unique answer to the question whether the belief is justified, we must specify which process is relevant to the belief on the occasion. For purposes of assessing reliability, the task of specifying which process is relevant is equivalent to that of individuating processes by output – i.e., identifying a unique class of beliefs in the actual world (and unique classes in nearby counterfactual worlds), usually called a reference class (or set of such classes for the different nearby worlds).[2] The reliability of the relevant process is the frequency of true beliefs in this reference class. The task is sometimes called the "generality problem" in honor of its focus on the extent of the reference class.

It is easy to see that we must avoid individuating processes too narrowly or too broadly (Feldman 1985). At one extreme, we must avoid individuating processes so narrowly that they produce single beliefs, since then processes that yield true beliefs will trivially be reliable, and the beliefs they yield will trivially be justified. At the other extreme, we must avoid individuating processes so broadly that, say, the generic perceptual process is the one relevant to any perceptual belief. For in this case, all perceptual beliefs will come out justified, contrary to intuition. A broad individuation is also ruled out if reliabilism is to offer a natural account of degrees of justification to supplement its account of justified belief. Such an account would say that a belief is justified to the degree that the relevant process on the occasion is reliable. But then relevant processes must be so narrowly individuated that each process yields only beliefs that are justified to the *same* degree, a degree identical with the reliability of the process. We must, then, avoid both very narrow and very broad processes.

Let me confess at the outset that I have no criterion of relevance to propose here, if what is meant by a "criterion" is a set of necessary and sufficient conditions. Some opponents of reliabilism have suggested that the view needs a criterion of relevance if it is to explain or be supported by our intuitions about examples of justified beliefs, and some have thought it an embarrassment for reliabilism that no adequate criterion has yet been proposed.[3] But I reject the need for a criterion.

For one thing, reliabilism may explain and be supported by our intuitions about justification even if we lack any theoretical account of individuation that might explain why we fasten on the particular processes we do. For we have intuitions about which processes are relevant. In judging whether a subject is justified in an inferential belief, we check to see which inferential process the subject exercises – e.g., whether it is induction from sufficiently many instances or affirming the consequent. We have the intuition that these are the relevant processes to consider. In the case of perceptual belief, we check which environmental conditions obtain – whether it is sunny or foggy – and whether the subject is careful and attentive in perception or quick and distracted. Here again we have intuitions about which processes are relevant. Reliabilism may explain why perceptual or inferential beliefs are justified or unjustified by relying on these intuitions.

Second, reliabilism may explain why we fasten on the particular processes we do without a criterion of relevance. It is enough to have a list of constraints on relevance for which some motivation can be provided. The constraints I have in mind characterize an aspect of the pragmatics of justified belief, rather than its semantics. The constraints are thus not strictly part of the concept of justified belief. I do not rule out semantical constraints, but I have none to offer here. (One might question the distinction between semantics and pragmatics for evaluative properties, but I will not go into the matter here.) The constraints that seem most likely to explain our intuitions describe the pragmatic conditions of epistemic evaluation. In particular, they describe the conditions that make evaluation feasible for us in our actual circumstances and the conditions necessary for epistemic evaluation to achieve its ends, especially the end of promoting and facilitating true belief. Epistemic evaluation functions to bring about true belief by promoting justified belief, thus enabling us to form more true beliefs, in number and proportion, than we would without evaluation. Some constraints describe the conditions necessary for epistemic evaluation to function in this way.[4]

The pragmatic conditions and ends of epistemic evaluation are rather fluid, so our constraints are bound to be vague. But there is no harm in this, so long as their vagueness roughly mirrors the vagueness of our intuitions about justification. To apply the constraints to examples we will often need to have in mind some proper class of processes, yet we will be unable to specify just which class it is appropriate to have in mind for a given example. Most of the constraints propose conditions that hold only ceteris paribus. But I will not attempt a complete list of constraints, so we will never quite know when other things are equal. As is always the case with ceteris paribus constraints, applying the constraints to examples in which other things are not equal requires balancing the constraints against one another. Most of the constraints will maximize some quantity, and balancing the constraints therefore involves comparing these quantities, but I will be unable to say just how they should be compared or even guarantee that they are comparable. For these reasons, applying the constraints to examples will require relying on our instincts about the nature of evaluation as conceived by reliabilism. Despite all this, our predicament is no worse than it is in other arenas ruled by ceteris paribus constraints – e.g., folk psychological explanations of action. Nothing here should prevent us from using our constraints to offer rough reliabilist explanations of our intuitions about justification. We explain our intuitions by judging which factors matter most and holding the other factors equal. We then apply the constraints that pertain to the important factors, rank-ordering them as best we can in light of our conception of the pragmatic conditions and ends of evaluation.

Let us proceed, then, with our list of constraints.

(1)*Salience Constraint.* The business of epistemology is in the first instance to characterize the property evaluators have in mind when they evaluate justified belief. That imposes a constraint on an account of justified belief: we must state the account in the terms in which evaluators think and talk. If we all have the same concept of justified belief, then our account of justified belief must employ terms common to all who evaluate. I would like to urge that an analogous constraint applies to relevant processes, though for a different reason. Neither the constraints on relevance nor the list of relevant processes are themselves part of our concept of justified belief – only of the pragmatics of justified belief – so the fact that our concept characterizes what all evaluators have in mind in evaluating justified belief does not yet entail that the constraints or list must be common to ordinary evaluators. The pragmatics of justified belief does, however, entail this. For the practice of evaluation is feasible only if evaluators can communicate their evaluations and teach others evaluative standards. To communicate their evaluations, evaluators must share their evaluative vocabulary. If we teach evaluative standards, we must agree to a large extent on which processes are relevant and on whether reliable relevant processes are exercised on given occasions. And this entails that we have in mind the same constraints on relevance and the same list of relevant processes. Evaluators must therefore share their vocabulary of relevant processes and the constraints on these processes. These requirements are reinforced by the point that justified belief is a deontic status, and the evaluation of such a status is designed to promote and facilitate its object. Toward this end, evaluators must be able to motivate subjects to conform to their evaluations, and this again requires a shared vocabulary of relevant processes and agreement on which processes are relevant. The pragmatics of evaluation entails something more. Evaluation will promote and facilitate justified belief only to the extent that evaluators are generally *accurate* in their beliefs as to whether subjects exercise relevant processes and relevant processes are reliable. (Perhaps pragmatics entails as well the absolute requirement that evaluators are generally accurate in these beliefs, but I will not press the claim.)

Thus we may lay down the Salience Constraint:

(a) Relevant processes are those in terms of which evaluators think and talk; and

(b) Ceteris paribus, relevant processes are individuated so as to maximize the accuracy of beliefs about whether subjects exercise reliable relevant processes.

I assume that the constraint requires maximizing among the systems of evaluation that are feasible for us. (If maximizing is judged too optimistic, it may be replaced without loss of explanatory power here and in the constraints below, with maximizing up to a criterion, provided the criterion is sufficiently high. I suspect it may also be replaced by satisficing, but I have not yet found a way to reformulate my applications of the constraints in terms of satisficing.) It should be noted that, since the constraint entails that the relevant processes maximize the accuracy of evaluators' beliefs about which processes are relevant, it also entails maximizing the accuracy of their beliefs about which processes conform to the constraint itself.

The constraint favors *broader* processes. For evaluators have more accurate beliefs about the reliability of broader processes. Broader processes yield more beliefs (or their negations), and so evaluators have a broader basis on which to assess their reliability.

(2) *Folk Process Constraint.* In speaking of what is generally true of evaluators, we must already have a fixed class of evaluators in mind. There is clearly an interaction between this class of evaluators and the processes that are deemed relevant under the Salience Constraint. If, for example, we have in mind the class of

all epistemic evaluators, we encompass virtually all mature human beings, and the relevant processes will have to be those recognized by ordinary psychology, including the processes we natively have the capacity to exercise and the processes and methods that we acquire the ability to exercise in virtue of common experience. But we might instead have in mind a smaller community of evaluators – e.g., a group of scientists who engage in a practice of evaluation referring to processes unknown to others (e.g., a process reflecting Neyman–Pearson statistics). One way to handle this freedom in the choice of the community of evaluators is to relativize the individuation of processes to given classes of evaluators. But while the individuation of processes is no doubt relativized to some degree, I do not believe it is relativized to arbitrary communities of evaluators. The evidence of intuition is that we have in mind very large classes of evaluators, encompassing a substantial portion of mature subjects belonging to a culture. Perhaps the explanation is that evaluation is feasible only when there are few options for relativization, and economical evaluation requires conditions that can be employed for a great variety of purposes, encompassing many circumstances. That militates in favor of evaluation that employs an ordinary vocabulary, referring to ordinary processes. Nevertheless, as we will see, the system of ordinary evaluation does seem to make provisions for extraordinary evaluation by a small community of evaluators when this evaluation is coupled in the right way with ordinary evaluation. And it allows extraordinary processes (methods) to be valued by members of a small community when these processes are coupled in the right way with ordinary processes. With certain important exceptions, then, relevant processes are *folk psychological processes*. Folk psychology is our common everyday system of psychological attribution and explanation. It is a pervasive and, for all we know about human psychology, ineradicable way of thinking about human beings. Attributions of folk processes figure centrally in our everyday explanations and predictions of cognitive and bodily behavior. They also figure centrally, I am now suggesting, in our epistemic evaluations. We may lay down the constraint:

> Relevant processes are (with extraordinary exceptions to be explained below) *folk* processes.

Processes are of course sequences of events arranged in a causal chain. I have not so far attempted to anatomize the relevant processes in terms of the events that compose them. Given the Folk Process Constraint, that difficult task may be left to the business of characterizing folk psychology itself. It is worth noting, however, that many folk processes are specified by the sequences of events that normally conform to inductive and deductive rules of inference. The temptation in epistemology to suppose that normal processes are necessary for justification may derive from the fact that in many instances, our only way of specifying folk processes is by ostension to normal circumstances.

In making the relevant processes folk processes, I am not yet rejecting Hume's use of the results of scientific psychology to judge how processes are individuated – to judge, for example, that what we call sense perception is an imaginative process – since Hume's use does not entail the relevance of processes that are not folk processes; it simply identifies certain folk processes with certain apparently different folk processes. But folk psychology does provide the resources to distinguish sense perception from imagination, and, as I will argue below, other constraints may entail the relevance of these processes so distinguished. In addition, the Salience Constraint favors individuating so that ordinary evaluators correctly individuate processes, and thus it presses against using surprising results of scientific psychology to distinguish relevant processes.

More importantly, the Folk Process Constraint contradicts Alvin Goldman's (1986) idea that the relevant processes include those described by scientific rather than folk psychology. Neither ordinary evaluators nor scientists ordinarily think in terms of such processes. Nor do we have the means to judge accurately whether such processes are exercised on given occasions or to assess accurately their reliability. True, they are processes we actually exercise, just as folk processes are, and so we can assess their average reliability, since it is the same as our overall frequency of true beliefs. But this is not the same as being able to assess the reliability of particular processes. We cannot generally gather the experimental data (reaction-time or error data) or know the theories necessary to discern which scientific processes are exercised or to assess their reliability. A proponent of scientific processes might dig in and reply that the practical limitations of evaluation should not be written into the account of justification, but should instead be taken only to excuse or justify erroneous evaluations of justification. While I would not deny the distinction between correct and justified evaluations of justification, I find counterintuitive an account of justification on which thinking about justification in the terms of the account and correct evaluations of justification are beyond the reach of most evaluators.

To say this is most emphatically *not* to deny that scientific psychology bears on epistemology. On the contrary, it may bear in several important ways (Schmitt forthcoming a). (i) Scientific psychology may tell us just which processes satisfy the Salience and Folk Process Constraints and in this way enable epistemologists to formulate a detailed account of relevant processes. As we have observed, the Salience Constraint itself entails that the relevant processes maximize the accuracy of evaluations, including beliefs about which processes are relevant and hence, we may now add, about which processes are folk processes. But it does not follow that evaluators judge precisely and with high accuracy which processes satisfy the constraints or are folk processes. Scientific psychology may discover just which folk processes evaluators have in mind when they evaluate justified belief. It may discover which processes evaluators are able to judge accurately. It may also discover which processes are folk processes. It is the business of attribution theory in social psychology to characterize folk psychology itself, and part of the characterization is the theory of folk processes. In addition, scientific psychology may aid the epistemological task of judging the reliability of folk processes. It may supplement and, within limits, correct our naive beliefs about whether these processes are exercised on given occasions, as well as our assessments of the reliability of these processes. It cannot overturn all or even the better part of these beliefs, since the very result that we are substantially wrong about whether a process is exercised or reliable would give us reason to doubt that it is a folk process. This is so, not only because folk psychology can succeed in explaining and predicting behaviour as well as it does only if its attributions are true, but more importantly, because epistemic evaluation can succeed as well as it does in facilitating the epistemic end of true belief only if our beliefs about whether processes are exercised and our assessments of the reliability of processes are correct. Even so, scientific psychology can provide limited correction of naive evaluation.

(ii) More profoundly, scientific psychology may study not only folk psychology, but folk *epistemology* as well. It may tell us how we naively evaluate justified belief and assess reliability. This information can help epistemologists gauge the nature of epistemic evaluation and thus derivatively the nature of justified belief. Significant work along these lines is beginning to appear (Neisser 1976, 1982; Rogoff and Lave 1984).

(iii) Scientific psychology may *transform* folk psychology as the result of education. Folk psychology is not a static, fixed system of attribution and explanation, but changes with the diffusion of new ways of thinking. Scientific concepts, principles, and modes of explanation diffuse into the general public and become folk property. Thus folk psychology was transformed early in this century by Freudian psychology. There are now many folk concepts ("id," "ego," "repression," etc.) that did not exist before Freud. And arguably folk psychology is now being transformed by information-processing cognitive psychology and by modes of psychological explanation based on analogies with computer programming. And it seems likely that folk psychology will be transformed in the future by developments in neurophysiology.

(iv) A final point, orthogonal to the preceding, is that scientific psychology may help epistemologists recommend improved institutions of epistemic evaluation. Just as scientific psychology leads to revisions of folk psychology that improve the predictive and explanatory power of folk psychology, it may equally lead to revisions in folk epistemology that improve the accuracy of folk evaluations, the reliability of the processes exercised as a result of evaluation, and ultimately the number and proportion of true beliefs. These, then, are some of the important ways scientific psychology may interact with epistemology and with the practice of evaluation even under the Folk Process Constraint.

To return to the constraint, the relevant processes are (with certain special exceptions) the perceptual, introspective, inferential, memorial, and fallacious processes recognized by folk psychology. These processes are further divided – the perceptual processes into visual, auditory, olfactory, etc. perceptual processes; the inferential into processes specific to inferential forms (induction, deduction – modus ponens, various forms of balancing evidence, perhaps hypothetico-deduction, hypothetico-induction, inference to the best explanation). The fallacious modes of reasoning include sweeping generalization, hasty generalization, wishful thinking, appeal to authority, appeal to pity, etc., and we would expect these (or folk psychological subprocesses of them – i.e., folk processes the output of which is a subset of these processes) to be among the relevant processes. The most helpful studies of fallacious reasoning for our purposes are to be found in the philosophical literature on critical thinking and the psychological literature on heuristics and probabilistic and deductive inference (Kahneman, Slovic, and Tversky 1982).

Folk psychology does not, however, recognize some of the bizarre, chimaerical processes that have been used to construct counterexamples to reliabilism. For instance, Steven Luper-Foy proposes a counterexample to reliabilism involving this rule of inference:

> For all *S*, *If*: *S* (believes that *S*) seems to see a table at some time, *or S* (believes that *S*) seems to see 12 centaurs pulling the sleigh of a fat, jolly elf at some time, *infer*: There is a table in front of *S* at that time.

> (Luper-Foy 1985: 212)

Luper-Foy claims that the inference in accordance with this rule is not justifying even though the rule is reliable. I doubt whether this rule specifies any particular inferential process. The complaint must be that *some* inferential process that conforms to the rule (i.e., is input–output coextensive with the rule in actual and nearby counterfactual worlds) and is thus reliable fails to be justifying. But there is no such folk process. If nearby worlds are sufficiently far from the actual world, then in some of them the subject will seem to see twelve centaurs pulling the sleigh of a fat, jolly elf, and infer by some process that there is a table in front of him. But no such process is a folk process. If, on the other hand, nearby worlds are not very far from the actual world, there will be no such inferences. In this case, some processes that conform to the rule may be folk processes, but there is no reason to deny that they are justifying when reliable. Of course folk psychology does make some provision for acquiring and following rules, but there is no reason to suppose that the folk process involved in following a rule will have the same extension as that rule: if its extension is broader, this will prevent us from inferring the reliability of the process from the reliability of the rule (see the next section). In any event, the Folk Process Constraint rules out counterexamples based on artificially concocted rules and processes. It is worth noting, too, that the constraint probably rules out processes with a single belief as output, since it is doubtful that any folk process yields a single belief.

The Folk Process Constraint sets up a system of perceptual, introspective, inferential, and memorial processes that work together to build our system of justified beliefs. That imposes a structure on justification. For the reliability required of inferential processes will have to differ from that required of noninferential processes: we cannot expect induction or deduction to be *unconditionally* reliable (i.e., generally yield true beliefs), only *conditionally* reliable (i.e., generally yield true beliefs given true inputs). We therefore require only conditional reliability of inferential processes, and we require unconditional reliability only of noninferential processes. Of course, if a sufficiently high proportion of inputs to induction and deduction were true, the distinction between conditional and unconditional reliability would collapse, and we could require unconditional reliability of inferential processes. But we cannot assume that so many inputs are true. On the other hand, if justified belief is to contribute to the end of true belief, it cannot merely be belief that results from a conditionally reliable inferential process, since that does not entail anything about the truth of the belief. If we wish to sanction true beliefs, we must require at least that a justified inferential belief results from a chain of conditionally reliable inferential processes initiated by an unconditionally reliable noninferential process.

The requirement of chains is considerably weaker than the simple reliabilist requirement that justified belief results from an unconditionally reliable process, since the conditionally reliable inferential processes in a chain of such processes will diminish the unconditional reliability of the initiating noninferential process (if the inferential processes have conditional reliability less than one). The simple reliabilist requirement in fact rules out justification by indefinitely long chains of conditionally reliable inferential processes, while the weaker requirement of chains allows this. I doubt whether intuition will decisively settle the issue between these two requirements. It is natural to doubt that we are justified in beliefs that result from indefinitely long chains of inductive inferences on the ground that they reduce reliability below any given threshold. But it is at least as natural to insist that we *are* justified because the inferential processes are after all conditionally reliable. Nor does the basic idea of reliabilism favor the simple over the weaker requirement here. Opting for the simple requirement does, however, entail a rather robust skepticism about general and theoretical justified belief.[5] I believe this gives an edge to the weaker requirement, so I will assume it.

(3) *Intrinsic Similarity Constraint*. The Folk Process Constraint suggests another constraint. Folk psychology employs folk processes to explain cognition and action. Explanations of this sort appeal in part to the intrinsic character of these processes – or more accurately, to the intrinsic character of their exercises – as well as to the intrinsic and representational character of the inputs to the processes. If we are to explain similar instances of cognition or action on several occasions by appeal to the *same* process, and in virtue of the intrinsic character of this process, we must assume that the exercises of the process have a similar intrinsic character on these occasions. Likewise, if we are to explain different instances of cognition or action by appeal to different processes in virtue of the intrinsic character of the processes, we must assume that the exercises of the process differ in their instrinsic character. The upshot is that, other things equal, folk processes are individuated so as to maximize the intrinsic similarity of the exercises of a single process and the intrinsic dissimilarity of the exercises of distinct processes (where maximizing dissimilarity simply means ensuring that the exercises of distinct processes are not similar – not that their exercises are as dissimilar as possible). Other things equal, folk processes are individuated as far as possible so that they are the same if and only if their exercises are intrinsically similar. Again, other things are rarely equal. Folk psychology distinguishes hallucinatory from perceptual processes even though their exercises are intrinsically similar. The proposal is that relevant processes be individuated according to the Intrinsic Similarity Constraint:

> Ceteris paribus, relevant processes are individuated so as to maximize the *intrinsic similarity* of the exercises of a *single* relevant process and the *intrinsic dissimilarity* of the exercises of *distinct* relevant processes.

The constraint does not say *how* similar the exercises of a relevant process must be, and thus it leaves vague just how narrowly processes are individuated. Clearly a narrow individuation will explain and predict more cognition and action than a broad individuation. Folk psychology no doubt leaves the individuation vague and arbitrary, to meet various explanatory and predictive purposes. Whatever degree of similarity may be required, it is clear that the constraint presses for a narrow individuation of processes.

(4) *Frequency Similarity Constraint.* It is plausible that folk psychology attributes folk processes to explain not only cognition and action but something else as well: the distribution of truth-values over beliefs. Attributing folk processes explains the similarities and differences in the proportion of true beliefs in certain stretches of belief. It is the use of folk processes in explaining these differences that bears most directly on the account of relevant processes. Why are my beliefs about the colors of objects in daylight true in similar proportion to yours? Why are my beliefs about arithmetical sums true in lower proportion than yours? The answer to the first question may be that we exercise the same visual perceptual processes, while the answer to the second may be that we exercise different arithmetical processes. Here we explain the similarities and differences between frequencies of true beliefs in given stretches of belief (e.g., my beliefs about the colors of objects in daylight and your beliefs about the same) by appeal to the folk processes exercised by the subjects.

The phenomenon to be explained here – the frequencies of true beliefs in certain stretches of belief – assumes a prior division of beliefs into stretches of belief. Beliefs are first divided by subjects, topics, environmental surroundings, and so on. The task is then to explain why two stretches of belief – e.g., the beliefs of two subjects on a certain topic in similar surroundings – have similar or different frequencies. The explanation is that the beliefs result from the same or different processes. To whatever extent possible, we explain these frequencies by appeal to the intrinsic character of the exercises of processes. But this explanation has its limits. Not all the similarities and differences in frequency can be explained by the intrinsic character of the processes; some are attributable to environment. Thus, folk psychology provides the resources for distinguishing veridical visual perception from hallucination even though these are intrinsically very similar. Still, it seems doubtful that environmental conditions play as significant a role in individuating folk processes as intrinsic character. And what matters for epistemological purposes is that processes are individuated so as to maximize the similarity of the frequencies of true beliefs in given stretches of belief belonging to one process and the dissimilarity of the frequencies belonging to different processes (where maximizing dissimilarity merely means ensuring that the frequencies are different, not that they are as dissimilar as possible). Let us, then, impose the Frequency Similarity Constraint:

> Ceteris Paribus, relevant processes are individuated so as to maximize the *similarity* of the frequencies of true beliefs assigned stretches of belief belonging to a *single* process and the *dissimilarity* of the frequencies of true beliefs assigned stretches of belief belonging to *distinct* processes.

The most important evaluative advantage of individuating processes by frequency is that evaluations will sometimes carry more information about the truth-values of the outputs than they would under the Intrinsic Similarity Constraint alone. That is, the Frequency Similarity Constraint allows intrinsically similar processes to be distinguished by frequency. And individuating processes by amalgamating stretches of belief with similar frequencies does not lose any information relevant to truth-values. Individuating in this way ascribes justified beliefs (and degrees of justification) to subjects under conditions in which the ascription is more closely correlated with the truth of the belief than it would be under the Intrinsic Similarity Constraint alone. Thus, it facilitates the use of epistemic evaluation to judge more precisely the truth-values of beliefs. At the same time, it increases the risk of error in evaluation and is thus in tension with the Salience Constraint.

The Frequency Similarity Constraint favors a narrow individuation of processes to the extent that the prior division of beliefs into stretches of belief is narrow and assigns different frequencies to the stretches. Other things equal, it distinguishes as many processes as there are stretches of belief with distinct frequencies. I have assumed that stretches of belief are defined by natural parameters like subjects, topics, and surroundings, but of course these may be so narrowly construed as to single out one belief. But, as I have already remarked, the Salience and Folk Process Constraints will militate against extremely narrow processes.

The Frequency Similarity Constraint will press for a narrow individuation of perceptual, introspective, inductive, and deductive

processes. Perceptual processes might be individuated by environmental conditions that affect the frequency of true beliefs. In the
case of visual processes, these conditions would include distance
from the object of the belief, lighting, clarity of atmosphere, and
resolution of the sense organs. By itself, the Frequency Similarity
Constraint favors individuating so that all exercises of a process
take place in the same environmental conditions, assuming that
the frequency in one set of conditions will differ from frequencies
elsewhere. (Processes might also be individuated, not by their
actual environmental conditions, but by the representation of their
conditions, thereby bringing the Intrinsic Similarity and Frequency
Similarity Constraints more in line.)

The constraint may entail sometimes individuating as narrowly
as the properties attributed by beliefs (the property of being a
dog, for the belief that Fido is a dog), assuming that the prior
division is also this narrow. Does this individuate too narrowly?
One might think so. Suppose Gina forms the belief that Buffo is a
Bedlington terrier as a result of exercising a visual process. Suppose
that the process she exercises forms beliefs in Bedlington terriers
only when the subject is presented with a Bedlington terrier. Then
on the present individuation we should say that Gina is justified in
believing that Buffo is a Bedlington terrier. But suppose that Gina's
exercise of this process is atypical of her. Suppose that in forming
beliefs about Bedlington terriers, she tends to exercise a process
that mistakes terriers for lambs (e.g., given a Bedlington terrier,
forms the belief that it is a lamb). One might deny that Gina is
justified in believing that Buffo is a Bedlington terrier. Accordingly
one might suggest that we ought to individuate processes broadly
enough to include beliefs about lambs as well as Bedlington terriers
in the output of the process that mistakes Bedlington terriers for
lambs. This broader individuation will make the process Gina
exercises unreliable and thus unjustifying.

I do not find this case for a broader individuation convincing.
We ought to observe straight off that individuating more broadly
here will not help unless we relativize individuation to particular
subjects, since we can repeat the example using any combination
of confusions in different subjects. But individuating as narrowly
as particular subjects would seem unlikely to pass the Salience
or Intrinsic Similarity Constraints. We might avoid a broader
individuation here by the device of metaprocesses, objecting to

154

Gina's belief on the ground that her process, though reliable, does not result from a metaprocess that selects reliable processes for exercise. We will return to this suggestion later in the chapter. In my view, it is best to respond to the objection to a narrow individuation by rejecting the claim that Gina is intuitively unjustified in her belief. I would speculate that any intuition that Gina is unjustified arises from overemphasis on the Intrinsic Similarity Constraint, employing it in preference to the Frequency Similarity Constraint. Once we restore balance to our thinking about the relevant process, we lose our intuition that Gina is unjustified. Thus, I do not find this a successful objection to individuating as narrowly as the properties attributed by beliefs.

At this point we should note that the Frequency Similarity Constraint favors individuating yet more narrowly than these properties. Suppose that Gina's belief that Buffo is a Bedlington terrier results from exercising a visual process that, when presented with a Bedlington terrier, forms the belief that it is a Bedlington terrier. Intuitively, Gina is justified in her belief. Suppose now that she also typically exercises a process that mistakes lambs for Bedlington terriers (i.e., given a lamb, forms the belief that it is a Bedlington terrier). The Frequency Similarity Constraint favors distinguishing the processes here – in which case Gina's belief that Buffo is a Bedlington terrier comes out justified, while the beliefs formed by the process that mistakes lambs for Bedlington terriers are unjustified. I do not find the individuation favored by the Frequency Similarity Constraint here compelling. I suspect that our intuitions waver at this point. Our uncertainty can, however, be explained by our constraints. An emphasis on the Frequency Similarity Constraint favors distinguishing the processes. The Intrinsic Similarity Constraint, on the other hand, favors amalgamating the processes, assuming that their exercises are intrinsically similar (as I think we must if we are to judge Gina's belief about Buffo unjustified). I doubt whether there is any way to resolve this conflict between the two constraints. For our purposes, it is enough to observe that the conflict may explain our wavering intuitions here.

Inductive inferences will be individuated by the number of observations and by the properties attributed by the inductively inferred belief. The import of the number of observations will vary with the property attributed, since the number of instances needed to secure a fixed frequency of true beliefs varies with the property – we need more instances of the color of a species of parrot than we do of the melting point of copper.

It is worth noting that the Frequency Similarity Constraint will favor individuating processes by what might be called the *style* in which these processes are exercised. By style I mean such things as the care with which the process is exercised, or the attention, energy, effort, alertness, thoroughness, completeness, methodicalness, systematicity, or persistence with which it is exercised. The Intrinsic Similarity Constraint already presses for an individuation at different degrees of style, if, as is plausible, distinctions in style affect the intrinsic character of the exercise of the process. The Frequency Similarity Constraint adds pressure in this direction, since different degrees are correlated with different frequencies of true output.

The Frequency Similarity Constraint sometimes favors individuating in such a way as to distinguish the processes that yield positive and negative existential beliefs affirming or denying the existence of the same objects. Visual perception forms both positive existential beliefs (that a spider is present) and negative existential beliefs (that no spider is present). (Perhaps positive beliefs of this sort result, not from visual perception alone, but from visual perception hooked to the deductive process of existential generalization. Negative beliefs perhaps result from a process that takes as input the presence or absence (or perhaps the withholding) of a positive existential belief and maps it into a negative existential belief or withholding of a negative existential belief.) Yet visual perception can differ sharply in its frequency of true positive beliefs and its frequency of true negative beliefs in a given domain. False positives tend to be more common than false negatives on some topics. For what may well be evolutionary reasons, we have a greater tendency to believe falsely that a spider is present than we do to believe falsely that no spider is present. Our tendency to overestimate the presence of spiders has obvious evolutionary value in a world in which there are poisonous spiders and little harm comes from overestimating the frequency of spiders. We may ask which process is relevant in evaluating positive beliefs: the process yielding only positive beliefs, or that yielding both positive and negative beliefs? If we say the former, we will judge positive beliefs as less justified than if we say the latter. The Frequency Similarity Constraint favors distinguishing the processes, since the frequencies of truths in the positive and negative outputs differ. Positive beliefs will then be less justified than they would be if the processes were not distinguished. Though the Frequency Similarity Constraint favors making the positive process relevant in the case of positive beliefs, this consideration is not decisive. Other constraints may press in the other direction. And there may be some ambiguity in our evaluation of the justification of positive beliefs. We do not clearly think the positive belief would be more justified than the negative.

I would add that the Frequency Similarity Constraint may handle an alleged counterexample to reliabilism proposed by Luper-Foy (1985: 210) involving a process that forms beliefs about water and has a high frequency of true beliefs on earth but a low frequency on another planet where water is, unbeknownst to the inhabitants, suddenly and surreptiously replaced with an indistinguishable fluid XYZ, so that most of the inhabitants' beliefs about water are false. Luper-Foy complains that reliabilism yields the counterintuitive result that earthlings' beliefs are unjustified because their process has a low frequency of true beliefs overall. But the Frequency Similarity Constraint favors distinguishing the earth process from the other planet process. And though the Intrinsic Similarity Constraint favors amalgamating these processes, the Salience Constraint joins the opposition to doing so. (The latter constraint has somewhat the effect that relativizing individuation to exercises by members of a given community of subjects would have in this case.) Reliabilism apparently does not entail that the earthlings' beliefs are unjustified.

(5) *Utility Constraint.* For a deontic status like justified belief, a chief purpose of evaluation is to promote and facilitate justified belief and ultimately true belief. The utility of a system of evaluation may therefore be measured by the true beliefs to which it would give rise, in number and proportion. This suggests a Utility Constraint:

> Ceteris paribus, relevant processes are individuated so as to maximize the utility of evaluating beliefs, measured in number and proportion of true beliefs.

Like the Salience Constraint, the Utility Constraint favors broader processes. Since evaluation competes with other belief-forming processes for resources of attention, memory, introspection, perception, and inference which would otherwise yield true beliefs, maximizing the utility of evaluation favors evaluative economy, hence individuating so that there are fewer relevant processes. It takes less education, attention, memory, introspection, etc. to keep track of fewer processes. A narrower individuation would have to merit its cost in lost opportunities for the formation of true beliefs.

This completes our list of constraints on relevance.[6] To consider further how the constraints may judge particular examples, it will be instructive to look at one of the very few existing attempts to formulate a criterion of relevance for reliabilism and apply it to an example. In *Epistemology and Cognition*, Alvin Goldman supports his criterion of relevance (for knowledge, rather than justified belief) by an example of perceptual belief:

> suppose (purely for illustrative purposes) that there is a template mechanism for forming perceptual beliefs. The mechanism takes feature inputs from the sensory systems and tries to match them to various templates, each template representing some category C, for example, the category of dogs, or the category of cars, or the category of chairs. Suppose the mechanism so functions that there is a value T such that if the input features match the template of category C to degree T or more, then the mechanism generates a belief that the stimulus object belongs to C.
>
> (Goldman 1986: 50)

The account of perception Goldman assumes here is pretty close to a naive explanation of perception, and the processes described are plausibly folk processes. We may assume, for purposes of discussion at least, that the processes all meet the Folk Process Constraint. In these processes, when the value *T* of the lower bound on a match is low, a degraded stimulus will match the template and yield the belief that the stimulus belongs to *C*, yet such a belief does not intuitively constitute knowledge even when true. But when the actual degree of match is high (say, .99), even though the lower bound *T* is low, the resulting belief that the stimulus belongs to *C does* constitute knowledge when the belief is true.

Goldman would explain the difference in our intuitions about knowledge in these two cases by appeal to a criterion of relevance, what might be called the *Narrowest Process Criterion*: the relevant process is the *narrowest* process that is *causally operative* in producing the belief.

Referring to the second case, in which the subject knows, Goldman explains:

> My proposed account would handle this case by noting that the mechanism's property of having T (say .70) as minimally sufficient is not causally operative in this case. The property of having this threshold value does not play a critical causal role in eliciting the belief. The degree of match in this case is actually .99. So the critical aspect of the mechanism's functioning that produces the belief is the propensity to produce a belief when the degree of match is .99. If *this* property, rather than the others, is included in the selected process type, an appropriate degree of reliabiilty is chosen that meshes with our knowledge ascription intuition.
>
> (Goldman 1986: 51)

Goldman proposes here that our intuitions about the two cases differ because the narrowest process differs in the two cases. In the case in which the match is low, the narrowest process involves that particular match, and such a process is unreliable: degraded stimuli lead to false beliefs categorizing the stimuli. On the other hand, in the case in which the match is high, the narrowest process involves that match and is thus quite reliable; so the belief is deemed justified by the Narrowest Process Criterion.

Goldman is certainly right to say that intuitively a low threshold for matching a template ought not to impugn the subject's justification for a perceptual belief in a case in which the match is close. And this intuition is most easily explained by ignoring the threshold *T* and focusing on the narrowest process. The Narrowest Process Criterion gets the right result in Goldman's cases. There are, however, two problems with this appeal to the criterion. One is that the criterion seems to be the sort for which some theoretical motivation is needed, yet there is no obvious motivation. There is no way to support the criterion by an appeal to the nature of evaluation. Our constraints certainly do not entail it. On the contrary, they allow for broader processes. If the nature of evaluation is our guide, relevance is bound to be a messier, more contextual affair than the criterion allows.

The second problem is that the criterion is thrown in doubt as soon as we turn to other cases varying in respects other than the degree of match with *C*. For example, imagine that the template for a feature *C* (say, the category of dogs) is itself degraded in such a way that a close match to the template makes it unlikely that the stimulus has *C*, while a distant match makes it more likely that the stimulus has *C*. For example, suppose that through colossal confusion, the subject's template for dog is in fact the normal template for cat. (I assume this is at least logically possible, even if the fit between the template and the category is a significant factor in determining which category the template represents; presumably someone might develop such a confused template by gradual degradation of an originally normal template for dog, making it plausible that it is still the template for dog despite its lack of fit.) Assume again a low threshold for matching. (Let us assume for simplicity that what matters is the actual frequency of true output and that there are many more dogs than cats. We may dispense with this fiction, but only at the cost of bringing in nearby worlds and other complicating factors.) Then the narrowest process in which the match is high is unreliable, while the narrowest process in which the match is low is reliable. Yet I think we would deny that *any* of the subject's beliefs resulting from the template are justified, even the ones resulting from a low match. If so, the relevant process is not the narrowest process. Our intuitions about these cases do not conform to the Narrowest Process Criterion. The relevant process in this example must encompass the high as well as the low matches, so that all the degrees of match fall under one broader relevant process. We must individuate the process no more narrowly than the template (and threshold). Our intuitions thus conform to the Narrowest Process Criterion in Goldman's example but not in the present example.

Why do unreliable high matches drag down reliable low matches in the present example, while unreliable low matches do not drag down reliable high matches in Goldman's example? The difference between these examples can be explained by our constraints. To be sure, several of our constraints treat the examples similarly. The Intrinsic Similarity and Frequency Similarity Constraints both favor distinguishing the high and low match processes, since exercises of these processes are intrinsically different, and their frequencies differ. In the example of the normal template with low threshold, these constraints would lead us to distinguish the processes and thus approve the reliable high match processes and disapprove the unreliable low match processes. But the Salience and Utility Constraints treat the examples differently. In Goldman's example, they provide little resistance to the narrow individuation. Subjects with normal templates can be fruitfully discouraged from setting a low threshold by disapproving their low match processes. In this way, the reliability of the processes they exercise can be improved. And discouraging the unreliable low matches is worth the effort given the large number of falsehoods produced by low matches. The upshot in Goldman's example is that our constraints favor the individuation entailed by the Narrowest Process Criterion.

When we turn to the example of the abnormal template, however, the Salience and Utility Constraints strongly oppose a narrow individuation. It would not be as useful to distinguish the high and low match processes for the abnormal template as for the normal one. Indeed, it would be counterproductive. Perhaps it would be feasible to make an exception of abnormal subjects, discouraging them from exercising unreliable high match processes and encouraging them to exercise reliable low match processes. But it would make more sense to encourage abnormal subjects to normalize their templates, assuming they are generally able to do so. Given the small number of abnormal subjects, a narrow individuation would not save many true beliefs. And it would have evaluative costs: distinguishing the degree of match; distinguishing abnormal from normal subjects (something not necessary for a narrow individuation of normal subjects' processes to be cost effective, given the very high proportion of normal subjects); and evaluating high and low matches for abnormal subjects in just the opposite way as for normal subjects, with the inevitable attendant confusion. The payoff of a narrow individuation in true beliefs would be too small to offset the cost. A broad individuation will encourage as many true beliefs in the end by encouraging abnormal subjects to modify their *templates* rather than their choice of match processes, bringing them in line with normal subjects and in the end make their processes just as reliable as they would be under a narrow individuation, with the advantage that the same individuation will apply to more subjects. This explains our intuition that the abnormal subject is not justified in any of the perceptual beliefs that result from the degraded template.

161

This example illustrates how our constraints may explain our intuitions about particular examples.[7] Our intuitions seem to have complex sources and seem to be influenced by contingent assumptions about the distribution of truth-values across beliefs and the evaluative limitations of subjects and evaluators. While I would not rule out a priori the possibility that a simple criterion might explain our intuitions, I think the prospect is dim. At the same time I see no need for a criterion. A reliabilist explanation may explain our intuitions by appeal to the epistemic end of true belief and the related pragmatic conditions and ends of epistemic evaluation.

Let me add two remarks about the implications of our constraints for skepticism. Our individuation of processes is rather more narrow than any that might give rise to Hume's consequent skeptical worry. Suppose that Hume is right in claiming that the operations that produce beliefs about body and causal powers are operations of the imagination. Then the Intrinsic Similarity Constraint favors the kind of broad individuation that would lead to skepticism. But folk psychology nevertheless distinguishes sensory and inductive operations from imaginative operations, and the Frequency Similarity Constraint also favors a narrow individuation, as does the Utility Constraint. Thus our constraints disarm the Humean worry. Nor can it be objected that our constraints beg the question against consequent skepticism by assuming that our assessments of the reliability of processes are in fact accurate, so that our constraints patently entail the reliability of our processes. The charge here is the converse of the charge of rubberstamping against the Humean review of reliability. If our assessments of reliability are accurate, it follows that our judgments of the truth of our beliefs must be accurate, and these coincide with the outputs of our processes, so that we must assess our processes as reliable. Moreover, our assessments of the reliability of our processes are often positive, so that the accuracy of our assessments entails the reliability of our processes. Thus our constraints beg the question against consequent skepticism. But in fact the Salience Constraint does not assume the accuracy of our assessments of reliability – only ceteris paribus maximizing of the accuracy of these assessments. Our constraints do not beg the question in this way. Nor does our disarming of Hume's consequent skeptical worry succumb to the objection that we beg the question because we use our assessments of accuracy to judge the individuation of processes, and the accuracy of our assessments already entails rejecting consequent skepticism. It is not true that assuming the accuracy of our assessments by itself guarantees a nonskeptical conclusion, since it does not by itself rule out a broad individuation (and indeed the Salience Constraint presses for breadth). Of course the Humean skeptical worry about broad individuation is not the only consequent skeptical worry; there is also the worry about shared underlying mechanisms. So disarming the former worry hardly rules out consequent skepticism.

It might be claimed that our narrow individuation undermines our ability to answer *local* skeptical challenges to the justification of beliefs. Reliabilism provides a natural framework for answering such challenges: we may show that a challenged belief is justified by demonstrating the reliability of the process that yields it, which we do in turn by relying on our beliefs about the truth-values of a sufficiently large number of unchallenged outputs of the process. The trouble with this is that a narrow individuation reduces the number of outputs on which we may rely in assessing reliability, quite possibly leaving too few unchallenged outputs to allow us to assess the process as reliable. But this assumes that reliability is assessed solely by relying on our beliefs about the truth-values of outputs. Once we recall that there are other grounds for assessing reliability, the trouble recedes. There are correlation beliefs. And narrowness is partly the effect of individuating processes along stylistic lines, and there is massive, unchallenged inductive evidence for the degree of reliability contributed by a particular style.

2 Metaprocesses

The version of reliabilism I have been developing is a very simple one, even considering the complexities of the constraints on relevant processes, and it is time to begin the long and arduous task of determining whether it needs to be complicated in any important way. I intend to resist all suggested complications. My interest in the remainder of this chapter is to consider, and ultimately reject, one key way of complicating reliabilism suggested by Alvin Goldman.

Goldman argues that reliabilism must be complicated to accommodate an important distinction between *native psychological processes* and *acquired methods* (or recipes, heuristics, techniques, algorithms, or skills). In his view, exercising a reliable native belief-forming process is sufficient for justified belief, but using a reliable acquired belief-forming method is not. Using a reliable method sufficient for justified belief only when the method is acquired and selected by suitable native acquisition and selection *metaprocesses*. Goldman applies the distinction between what is native and acquired directly to processes and methods, but strictly speaking what is native or acquired is the *capacity* to exercise the processes and methods. This point would affect certain ways of individuating methods and processes to be mentioned below, but not the one we will propose, since ours does not depend on the distinction in question. Goldman regards both the native acquisition and selection metaprocesses as pertinent to the justification of the belief that results from the use of an acquired method, but I would urge to the contrary that the most pertinent native metaprocess is not one that leads to the acquisition or selection of the method *itself*, but rather one that leads to the *use* of the method to form the belief on that occasion. Goldman tentatively suggests that a suitable metaprocess will be one that is metareliable – that is, one that generally acquires (or selects) reliable methods (or, as I would prefer to say, one that generally leads to uses of reliable methods). On such a modified reliabilism, evaluating justification would no longer involve merely assessing the reliability of a method but also the metareliability of a metaprocess.

Does reliabilism really need to be amended in this way? Goldman takes the following example to show that it does:

Suppose Gertrude's mathematical education is seriously deficient: she has never learned the square root algorithm. One day she runs across the algorithm in a pile of papers written by someone she knows to be a quirky, unreliable thinker, and no authority at all on mathematical matters. Despite this background knowledge, she leaps to the conclusion that this rule for deriving square roots (the rule so labeled) is a sound method. She proceeds to follow, and form beliefs in accordance with, this algorithm. She forms beliefs in propositions of the form "x is the square root of y." Are these beliefs justified? Clearly not, for Gertrude has no adequate grounds for trusting the result of this algorithm. She herself has inadequate understanding to realize that it works correctly; nor has she checked to see that the answers are right; nor does she have good inductive grounds for supposing that a random algorithm in this room is correct. So her belief is unjustified; yet she has used a correct algorithm to arrive at her belief.

(Goldman 1986: 91)

This example is supposed to show that a reliable method yields a justified belief only if the subject employs a suitable native metaprocess leading to the use of the method. Goldman concludes:

Ultimately, the question of justifiedness must rest on some unlearned process, or some psychologically basic processes that are never themselves encoded or stored as recipes, algorithms, or heuristics. These processes are just executed, not "applied" in the way that an algebraic or statistical technique is "applied".

(Goldman 1986: 92)

Goldman's example clearly has force. I share his intuition that Gertrude is unjustified in this example. And there is certainly some psychological distinction between native processes and acquired methods, though the distinction is rather obscure. Are native processes those such that one's capacity to exercise them does not derive from prior (noninnate?) cognition or belief? Or are they those one has a capacity to exercise in the absence of prior (noninnate?) cognition or belief (apart from inputs)? Neither account seems satisfactory. Consider visual processes leading to color beliefs. Though intuitively native, one's capacity to exercise them derives from having (noninnate) concepts of various colors, as well as from various perceptually acquired beliefs (e.g., that color vision in dim light is unreliable), and one cannot exercise them without having these concepts and beliefs. Moreover, it is consistent with Piagetian developmental theory, and many post-Piagetian theories (Siegler 1981) as well, that there are no cognitive belief-forming processes the capacity for which does not derive from prior cognition. Thus on either account of native processes, there are no native processes. If there were no native processes, then Goldman's view would strictly imply that a metaprocess is always needed for justification. In this case, Goldman's view would need correction, since it is implausible that a metaprocess is required for many perceptual, deductive, and inductive processes. While neither account of native processes is correct, I have no alternative account to offer.

Still, obscure as it is, there is some distinction between native processes and acquired methods. And in any case Goldman is correct in thinking that using a reliable method is not always sufficient for justified belief.[8] But should we conclude that using a reliable acquired method never suffices for justified belief, or that a native metaprocess is always required when an acquired method yields a justified belief? Should we complicate reliabilism to accommodate these conclusions? That depends on the diagnosis of our intuition that Gertrude is unjustified and on our reaction to other cases.[9]

Goldman's stated diagnosis of the case is in fact at odds with his suggested requirement of a metareliable metaprocess. According to Goldman, Gertrude's square root belief is unjustified because she "has no adequate grounds for trusting the result of this algorithm" – that is, she is not justified in believing that her method is reliable. That diagnosis does not even suggest the requirement of a native acquisition process, still less a metareliable metaprocess. Rather it assumes (one half of) what we earlier (chapter V) called *reliabilist iterativism*, applied to beliefs that result from acquired methods: a subject is justified in believing *p* only if she is justified in believing that her belief results from a reliable method. All that is required is that the subject be justified in believing that the method is reliable, where the justification for the belief that the method is reliable ultimately traces to a reliable native process. No metaprocess is required; the subject's justified belief that her method is reliable need not even give rise to the use of the method.

Neither reliabilist iterativism nor the requirement of a meta-reliable metaprocess fits naturally with reliabilism. We have already rejected the responsibilist argument for a fully general reliabilist iterativism (chapter V). Nor, once we have agreed that reliability is necessary for justification, can that argument be restricted so as to establish a partial reliabilist iterativism. True, the partial reliabilist iterativism here escapes a main challenge to the fully general reliabilist iterativism, since it does not apply to native processes and so does not require immature subjects to be justified in believing their processes reliable. But the question remains why it should apply to acquired methods but not native processes. The reader will recall from the Introduction and chapter V the familiar reasons for valuing reliably formed beliefs regardless of whether they are positively evaluated. We can and do exercise many reliable processes without justified positive evaluation. Since we wish to recognize the contribution a belief makes to the epistemic end of true belief, and reliably formed belief makes such a contribution regardless of whether the subject is justified in believing that it results from a reliable process, we value it apart from such evaluation. It is true that in forming beliefs as a result of epistemic advice, we necessarily evaluate the belief positively. But it does not follow that it is pointless to value reliably formed belief apart from justified positive evaluation. For evaluation here is merely a means to the end of reliably formed belief: the two are valued for different reasons and not naturally combined in a single status. In any event, this advisory argument is fully general and does not discriminate between native processes and acquired methods. The requirement of a metareliable metaprocess faces the same question. Why should a justifying acquired method need a metareliable metaprocess when a justifying native process does not? I do not deny that there is an answer to this question; rather I believe the answer will show that the epistemological interest of the distinction between native processes and acquired methods is derivative from other considerations, and these considerations may follow directly from our unmodified reliabilism.

One reason to resist the fundamental epistemological significance of the native process/acquired method distinction is that it is not intuitively plausible that justification requires *both* a metareliable metaprocess *and* a reliable method. The metaprocess and the method may work together to make a belief justified, in such a way that the strengths of one may atone for the deficiencies of the other. For one thing it seems possible for a belief to be justified when the method is unreliable, provided that the *metaprocess* is reliable. Here is an example:

> Elmo uses an unreliable square root algorithm, but does so because he has been instructed to do so by someone he justifiably believes to be an authority on arithmetic.

Intuitively Elmo is justified. One reason might be that he *infers* the results of his computation from the justified belief that his instructor is an authority. But it is not obvious that he must make such an inference in order to be justified. Indeed it is not clear that he even need justifiably believe that his instructor is an authority – at least, this would not seem to be necessary for simple arithmetical beliefs. Children are presumably justified in the arithmetical beliefs they acquire from instruction even though they do not have evidence of the reliability of their instructors on arithmetical topics. It would seem enough that Elmo is justified because his belief results from a metareliable instructional metaprocess that is noninferential in character.

A second reason for doubting that justified belief requires both a metareliable metaprocess and a reliable method is that it seems possible to be justified as a result of using a reliable method – or at least an acquired process – *without* a metareliable metaprocess. Consider this (admittedly preposterous) example:

> Hermione is unusual in being natively deficient in deductive reasoning: she does not natively exercise the modus tollens process. One day, however, she falls down the stairs, bangs her head on the banister, and ever after exercises the modus tollens process.

I am inclined to think that Hermione's modus tollens beliefs are justified even though the exercise of modus tollens is not one that results from a native process or metareliable metaprocess. If this intuition is correct, then justified belief can result from an acquired process. One might be tempted to conclude that what matters is not whether a process or method is native or acquired, but whether it is a process or method: a process does not need a metareliable metaprocess to be justifying. The modus tollens process is a *process*, so it need not be prefaced by a metaprocess. But even if we can muster a sufficiently robust idea of the difference between processes and methods for this purpose, it seems that we retain the intuition that Hermione is justified when we replace the process of modus tollens with simple methods (whether native or acquired) like those that compute sums or products. So it seems that it is possible for methods to be justifying without resulting from a metareliable metaprocess.

Moreover, the distinction between metaprocess and method may not be as significant for justification as it first seemed from the example of Gertrude. The example of Hermione shows that a *cognitive* metaprocess, whether metareliable or not, is not always necessary for justification by a reliable method. Whether a metareliable cognitive metaprocess is necessary for justified belief in a given case, and whether it is sufficient, as in the example of Elmo, may depend on the circumstances.

When, then, is a metareliable metaprocess necessary or sufficient for justified belief? Ultimately I wish to answer by appeal to our constraints on relevant processes. But let us begin with a simple (though not quite correct) idea that fits the examples of Gertrude and Hermione: justified belief requires a metareliable cognitive metaprocess just when the subject's belief results from the use of a method that derives from some cognitive metaprocess. That is, when a cognitive metaprocess is employed, it is pertinent to justified belief and must be metareliable if the subject is to be justified. Hermione acquires the modus tollens process noncognitively – by a bump on the head. Her belief does not ultimately derive from any cognitive metaprocess. So her belief may be justified even though she does not employ a metareliable cognitive metaprocess. In this she differs from Gertrude, who uses a method that derives from a cognitive metaprocess and must therefore employ a metareliable metaprocess. Perhaps, then, methods whose use derives from a cognitive metaprocess must result from a metareliable metaprocess, while methods whose use does not need not. The idea is that the crucial distinction is not between native processes and acquired methods, but between processes whose use is not cognitively derived and processes whose use is cognitively derived – the distinction earlier mentioned and rejected as an account of the difference between native processes and acquired methods.

This simple idea might devolve from an equally simple fact about relevant processes: relevant processes are cognitive processes. So in evaluating the justification of a belief we trace back no farther than the beginning of the cognitive process. Thus, the only process that can be relevant in Hermione's case is the noncognitively derived modus tollens process, while in Gertrude's case the metaprocess may be relevant as well. In one respect, the irrelevance of noncognitive metaprocesses does follow from the way we have characterized justified belief: they cannot be *part* of the justifying process, since relevant processes are cognitive processes. Hermione's metaprocess – the bump on the head – is in this respect irrelevant. And if the relevance of this noncognitive metaprocess could be entirely excluded, it would be plausible that the modus tollens process is the relevant process and Hermione's belief is justified. Unfortunately the present idea is not fully motivated by the simple fact that relevant processes are cognitive. For one thing, we cannot assume that a metaprocess necessary for justification must be *part* of the justifying process. It might be merely a necessary condition of justification – in which case the fact that relevant processes are cognitive does not exclude requiring noncognitive metaprocesses. For another, the irrelevance of noncognitive metaprocesses patently does not explain why Gertrude's cognitive metaprocess *is* relevant: it leaves open which cognitive metaprocesses (if any) are relevant.

Nor is it obvious that a *cognitive* metaprocess must always be metareliable if it is to lead to the use of a justifying method. If a person picks up a simple reliable arithmetical algorithm or the modus tollens process from a nonauthoritative source (to give the metaprocess a name, call it gullibility), it is not so clear that these are unjustifying, even though their exercise results from a cognitive metaprocess that is not always metareliable. We must find a principled ground, not only for rejecting noncognitive metaprocesses as irrelevant, but for treating cognitive metaprocesses as relevant to justified belief in some circumstances but not others.

Might we explain our intuition by appeal to constraints on relevant processes? Might our constraints entail that the presence or absence of a metareliable metaprocess determines the individuation of methods (or processes) in such a way as to explain our intuitions? (It will not matter for purposes of explaining our intuitions whether the metaprocess is *part* of the justifying process or simply a condition of a justifying method.) Perhaps we should observe first that the Narrowest Process Criterion of relevance is not consistent with our intuitions about the above examples. It conforms well enough to our intuition about Hermione, since Hermione's narrowest process is the modus tollens process, and so Hermione is justified on this criterion. But the criterion runs afoul of our intuitions about Gertrude and Elmo. For Gertrude's narrowest process is the reliable square-root algorithm, and so her calculation would be incorrectly labeled justified on the Narrowest Process Criterion. And Elmo's calculations result from an unreliable algorithm and so would be incorrectly labeled unjustified. To explain our intuitions about these cases we must

170

appeal to constraints on relevance that are flexible enough to make a broader process relevant in some cases and the narrowest process relevant in others.

Our constraints on relevant processes may help here. The Intrinsic Similarity and Frequency Similarity Constraints as usual favor a narrow individuation, which, as we have just noted, judges the examples of Gertrude and Elmo incorrectly. But the Utility Constraint strongly favors a broader individuation, at least in many cases. People are just not able to use reliable square root algorithms or complex logical inferences unless their use derives from a metareliable cognitive metaprocess. Subjects who do not employ such metaprocesses do not arrive at reliable complex algorithms or complex inferences, only unreliable ones. Yet it is necessary for people to exercise such algorithms if they are to form beliefs reliably on a broad range of topics. Native perceptual and inferential processes, unsupplemented by methods, pronounce only on a limited range of topics. So if epistemic evaluation is to promote the use of reliable complex algorithms, it must often approve the use of such algorithms when they result from metareliable cognitive metaprocesses and often not approve the use of them when they do not result from metareliable cognitive metaprocesses, as in the example of Gertrude. It is clear that a system of evaluation that approves precisely the reliable complex algorithms that result from metareliable cognitive metaprocesses and does not approve precisely the unreliable ones is not feasible. In other words, no matter how hard we try in assessing the reliability of algorithms that result from such metaprocesses, we are bound to approve some unreliable algorithms and fail to approve some reliable ones. And similarly, we are bound to approve some unreliable algorithms that do not result from metareliable cognitive metaprocesses and fail to approve some reliable ones. It may, however, be feasible to distinguish many of the reliable and unreliable algorithms among those that result from, and among those that do not result from, metareliable cognitive metaprocesses. The question is whether we should institute such a partial system or instead approve wholesale all complex algorithms, reliable and unreliable, that result from metareliable cognitive metaprocesses, and not approve all such that do not result from these metaprocesses. Considerations of cost suggest wholesale approval. A partial system fails to promote, and indeed risks undermining, the employment of metareliable cognitive metaprocesses. Evaluative efficiency favors a wholesale system. In other words, the Utility Constraint favors a broad individuation, amalgamating all the complex algorithms in the presence of a metareliable cognitive metaprocess into a single reliable process, and amalgamating some of those that do not so result into a single unreliable process. This individuation entails the requirement of metareliable cognitive metaprocesses for justifying complex algorithms. Complex algorithms and inferences will justify even when unreliable, so long as they result from a metareliable cognitive metaprocess. And they will fail to justify even when reliable if they do not result from a metareliable cognitive metaprocess.

We have so far been speaking of *complex* methods and inferences, and I should explain why I have limited the discussion to these. The reason is that matters are quite different when we turn to simple methods and processes. We judge the use of a simple reliable deductive inferential process like the modus tollens process justifying even if it derives from an unauthoritative source or from some other cognitive metaprocess that is not metareliable. The same is true of simple arithmetical algorithms. The explanation for our judgment would seem to be that we are able to and do exercise reliable processes of these sorts without employing metareliable cognitive metaprocesses or at least without the imposition of the requirement that we employ such metaprocesses, and thus considerations of evaluative cost do not entail that justifying processes must result from such metaprocesses. Thus, we approve Hermione's exercise of the modus tollens process despite the fact that it results from a bump on the head and not a metareliable cognitive metaprocess. That is to say, the Utility Constraint favors individuating processes narrowly here.

It would be possible to approve native exercises of the modus tollens process while not approving acquired ones that do not result from a metareliable cognitive metaprocess. Similarly, it would be possible to fail to approve native exercises of simple unreliable processes while approving acquired ones that result from a metareliable cognitive metaprocess. It would be possible, in other words, to individuate native exercises of simple processes narrowly – at the processes themselves – while individuating the acquired exercises at the metareliable cognitive metaprocesses. But this would require dividing simple processes at the juncture between their native and acquired exercises, an individuation that may well be inconsistent with the Folk Process Constraint and would certainly be opposed by the Intrinsic Individuation and Frequency Similarity Constraints. More importantly, this individuation would put us to some trouble for little gain. The number of acquired exercises of these processes is small; approving these exercises would have little tendency to make us cavalier in acquiring complex processes, and if we did not approve the acquired exercises of simple reliable processes, we would not approve the true beliefs that result from them. So it is doubtful that we should distinguish native and acquired exercises of simple processes. The Utility Constraint favors individuating narrowly both the native and the acquired exercises of these processes.

Similar remarks may be made about simple arithmetical algorithms. Though these algorithms are not native but acquired, almost everyone who learns them acquires them from an authoritative source. Social mechanisms guarantee their reliability without the use of a metareliable cognitive metaprocess. Indeed we learn these algorithms at an age when such metaprocesses are not even available. So requiring a metareliable cognitive metaprocess would get in the way of learning the algorithms. We could of course refuse to deem arithmetical calculations justified until such time as the subject employs a metareliable cognitive metaprocess that sustains the use of the algorithm she has already acquired by social means. But withholding approval here may do more harm than good. In addition one is apt to be corrected rather quickly if one uses an unreliable arithmetical algorithm. There are social mechanisms for replacing unreliable algorithms with reliable ones, again without employing a metareliable cognitive metaprocess.

In individuating simple and complex algorithms differently, I am assuming that our constraints are relativized to very large communities of evaluators, so that social mechanisms that guarantee the reliability of complex algorithms without the use of metareliable cognitive metaprocesses are not generally available. The exact point at which they are to be individuated differently will depend on the exact community of evaluators to which the constraints are relativized. A community of sophisticated evaluators may be able to use reliable complex algorithms without a metareliable cognitive metaprocess because there are social mechanisms that guarantee reliability. Where one draws the line between simple and complex algorithms is in part a matter of the size and sophistication of the community of evaluators to which the constraints are relativized. It may also be a matter of the psychological abilities of subjects: subjects may simply be psychologically unable to use algorithms beyond a certain level of complexity without employing a meta-reliable cognitive metaprocess; they may be unable to learn square-root algorithms by rote instruction from teachers whose reliability they are willing to take for granted; sophisticated psychological abilities bring with them critical tendencies and justificatory demands.

These reflections raise the profound question whether meta-reliable *social* metaprocesses may be necessary for justification where metareliable cognitive metaprocesses are not. But the case of Hermione shows that even metareliable social metaprocesses are not universally required. This is, however, a large question that takes us straight into the deepest waters of social epistemology, an arena beyond the scope of this book.

In sum, where the difference between native processes and acquired methods is epistemically significant, its bearing can be explained by appeal to the needs of epistemic evaluation as embodied in our constraints on relevance. We can explain our intuitions without requiring a metareliable cognitive metaprocess for all acquired methods, or even distinguishing native processes and acquired methods in a fully general way in our account of justified belief.

174

CHAPTER VII

Justification and Evaluation

We have so far developed a simple and uncompromising version of reliabilism, one that makes no concession to internalism. Not only does it impose a condition reflectively inaccessible to the subject, but, apart from what is admitted under the constraints on relevant processes, it makes no allowance for the effect of the subject's evaluations of a belief on the justification for that belief. Many will find this deeply unsatisfactory. For there is an intuitive case that the subject's evaluations affect justification. We have already argued (chapter V) that the subject's *positive* evaluation of a belief is not intuitively *sufficient* for justification: the subject's being justified in believing that her belief *p* is reliably formed does not entail her being justified in believing *p*. But some have claimed that the subject's positive evaluation is nevertheless intuitively *necessary* for justified belief: the subject must be (propositionally) justified in believing that her belief is reliably formed. And it is widely agreed that justified belief is intuitively *undermined* by justified *negative* evaluation: the subject must not be (propositionally) justified in believing that her belief is not reliably formed. These intuitions oppose the sufficiency of reliability for justification and threaten to return us to perspectival internalism.

1 Does justified belief require positive evaluation?

Laurence BonJour supports an affirmative answer to our title question with this example:

> Norman, under certain conditions which usually obtain, is a completely reliable clairvoyant with respect to certain kinds of subject matter. He possesses no evidence or reasons of any kind for or against the general possibility of such a cognitive

power or for or against the thesis that he possesses it. One day Norman comes to believe that the President is in New York City, though he has no evidence either for or against this belief. In fact the belief is true and results from his clairvoyant power under circumstances in which it is completely reliable.

(BonJour 1985: 41)

BonJour denies that Norman is justified in believing that the President is in New York City, despite the fact that Norman's belief is reliably formed (or as BonJour would perhaps prefer, reliable). The problem is that Norman fails to be justified in believing that his belief is reliably formed. Thus, reliability is not sufficient for justified belief. The subject must also be justified in believing that his belief is reliably formed.

I agree with BonJour that reliabilism does not conform to his intuition. But I doubt whether many will share that intuition. In any case, we ought not to share it. For consider the following example:

> The Andromedans exercise reliable clairvoyant processes. They know these processes to be reliable. Clairvoyance plays a role for the Andromedans much like the role perception plays for us: it is their primary way of gathering information about their local environment. However, one Andromedan, a fellow named Abnorman, has reliable *perceptual* powers in addition to the normal clairvoyant powers. These perceptual powers do not yield beliefs about matters to which clairvoyant powers apply, so Abnorman has no nonperceptual evidence for or against the reliability of his perceptual processes.

If we judge Norman's *clairvoyant* belief unjustified because of the absence of a justified positive evaluation, then we must do the same for Abnorman's *perceptual* beliefs. Yet we are hardly tempted to do this. On the contrary, most of us will, I think, have the strong intuition that Abnorman's perceptual beliefs are justified. Of course in making this judgment it is possible that we are covertly assuming that Abnorman *is* justified in believing that his perceptual beliefs are reliably formed in virtue of his being able to infer the reliability of perception from his perceptual beliefs themselves. But this cannot help BonJour, since the inference to the reliability of perception can be justifying only if the perceptual beliefs are already justified. Nor will it help BonJour to claim

176

that in judging Abnorman's perceptual beliefs justified, we are mistakenly importing our habitual ascription of justification to perception. For if this is so, BonJour's intuition that Norman's clairvoyant belief is unjustified is open to an analogous charge: he is simply importing his habitual judgment that clairvoyant beliefs are unjustified. At any rate, it seems clear that most of us will prefer our intuition that Abnorman's perceptual beliefs are justified to BonJour's contrary intuition that Norman's clairvoyant belief is unjustified. We ought to reject BonJour's intuition.

Nor is reliabilism consistent with that intuition. It is not possible to assimilate the example of Norman to that of Gertrude in the preceding chapter, attributing Norman's lack of justification, despite his exercise of a reliable clairvoyant process, to the relevance of an unreliable amalgamated process analogous to the absence of a metareliable metaprocess. The proposal would be that we amalgamate exercises of reliable processes when the subject fails to be justified in believing that he exercises a reliable process, with exercises of unreliable processes. If sufficiently many exercises of unreliable processes were amalgamated, the unamalgamated process would turn out to be unreliable. But this way of accommodating BonJour's intuition is unavailable. For processes exercised when the subject fails to be justified in believing that his belief is reliably formed are *not* generally unreliable. Immature subjects natively exercise reliable processes without being justified in believing that their beliefs are reliably formed. So the amalgamated process will not be unreliable. Only an individuation that includes not only such processes but a large number of unreliable processes would entail that the amalgamated process is unreliable. This would require a very much broader individuation than we employed in our earlier handling of the example of Gertrude. Yet such an individuation would not conform to our constraints on relevant processes. It would be opposed by the Intrinsic Similarity and Frequency Similarity Constraints. And it is doubtful that the Salience or Utility Constraints would countervail in favor of such an individuation. Nor is there any great need to encourage subjects always to exercise processes when they are justified in believing that their beliefs are reliably formed. For they natively exercise reliable processes, and they can as easily be discouraged from exercising unreliable native processes like wishful thinking, by discouraging the exercise of processes when they are justified in believing that their beliefs are not reliably formed, as by encouraging them to exercise processes only when they are justified in believing that their beliefs are reliably formed. (Not to say that discouragement is always easy or even feasible: it is hard to get people to see that beliefs that result from quick and dirty heuristics are not reliably formed, and it is perhaps impossible to get them to stop using these heuristics.) And we must also take into account the cost of having to judge that the subject is justified in believing that his belief is reliably formed – not in general a high cost but a cost none the less. In all, there is little prospect of accommodating BonJour's iterativist intuition by individuation.

On the contrary, reliabilism may well entail that Norman's belief is justified. Whether it does depends on the exact nature of clairvoyance. If clairvoyance is intrinsically like perception, then our constraints will favor an amalgamation with perception: the Intrinsic Similarity and Frequency Similarity Constraints favor it, and the Utility Constraint may too. If, on the other hand, clairvoyance and perception are intrinsically dissimilar, then we must know more about what clairvoyance is like to decide its fate. Does it involve no cognitive process at all, just a spontaneous belief, perhaps accompanied by a feeling of confidence? In this case, reliabilism will not ascribe justification. But then, so understood, clairvoyance is not intuitively justifying.

It is tempting, however, to argue that reliabilism entails the weaker iterativist requirement that *mature* subjects are justified in believing that their beliefs are reliably formed. The argument is that if a belief is reliably formed, a mature subject will have sufficient evidence to be justified in believing that it is reliably formed merely in virtue of having exercised the process that forms the belief often enough to ensure that he would be justified in believing that the belief is not reliably formed if in fact it were unreliably formed. Alvin Goldman puts it this way:

> BonJour describes this case as one in which Norman possesses no evidence or reasons of any kind for or against the general possibility of clairvoyance, or for or against the thesis that he possesses it. But it is hard to imagine this description holding. Norman *ought* to reason along the following lines: "If I had a clairvoyant power, I could surely find *some* evidence for this.

I would find myself believing things in otherwise inexplicable ways, and when these things were checked by other reliable processes, they would usually check out positively. Since I lack any such signs, I apparently do not possess reliable clairvoyant processes."

(Goldman 1986: 112)

The mature subject will always have sufficient evidence to be justified in believing that the belief is not reliably formed, and so the iterativist demand could be satisfied for mature subjects.

This attempt to reconcile reliabilism with reliabilist iterativism for mature subjects does not succeed in the end. Let us set aside the difficulty that even if the subject is justified in believing that clairvoyance is reliable, it does not follow that he is justified in believing that his belief is reliably formed, since he may not be justified in believing that it *results from* this process. The chief difficulty is that the evidence for the reliability of clairvoyance that Goldman describes need not be as widely available as it might at first seem. It is not hard to construct an example, not much more artificial than BonJour's, in which the subject is justified in believing *p* on reliabilism, even though he cannot reason as Goldman recommends.

The following example will do:

> In Arnold's community, half the individuals exercise reliable clairvoyant processes. The other half exercise processes that are cognitively intrinsically like these reliable clairvoyant processes (though perhaps differing in their underlying neurophysiological mechanisms) but are in fact unreliable. This is well verified by sense perception. But there is no way to tell which half an individual belongs to, apart from verifying the frequency of truths in his or her beliefs by sense perception. Individuals belonging to both halves vary in whether their processes form beliefs about past, present, or future events. A very few individuals form beliefs about future events, and Arnold is one of these. However, his processes happen to be genuinely clairvoyant and thus reliable.

Given these circumstances, it seems Arnold must lack sufficient evidence for any conclusion about which half he belongs to. He lacks sufficient evidence for the belief that his beliefs result from

179

reliable clairvoyant processes and for the belief that they do not. And thus he is unjustified in believing that the beliefs are reliably formed. Arnold exercises a reliable process without being justified in believing that his beliefs are reliably formed. It may be true that Arnold *would* be justified in believing that his beliefs are reliably formed by induction from his own output beliefs, except for the fact that he has sensory evidence that there is a fifty percent chance that these beliefs are not reliably formed. But even if this is so, it does not show that Arnold does not exercise a reliable process. It does not show that there is counterevidence to Arnold's belief *p* or that Arnold is justified in believing that his beliefs are not reliably formed – conditions that would entail that his process is unreliable on the account of undermining by counterevidence and justified negative evaluation I will offer below. It shows only that Arnold is *not* justified in believing that his beliefs are not reliably formed.

In the end, reliabilism is not consistent with the iterativist intuition that Norman and Arnold are unjustified in their clairvoyant beliefs. The reliabilist must reject this intuition as incorrect. Rejecting the intuition is in any case the right thing to do. We cannot maintain the intuition consistently with strong intuitions we have about other cases. And a fully general requirement of justified positive evaluation is objectionable on grounds independent of reliabilism. It is inconsistent with justified immature belief. And it entails a troubling regress of justification. So the iterativist intuition presents no difficulty for reliabilism. We have no reason to budge from our simple and uncompromising reliabilism.

Of course, denying that justification requires justified positive evaluation is consistent with the plausible idea that mature justified belief is in fact often accompanied by justified positive evaluation of processes and beliefs. We must, however, wait for the final chapter to discuss the role of justified positive evaluation in bringing about justified belief.

2 Is justified belief undermined by negative evaluation?

While our intuitions do not genuinely support the requirement of justified positive evaluation, they do favor the claim that justified *negative* evaluation *undermines* justification. Consider this example:

Burl comes to believe that the flowers are jonquils via a normal process of vision. He sits close to the flowers in a well lit room, trains his physiologically normal eyes on them, and forms the belief as a result of exercising a normal visual process. Yet Burl possesses substantial evidence for another belief, that his (relevant) visual process is unreliable. In particular Burl has just had the first of a series of cataract operations, and he has been led to believe that after the first operation, his vision will remain unreliable. But in fact the operation has been far more successful than the ocular surgeon had expected, and Burl's vision is now normal. Nevertheless, when the bandages first come off, Burl forgets that his vision is supposed to be unreliable, and he forms the belief that the flowers are jonquils.

Intuitively Burl's belief that the flowers are jonquils is unjustified. His justification for believing that the flowers are jonquils is undermined by his being justified in believing that his visual belief is not reliably formed. Justified negative evaluation of the belief p undermines the justification for believing p.[1] Yet reliabilism apparently entails that Burl's belief is justified, since his visual process is reliable. The lesson of the example is supposed to be that reliabilism needs to be supplemented with a condition that rules out undermining by the subject's being justified in a negative evaluation of his own belief. What is needed is a local requirement of "nonnegative" coherence between the belief p and any justified evaluation of the belief p that the subject might make.

At one time I found examples of this sort convincing counter-examples to reliabilism, and I attempted to add a condition to the view designed to handle them. I confess I have since lost confidence that these examples force any revision, both because I am no longer entirely confident that the intuition that Burl is unjustified in believing p is correct, and because I no longer think it obvious that reliabilism must be amended if it is to accommodate the intuition.

Let us review first the ways reliabilism might be modified to handle our intuition. This matter is almost entirely unexplored in the literature, and it is worth considering in detail. I will return in the end to our unmodified reliabilism and argue that it handles our intuition at least as well as any modified version:

181

(1) *Nonnegative iterativism*. We might modify reliabilism by adding one half of what we may call "nonnegative iterativism":

> *S* is justified in believing *p* only if *S* is not justified in believing that *S* is not justified in believing *p*.

Nonnegative iterativism accommodates our intuition about Burl, if Burl's being justified in believing that his belief is not reliably formed entails that he is justified in believing that he is not justified in believing *p* (as it will if reliable formation is necessary for being justified in believing *p*). But this accommodation of undermining by justified negative evaluation comes at considerable expense. Perhaps the most serious problem is that the condition offers no *explanation* of why justified belief is undermined by a justified negative evaluation. It simply says that being justified in a negative evaluation undermines justification for believing *p*. Moreover, it sits poorly with the requirement of reliability: it offers no explanation in terms of reliability, the epistemic end of true belief, or the pragmatic conditions of evaluation.

Another point against nonnegative iterativism is that it does not handle undermining by counterevidence against *p*, as in this example:

> Curly forms the belief that the flowers are jonquils via a normal process of vision in standard conditions. However, before he forms this belief, he acquires substantial evidence that the flowers are daffodils of another kind. Curly has good evidence, for example, that these flowers are daffodils, that jonquils do not grow nearby, and that there are no florists in the vicinity who deliver flowers grown elsewhere. He nevertheless ignores this counterevidence and forms the belief that these flowers are jonquils.

Curly's belief is unjustified because he possesses counterevidence against it. Curly's perceptual process is intrinsically just like Burl's, and thus reliable if Burl's is, so this example must also be a counterexample to unmodified reliabilism, if the example of Burl is. But it is no less a counterexample to reliabilism supplemented with nonnegative iterativism. Nor can we handle the example of Curly by constructing a condition parallel to nonnegative iterativism, since the format of nonnegative iterativism depends on specifying a particular proposition that the subject must not be justified in believing, and there is no one propositional content that counterevidence must have. A very different kind of condition would be needed to accommodate the example of Curly. And we might hope that once we find such a condition, a parallel condition would handle the example of Burl. Nonnegative iterativism, then, seems an unpromising approach to undermining by negative evaluation.[2]

(2) *Holistic reliabilism.* It is an appropriate moment to bring up the intriguing idea of holistic reliabilism, a version of reliabilism with some outstanding virtues, and one that may be able to handle the example of Burl quite naturally.[3] On this view, justified belief is defined in terms of the reliability, not of a single process, but of a whole system of processes – *holistic reliability* as opposed to atomistic reliability:

S is justified in believing *p* just in case S's belief *p* results from a process belonging to some *select* system of processes that is *holistically reliable* (alternatively: the select system that is most holistically reliable).

In a holistically reliable system of processes, the members of the system work together to achieve holistic reliability. This means that a reliable process may fail to be justifying (at least on an occasion) because it (or its exercise on that occasion) does not contribute to the holistic reliability of a select system of processes. And of course unreliable processes may be justifying, so long as they contribute to the holistic reliability of some select system. Selectness plays a role here analogous to relevance in unmodified reliabilism – e.g., it prevents justified beliefs from being simply true beliefs.

Holistic reliabilism would handle the example of Burl by treating as unjustified his exercise of his visual process despite its reliability, on the ground that the exercise of a process, even a reliable one, when the subject is justified in believing the process exercised to be unreliable, does not contribute to the holistic reliability of any select system of processes. On this proposal, any select holistically reliable system will have to exclude exercising a visual process in circumstances in which the subject is justified in believing that his belief is not reliably formed. The obvious problem the proposal faces is that Burl's process is surely included in *some* holistically reliable system. Indeed, a system that includes the process may have a higher holistic reliability than one that does not, since the process is after all reliable (and forms true beliefs on occasions such as these). So the qualification that we consider only *select* holistically reliable systems must clearly do some important work here. The solution to the problem must be a utility constraint on select systems analogous to our Utility Constraint on relevant processes: the select systems must be ones that are not too costly to employ. Even though sanctioning Burl's visual process on this occasion would entail a higher holistic reliability for the system, allowing subjects to exercise *reliable* processes when they are justified in believing that their beliefs are not reliably formed would in the end be too costly, since there would be no way to sanction such processes and at the same time discourage the exercise of *unreliable* processes when subjects are justified in believing that their beliefs are not reliably formed. Because subjects are generally justified in believing correct propositions about whether their beliefs are reliably formed, and because they are unable to exercise only the reliable processes among those they exercise when they are justified in believing that their beliefs are not reliably formed, it is cost effective to forbid the exercise of *all* processes subjects exercise when they are justified in believing this, including the reliable ones. Only a system that excludes the exercise of all such processes will be both cost effective and holistically reliable. I find this a plausible story, though no more plausible than the one I will later tell to show that unmodified reliabilism can also handle undermining by justified negative evaluation.[4]

Holistic reliabilism does face a number of significant difficulties, of which I have space to mention only the most troubling. Just as the view disapproves some reliable processes, it may approve some unreliable processes that are intuitively unjustifying. Unjustifying processes may be sanctioned because they work together with other processes to achieve holistic reliability. It may be that human beings are able to exercise the reliable processes they do only because they occasionally indulge in unreliable time- and energy-savers like quick and dirty heuristics or even irresponsible cognitive recreation and ego-boosting like wishful thinking and self-deception. If holistic reliabilism is to avoid approving intuitively unjustifying processes, we must not conceive of these processes as working with other intuitively justifying processes to achieve holistic reliability. We must restrict select systems yet further, so as to exclude unjustifying processes that causally contribute to the exercise of justifying processes. We might say that wishful thinking and the quick and dirty heuristics are merely *instrumental* to exercising the justifying processes, and thus contribute to holistic reliability merely instrumentally – so do not count as members of a select system. The danger of this suggestion, however, is that it will deprive holistic reliabilism of its ability to handle undermining by justified negative evaluation: it raises the question whether processes that lead to beliefs about the reliability of processes are merely instrumental to exercising the latter processes. Some of the processes that must belong to a select system to handle undermining by justified negative evaluation are instrumentally related to the exercise of other processes in the system. It might be replied that wishful thinking differs from these justifying processes in *merely* contributing to holistic reliability instrumentally, while these processes, being reliable, contribute directly. But surely holistic reliabilism will want to admit as members of the select system processes that do not make a direct contribution to holistic reliability because they are not belief-forming processes, only metaprocesses. Without admitting metaprocesses, holistic reliabilism cannot explain why some uses of a reliable method are justifying and others not: a system without metaprocesses will sanction all uses of a method or none. Holistic reliabilism might admit metaprocesses by treating them as fused with methods, but then the question will arise why wishful thinking and the quick and dirty heuristics are not to be treated as fused with reliable processes. So it is not clear how holistic reliabilism can avoid approving wishful thinking. Despite this problem, the view must be taken quite seriously. I regret I must leave the matter for more leisurely exploration on another occasion.

(3) *Comparative reliabilism.* In earlier work (1984) I proposed a way of amending reliabilism to handle undermining by justified negative evaluation. On comparative reliabilism, a belief is justified only if it results from the exercise of a process that is not merely reliable, but at least as reliable as any competing processes. To be exact, S is justified in believing p just in case

(a) *S*'s belief p results from the exercise of a reliable belief-forming process R (that is, a belief-forming process with reliability greater than the lower bound r_0 necessary for reliability); and

(b) there is no belief-withholding process R', available to S on the occasion of exercising R, that withholds the belief p and has reliability at least that of R.

The first clause here is simply the requirement set by reliabilism. The second clause requires that there be no competing process at least as reliable.[5]

Comparative reliabilism clearly has merit as an account of justified belief. But I am no longer convinced that it handles undermining by negative evaluation. It is worth examining whether the view can handle such undermining, both because it does handle undermining by counterevidence against p and because a close look at how it handles undermining by negative evaluation can reveal some similarities and differences between these two kinds of undermining.[6]

Let us say a few words at the outset about the nature of belief-withholding processes and their reliability. Talk of withholding a belief, unlike that of forming one, is ambiguous: it may refer to the *process* (or act) of withholding, analogous to the process (or act) of forming a belief, or it may refer instead to the *product* of that process, the state of withholding, which is a cognitive attitude analogous to a belief, though not a propositional attitude. Withholding the belief that Buffo is a Bedlington terrier, as a state, is not the same as *believing* that Buffo is *not* a Bedlington terrier, nor is it the same as *not* believing that Buffo is a Bedlington terrier. The first of these is a propositional attitude, while the second is not a representational state at all. Withholding the belief that Buffo is a Bedlington terrier is a representational state but not a propositional attitude: it takes as its object the (nonexistent) *belief* that Buffo is a Bedlington terrier, not the proposition that Buffo is a Bedlington terrier. To disambiguate withholding language, I will talk of withholdings when I wish to refer to the representational state, and I will talk of belief-withholding processes when I wish to refer to the process of withholding.

It is natural to think of folk processes as a combination of belief-forming and belief-withholding processes – that is, as yielding withholdings as well as beliefs. Folk perceptual processes not only form beliefs, but withhold them as well. If I view a bird from afar, my perceptual process may form the belief that it is a great horned owl or withhold this belief, depending on the exact distance and lighting. And the same may be said of folk inferential processes: my inductive inferential process may form or withhold a belief in the inductive generalization that all beavers have flat tails depending on whether there is a sufficiently large observed sample of beavers. Moreover, our constraints on relevant processes would seem to allow mixed belief-forming and belief-withholding processes. Assuming we can make out a conception of the reliability of belief-withholding processes that allows comparison with that of belief-forming processes, the Frequency Similarity Constraint favors individuating processes in a way that cuts across beliefs and withholdings where their reliabilities are the same. Only the Intrinsic Similarity Constraint would oppose this (since, presumably, exercises on occasions of withholding differ intrinsically from those on occasions of forming).

How do we measure the reliability of a belief-withholding process? Consider first a pure belief-withholding process. The natural approach is to say that the end of withholding beliefs is to withhold false beliefs, just as the end of forming beliefs is to form true beliefs. And thus it is natural to define the reliability of a belief-withholding process as its frequency of false beliefs withheld, just as we define the reliability of a belief-forming process as its frequency of true beliefs formed. The reliability of a *mixed* belief-forming and belief-withholding process will simply be the average of the reliability of the belief-forming portion of its output (i.e., the frequency of true beliefs) and the reliability of the belief-withholding portion of its output (i.e., the frequency of false beliefs withheld) weighted by the relative size of the contributions of these portions to the total output of the process. A mixed process also counts as reliable when its reliability exceeds r_0.[7]

Comparative reliabilism has two important merits. First, it imposes a condition of obvious value. It is valuable for subjects to exercise a process more reliable than any competing process available to the subject. Exercising such a process may make a greater contribution to the end of true belief than exercising a merely reliable process. Whether exercising such processes ought to be encouraged is a difficult question. Exercising reliable processes will lead in the long run to a large number and a high proportion of true beliefs. Exercising comparatively reliable processes will lead to at least as large a number and as high a proportion, assuming the same lower bound r_0 on reliability set by reliabilism. The overall effect of encouraging exercising comparatively reliable processes on the number and proportion of true beliefs can, however, be simulated by reliabilism simply by raising the lower bound r_0 it sets on reliability. It is by no means clear at this point how comparative reliabilism and reliabilism differ in their implications for the epistemic end of true belief, or whether the difference between them is significant.

Second, comparative reliabilism accommodates and explains our intuition that counterevidence against p undermines justification. Consider first an example of the undermining of inferential justification by counterevidence:

> On the basis of a large body of evidence, Miss Marple forms the belief that Duncan Maybury stole the brooch. But uncharacteristically, she overlooks substantial counterevidence against the conclusion, counterevidence that is already in her possession. In fact this counterevidence outweighs the evidence for the conclusion.

Miss Marple is not justified in her conclusion, even though (assuming that this example is not handled by reliabilism) she exercises a reliable process R. Comparative reliabilism would say that she is not justified because there is an available competing process R' at least as reliable as R that withholds her belief p. Suppose, for an obvious choice, that R' is a process that involves taking into account not only the evidence for p but the available counterevidence against p as well. Is R' as reliable as R?

There are many factors that affect the reliability of processes taking representations of evidence and counterevidence as input. Perhaps a look at a few of these features will do for illustration. Other things equal, normal inferential belief-forming processes will be more reliable to the extent that the input evidence for p is greater than the input counterevidence – or more accurately, to the extent that the evidence represented in the input exceeds the counterevidence represented in the input beyond a certain threshold of difference. (For simplicity of exposition I will drop the talk of "representation.") And, other things equal, a belief-withholding process will be more reliable to the extent that the input counterevidence for p exceeds the input evidence (again, beyond a certain threshold of difference). Other things equal, too, both belief-forming and belief-withholding processes are more reliable the greater the sum of the input evidence and counterevidence, and the greater the portion of available evidence and counterevidence they take as input.

To apply these observations to the example of Miss Marple, the belief-withholding process R' takes as input both the evidence that enters R and also counterevidence that does not enter R. Now R is more reliable to the extent that its input evidence exceeds its input counterevidence. But it is less reliable to the extent that it fails to take as input the available counterevidence. And it is also less reliable to the extent that its sum of evidence and counterevidence is less.

It is reasonable to think that R' will be as reliable as R – indeed more reliable. The reliability of R' will be at least that of R if evidence and reliability are related in the following way: the positive contribution to the reliability of R' due to a greater sum of input evidence and counterevidence, together with the positive contribution to its reliability due to a larger ratio of this sum to the quantity of available evidence and counterevidence, is at least as great as the positive contribution to the reliability of R due to the greater quantity of evidence for p. As with all questions about reliability, it is an empirical question (granted a specific conception of evidence) whether this condition is satisfied. But it seems a reasonable bet that it is. Certainly we think that adding available counterevidence to a fixed quantity of evidence *increases* the reliability of a belief-forming process down to the threshold of evidence minus counterevidence necessary for justified belief. And it is plausible to suppose that this increase continues below the threshold if only the process withholds belief below the threshold instead of forming it. In this case R' will turn out to be *more* reliable than R, and thus the availability of R' will undermine Miss Marple's justification. Perhaps this illustration is enough to make it plausible that comparative reliabilism can explain how available counterevidence that does not serve as input to the process R can undermine justified belief, at least in the case of inferential belief.

The story to be told about perceptual belief runs along similar lines. It will help for our discussion of undermining by negative evaluation if we look at the matter in detail. Curly sees the flowers and forms the belief that they are jonquils, yet there is

189

counterevidence that undermines his justification. A folk picture of perceptual processing would go something like this. A normal visual process takes as input transductions of sensory stimuli, applies perceptual schemata to form sense impressions, then applies conceptual schemata to form beliefs. The perceptual schemata endow the sense impression with features that represent spatial dimensions, sizes, shapes, colors, textures, and other visual properties. We may think of the process as employing the conceptual schemata to convert these representations into representations of objects with nonvisual properties – having petals, having a stem, being a flower, etc. Various accounts may be given of how the process forms beliefs. Let us make do, as we have before, with a *feature* account. On this account, the process involves matching the values of dimensions, sizes, shapes, and so on with threshold values specified by the conceptual schemata for each of a number of nonvisual properties ascribed to an object. When the values meet threshold for a property ascribed to an object, then the process forms a belief attributing that property to that object. When they fail to meet threshold, then the process either withholds belief or fails to form or withhold belief.

On this account, the reliability of forming beliefs will increase (up to a point) with the difference between the input values and the threshold values, while the reliability of withholding beliefs will decrease with this difference. Reliability will also vary with other properties of the process. For example, the process will include representations of the subject's relation to the environment – distance, orientation, clarity of atmosphere, illumination, presence of opaque objects, and so on. These representations will normally enter into both the formation of the sense impression and the formation of beliefs. The reliability of the process will vary depending on how such representations are employed. The reliability of forming beliefs, for example, will increase with clarity of atmosphere and illumination (up to a point) and decrease with distance, and the reliability of withholding will do the reverse.

I have described the operation of the simplest normal perceptual process, but there are more complex normal processes as well. These have provisions for employing background beliefs. In particular, they can take as inputs beliefs about the environment, the subject's physiology and psychology, and the objects of belief, combine these with their processing of the sense impression, and yield beliefs or withholdings. In the simplest such case of withholding, the conceptual schema is applied to the sense impression, and the values represented meet the threshold for the feature "jonquil" ascribed to the flowers, but the subject already believes (justifiably) that the flowers are daffodils of another kind (e.g., because he deduces this from his belief that no jonquils grow nearby), and thus the perceptual process withholds the belief that the flowers are jonquils. In more complicated cases, the subject does not already believe that the flowers are not jonquils, but has some counterevidence against this proposition. The process weighs this counterevidence against the difference between the values represented in the sense impression and the threshold values (and other pertinent values). When the quantity of counterevidence is greater than this difference (above a specified threshold), the process withholds the belief that the flowers are jonquils. It is plausible that a perceptual belief-withholding process will be more reliable the more counterevidence there is against p and the less the difference between the values. The reverse is true for a perceptual belief-forming process.

Given this description of the perceptual process, it is not difficult to tell a story about the comparative reliability of the withholding process that parallels the story we have already told in the case of inferential belief. If the counterevidence available to Curly is substantial enough, then its quantity will be enough greater than the difference between values that the reliability of R' will overcome any advantage that R might have in virtue of its not taking any counterevidence as input. The belief-withholding process R' will be at least as reliable as, if not more reliable than, R. So Curly's perceptual justification for believing that the flowers are jonquils will be undermined.

All this seems to show that comparative reliabilism handles undermining by counterevidence. We must return now to my old proposal that it could handle undermining by justified negative evaluation as well, and in a parallel fashion. The available belief-withholding process in this case is also inferential, taking justified negative evaluation as input. We may conceive of it on the model of the normal perceptual belief-withholding process: its exercise has part of the exercise of R as a segment or part (perhaps up to the formation of the belief p). (Or its exercise may take the exercise of R as an input, or involve only contemplating or imagining, or otherwise simulating its exercise far enough to judge whether R yields the belief on this occasion.) The rest of the belief-withholding process involves an interaction between the negative evaluation and the part or segment of the exercise of R in such a way that the completion of the exercise of R is preempted. In some cases the negative evaluation will directly preempt the completion; in other cases, it will preempt it as a result of the weighing of features of R, such as the quantity of evidence for p, against features represented in the negative evaluation, such as the degree of unreliability attributed to R.[8]

One might complain that it is obscure just how such belief-withholding processes work (Feldman 1985). But it seems certain that these processes are recognized by folk psychology and that any obscurity here lies in folk psychology itself. This is not an obscurity the comparative reliabilist is obligated to clear up. The belief-withholding processes pass the test of the Folk Process Constraint. We must ask, however, whether they are deemed relevant by the other constraints on relevant processes, and whether they are as reliable as the processes undermined, as well as available on occasions of undermining.

The exercise of the belief-withholding process R' that takes the justified belief that the belief p is unreliably formed as input, together with an incomplete exercise of R, does employ more information than the exercise of R, but there does not seem to be a clear case for individuating processes so that this process comes out reliable (at least not for every R undermined by justified negative evaluation). It is natural to individuate R' in such a way that its output overlaps with that of R. (This will, however, require reformulating our constraints, which assume a disjoint individuation of processes.) R' yields the same beliefs that R does on occasions when there is no justified negative evaluation, since it allows the completion of the exercise of R, and thus it has the same frequency of true beliefs on these occasions. Where it differs from R is in taking the justified negative evaluations as input on occasions when there is such input, and withholding the belief p on such occasions. Of course on these occasions R yields the belief p.

Unfortunately, this way of individuating R' will not make R' as reliable as R. For we would not expect R's frequency of true beliefs on such occasions to differ from its frequency on other occasions, hence from its overall frequency. There is no reason to suppose that R will have a lower frequency of true beliefs on the occasion just because subjects are justified in believing that their beliefs are not reliably formed. When processes deviate from their overall frequency of truths on such occasions, the deviation will be random. But then R''s frequency of false withholdings on such occasions will be lower than R's frequency of true beliefs on such occasions, and thus R' will be overall *less* reliable than R.

A more promising approach would be to individuate R' so as to assimilate it to undermining by counterevidence against p. Both R' and the competing processes on occasions of counterevidence take inputs beyond those taken by R and yield withholdings on some occasions. If R' could be individuated so as to be identified with one of these competing processes, then its reliability might exceed that of R. The frequency of false beliefs withheld of the competing processes on occasions of counterevidence is greater than R's frequency of true belief on these occasions. So if the number of occasions of counterevidence were large in proportion to the number of occasions of justified negative evaluation, R' would have as great a reliability as R. It is not at all easy, however, to judge the prospects for this approach. It is unclear whether our constraints on relevant processes will favor such a broad individuation of R'. The Utility Constraint does favor such an individuation, since assimilating undermining by negative evaluation to undermining by counterevidence would associate the prohibition of exercising belief-forming processes in the face of counterevidence with the prohibition of exercising processes when subjects are justified in believing that their beliefs are not reliably formed, and would thus make the two prohibitions mutually reinforcing. The Intrinsic Similarity Constraint, on the other hand, offers a bit of resistance to this individuation, since the exercises of R' are intrinsically somewhat different from the exercises of competing processes on occasions of counterevidence. The Frequency Similarity Constraint offers more resistance, since R's frequency of false beliefs withheld is much lower than that of the competing processes on occasions of counterevidence.[9] I do not see a clear case here for saying that comparative reliabilism entails that Burl's belief p is unjustified.

193

So much for comparative reliabilism. It is time to return to our unmodified reliabilism. I would argue, albeit tentatively, that it does conform to our intuition about Burl. For our constraints on relevance assimilate the example of Burl to the model of meta-processes and complex methods we developed in the preceding chapter. They treat Burl's being justified in believing that his visual process is unreliable as analogous to a metaprocess and the visual process itself as analogous to a method.

The proposal is that our constraints amalgamate into a single process the exercises of many visual processes on occasions of justified negative evaluation. Suppose the visual process Burl exercises is an amalgamated process the output of which is a set of (intrinsically?) similar exercises of visual processes on occasions when subjects are justified in believing that their beliefs are not reliably formed. Subjects are usually correct when they are justified in believing this. Hence the exercises of visual processes on such occasions can be expected to have a low frequency of true output. The amalgamated process will therefore itself be unreliable, even though it has as output exercises of some reliable (though on the occasion irrelevant) processes like a normal process of vision. Burl's visual process in the presence of his justified belief that his process is unreliable will then be the unreliable amalgamated process. Thus, if our constraints make the amalgamated process relevant, Burl's belief will be unjustified.

It is worth pausing for a moment to note a number of implications of the present proposal. First, we cannot treat the amalgamated process Burl exercises as the fusion of the visual process with the process that leads to the belief that his belief p is not reliably formed. For even if Burl does exercise the process in virtue of which his negative evaluation is (propositionally) justified, this process need not be causally related to his exercise of the visual process in such a way that the exercises of the two processes can be regarded as parts of the exercise of a single fused process. There need be no fused process. Second, the amalgamated process will be relevant on all occasions of its exercise. The processes from which it is amalgamated will either have to be regarded as irrelevant on the occasions of these exercises, or they will have to be truncated so as to excise these exercises. On the former approach, relevance will no longer apply to processes but to their exercises. Our constraints on relevance will have to be rewritten, since they assume that relevant processes are disjoint. And we will of course have to explain why the amalgamated process is relevant on all occasions of its exercise while the normal visual process is not. On the latter approach, relevance will continue to apply to whole processes, rather than being divided among their exercises; processes will remain disjoint; and we may retain our constraints as currently written. But the truncated individuation raises the question whether we are still dealing with folk processes, and in any case we will now have to explain why some processes are truncated and others amalgamated. Obviously, the answer to the last question will have to lean heavily on our constraints on relevance. Neither of these approaches is entirely happy – the choice between them needs further exploration – but the latter entails less revision of our account, less explanation of the approach, and is formally easier to manage, so I will adopt it here.

A third point is that on the present proposal, Burl's justified belief that his belief is unreliably formed, while correct, is so for the wrong reason. He is correct in believing that the process he actually exercises is unreliable. But this is not because it is the unreliable visual process he thinks it is. Rather it is because it is the amalgamated process. In undermining, the subject is not mistaken in believing that the exercised process is unreliable, but rather mistaken about what that process is. Note too that, on the present proposal, the undermining negative evaluation concerns a process different from the one relevant on the occasion, indeed different from any actually exercised. Even so, the process Burl is justified in believing to be unreliable is presumably the process that *would* be relevant on the occasion if it were actually exercised.

It is an intriguing question whether the process the subject is justified in believing to be unreliable in undermining negative evaluation can ever be the relevant, amalgamated process the subject actually exercises. On the present proposal, merely by being justified in believing that one exercises an unreliable process, one ensures that one exercises an unreliable process. The question is whether one could be *justified* in believing that one exercises the amalgamated process. If one could be justified in believing that one exercises it merely by believing that one exercises it, then there would seem to be no obstacle to being justified in believing this proposition. But of course mere belief is not enough for justification. It seems that to be justified in believing this proposition, one would have to be justified in believing that one exercises a process that is reliable, though this process is irrelevant merely because one is justified in believing that one exercises an unreliable process. But it is hard to see how one could be justified in such a belief. The matter is perplexing, but nothing central hangs on it, so I will not try to resolve it.

Let us turn to the key question. Do our constraints entail the relevance of the amalgamated process? The reader will recall that the case for amalgamating complex algorithms was made largely by appeal to the Utility Constraint. It is not feasible to individuate at the particular complex algorithms rather than at the metaprocesses that lead to their use because subjects are not generally able to exercise reliable complex algorithms except when these algorithms result from metareliable cognitive metaprocesses. It might be feasible to individuate at some particular complex algorithms and not others, amalgamating these others, but considerations of evaluative efficiency favor individuating at the metaprocesses for all complex algorithms. It must be admitted that there is no equally powerful analogous argument for broadly individuating Burl's visual process. It is not true that subjects are unable to exercise reliable visual processes unless they avoid exercising processes whenever they are justified in believing that their beliefs are not reliably formed. We do not have to get subjects to avoid exercising unreliable visual processes by encouraging them to evaluate those processes and avoid exercising the ones they deem unreliable. Subjects *natively* exercise reliable visual processes and avoid exercising unreliable ones. In this regard, the case of visual processes is different from that of complex algorithms.

Even so, there is much profit to be had from encouraging subjects not to exercise processes when they are justified in believing them unreliable. And the cost of requiring the absence of justified negative evaluation is substantially less than that of requiring justified positive evaluation. Requiring the absence of justified negative evaluation entails only that the subject weeds out processes which she is justified in believing unreliable, while requiring justified positive evaluation entails that the subject must be justified in believing the process reliable whenever she exercises it. It is true that there is no difference in the cost of the regulation needed to ensure conformity to these requirements. But there is a difference in the cost of conformity itself: the requirement of the absence of justified negative evaluation does not require one to be justified in believing that the process is reliable, while the requirement of justified positive evaluation does. And there is another difference in cost. The requirement of justified positive evaluation strongly encourages subjects to acquire justification for believing in the reliability of processes in tandem with acquiring beliefs about other topics, while the requirement of the absence of justified negative evaluation merely encourages subjects not to acquire justification for believing in the unreliability of processes. Of course acquiring justification for believing in the reliability of processes is laudable when beliefs about reliability are desired. But there is nothing especially laudable about acquiring justification concerning reliability *in tandem with* beliefs about other topics. And when beliefs about reliability are desired, the evaluation of justified belief will itself encourage acquiring justified beliefs about this matter. We need not encourage it by imposing the additional requirement of justified positive evaluation.

It seems likely, then, that the Utility Constraint will warrant individuating in such a way that reliabilism entails undermining by justified negative evaluation. I would add that the constraint makes a stronger case for this individuation applied to some processes than applied to others. More sophisticated processes whose exercise results from evaluation by the subject may profit more from, or even require, the encouragement provided by this kind of individuation. Perhaps we need such encouragement to learn to exercise reliable color vision processes.

This is the best reliabilist case I can make for undermining by justified negative evaluation.[10] I believe it succeeds, though obviously it needs more development, and it is clear even now that it will never be anywhere near decisive. But in the absence of a potent argument for undermining by justified negative evaluation, we would do best to let the chips fall where they may. I would rather contradict our intuitions about examples than add theoretically unmotivated and unexplained conditions to our account of justified belief.[11]

In this chapter, I have argued that reliabilism accommodates whatever truth there may be in the idea that justified negative evaluation undermines justification. The view does not entail, however, that justified belief generally requires justified positive

197

evaluation, though such evaluation may often appear as a component in justifying processes and, as I conceded in chapter VI, may be necessary in many metaprocesses that give rise to justifying methods. Reliabilism imposes only a modest requirement of evaluation. We value reliably formed beliefs whenever they occur, regardless of the presence of evaluation.

CHAPTER VIII

The Value of Evaluation

Justified belief does not entail evaluation. Nevertheless, evaluation may play an extensive role in *bringing about* justified belief and true belief. It may do so by *promoting* (doxastically) justified belief – by making subjects want to believe what is (propositionally) justified. And it may do so as well by *facilitating* (doxastically) justified belief, making it feasible and easy for subjects to exercise reliable processes.[1] It goes without saying that evaluation is an important *theoretical* activity, one of the chief theoretical activities of daily cognitive life. The present question is the *instrumental* value of evaluation. Just when – for which kinds of beliefs and processes and uses of evaluation – is evaluation desirable for bringing about justified and true belief? When is it better to evaluate and when not?

We have already briefly discussed the role of evaluation in epistemically responsible belief (chapter V), in metaprocesses (chapter VI) and in the revision of beliefs (in chapter III). We have also laid down the Utility Constraint on relevant processes. We have used this constraint to argue for the requirement of metareliable cognitive metaprocesses in cases of complex algorithms and processes, and this sometimes involves evaluation. However, the constraint merely favors, and does not mandate, individuating processes so as to maximize utility. Even if, as I have claimed, our system of evaluation meets the Utility Constraint, it does not follow that evaluation maximizes utility over the totality of evaluations, still less does it follow that it does so over given types of processes or uses of evaluation. I will not focus here, however, on whether evaluation maximizes utility over the totality of evaluations or over given types of processes or uses of evaluation. That would require some idea of the feasible alternatives to our system of evaluation, since maximization must be understood relative to competing systems; yet it is doubtful that we have any idea of these alternatives at the present time. It seems best, then, to focus, not on whether evaluation maximizes utility, but on whether it has absolute utility for given types of processes or uses of evaluation. We must ask when – for which types of processes and which uses of evaluation – the benefits of evaluation exceed its costs. I wish to suggest that benefits may exceed costs for fewer uses of evaluation than many have thought, fewer even than reliabilists have tended to think.

1 The utility of evaluation

For purposes of this chapter, we may define an *evaluation* as a *belief* as to whether a given belief is reliably formed or a given process is reliable. This contrasts with our usage in chapter VII, where a justified evaluation amounted to being propositionally *justified* in believing that a given belief is reliably formed. I will focus here on the evaluation of processes as reliable, though the evaluation of beliefs is also of key interest.

It will help to be clear at the outset just what counts as the utility of evaluation for a fixed kind of belief, process, or use of evaluation. It is measured by the *number* and *proportion* of actual *true beliefs* that result from evaluation, either by promotion or facilitation. Note that this measure is not quite the same as the average reliability and the total power of the processes exercised as a result of evaluation (where the power of a process is its capacity to produce true beliefs measured in numbers, or its capacity to produce beliefs with true information). In the case of a fixed kind of belief or use of evaluation, the former measure will correlate with the latter. But in the case of a fixed kind of process, it will not, since the average reliability and total power is determined strictly by the processes and not by any effect of evaluation on how frequently or in what ways they are exercised. Thus we will not learn anything about the utility of evaluation for a fixed kind of process by comparing the average reliability and total power of the processes when evaluation is used with that when it is not used: the two figures will be the same. Induction, for example, will do just as well regardless of whether it is evaluated. I will say more about whether we ought to focus on fixed kinds of belief, processes, or uses of evaluation in a moment.

The utility of evaluation is diminished by its cost, which is correlated to some extent with the resources consumed in evaluating. Evaluation after all consumes cognitive resources – time, energy, memory storage and retrieval capacity, reasoning capacity, etc. – that would otherwise be spent exercising processes, some of which would be reliable.

It would be nice if natural kinds of beliefs (defined by topic) or processes (folk psychologically described) were systematically correlated with the utility of evaluation, so that we could list the kinds for which evaluation is desirable. But I see little reason to expect a systematic correlation. The accuracy of evaluation does correlate with certain features of topics and processes: it goes down with the complexity of the process, the number of inputs, and the duration of exercise. In the case of problem-solving processes, it correlates, as we will see, with the difficulty of the problem. At the same time, the effort of evaluation is greater the more complex the process, and this increases the cost. Nevertheless, evaluation is more likely to enhance the average reliability of complex processes than simple ones. The upshot is that the benefit for simple processes will be significantly offset by the cost of evaluating a process when it is less likely to enhance reliability. In short, there is no reason to expect systematic conditions of valuable evaluation in terms of natural kinds of beliefs or processes. The most we can hope for are crosshatching rules of thumb keyed to features of topics and processes – as well as subjects and environments. What might be true, however, is that certain *uses* of evaluation correlate with utility. We will therefore focus on uses, rather than kinds of beliefs or processes. Our task will be to associate uses of evaluation with utility. I will begin with some observations about the effort involved in certain uses and the likelihood that these uses will enhance the number and proportion of true beliefs, and turn in section 2 to the topic of accuracy.

Before we proceed, let us make some general observations about the resources consumed by evaluation. One key factor that affects the kind and quantity of resources consumed is whether evaluation and its use, or the processes that lead to these, are conscious and controlled or instead unconscious and automatic. Conscious and controlled processes, according to the orthodox economics of cognition, share limited resources to a far greater extent than do unconscious and automatic processes (Schneider and Shiffrin

201

1977). They share the limited storage and processing capacity of
short-term memory, a retrieval capacity from long-term memory
limited by the amount of information that can be gotten per unit
time (though not by the topics of information), and a similarly
limited capacity to store information in long-term memory. If
evaluation and its use were unconscious and automatic, it would
consume fewer resources than if it were conscious and controlled.
I doubt whether we currently know enough about evaluation to
ascertain how much evaluation is conscious or unconscious and
automatic. It must be noted, however, that even unconscious
and automatic processes are limited in their information-handling
capacity. Even if evaluation is unconscious and automatic, it will
consume resources that would otherwise go to exercising processes,
some of which are reliable.

There is a related way in which evaluation might save resources:
it might involve something other than belief or processing other
than central processing – subdoxastic states (Stich 1978) or the
nondoxastic states involved in peripheral, modular processing
(Fodor 1983). These states are available to conscious inspection,
if at all, only with difficulty, and they are also to some degree
informationally isolated from long-term memory and, in the case
of modular states, from central processing. In general, the processing associated with these states trades access to information
in long-term memory for speed and accuracy within narrowly
defined circumstances. Their inputs from and outputs to long-term
memory, when they exist, are restricted by topic. Evaluation would
consume fewer resources if it involved these states rather than
belief. However, on reliabilism, accurate evaluation is bound to
depend on substantial memorial resources, since it relies on beliefs
about the outputs of processes, beliefs about which outputs are
true, and correlation beliefs. There is no limit in principle to
the topics of the correlation beliefs even for a given narrowly
individuated process, and so it is doubtful that evaluations would
be accurate if they were informationally isolated subdoxastic or
nondoxastic states. Versions of internalism skirt this obstacle to
identifying evaluations with these states because they do not entail
that evaluation requires input on as wide an array of topics.
But they do run up against another difficulty where evaluations
that are claimed necessary for justification are concerned: they
are supposed to express the view that subjects possess their

justification, and the further the evaluations veer from conscious, controlled beliefs, access to long-term memory, and central processing, the less plausible is the claim to capture the *subject*'s possession of justification. Internalists must face the problem of the cost of evaluation as surely as reliabilists do.

There is yet another way that evaluation might save resources. Over time subjects accumulate beliefs as to which processes, psychologically described, are reliable. These beliefs enable the subject to infer from the fact that a belief results from a certain process, psychologically described, that it is justified. Subjects are thus able to infer whether given beliefs are justified without relying on beliefs as to whether the given beliefs are reliably formed. That enables the subject to make do with fewer beliefs and thus saves resources, whether the beliefs that given beliefs result from processes are conscious or not. Of course this shortcut evaluation has its costs. And subjects must still review the reliability of processes periodically and must assess the reliability of new processes if the system of evaluation is to be maintained.

With these points in mind, we may now consider the utility of evaluation in its various uses:

(1) *Evaluation as part of a metaprocess that results in the use of a method.* As we observed in chapter VI, the evaluation of a method as reliable may enter into the justifying process as part of a metaprocess that leads to using the method: assessing a square root algorithm as reliable may lead to the use of the algorithm. Employing evaluation here does not add new processes, and so does not increase the power or average reliability of the processes we actually exercise or have the capacity to exercise (unless processes are individuated at methods – an improbable individuation, as I argued in chapter VI). It does, however, increase the reliability and power of our complex *methods*. And thus it increases the number and proportion of true beliefs.

(2) *Evaluation as justifying surrogate for the exercise of another justifying process.* An evaluation of a process R can be employed in lieu of the exercise of R on an occasion when the subject knows what belief would result from exercising R on the occasion. In this case the process of which the evaluation is part serves as a *surrogate* for the exercise of R. Thus, if one is justified in believing that looking would reveal a crimson sunset, then one need not look

in order to be justified in believing that there is a crimson sunset. One can be justified on the basis of an inference from the premise that looking is reliable and would yield the belief. The evaluation of the process serves as a surrogate for looking.

The surrogate process is presumably an inference taking this form:

> Process R (looking at the sunset) is reliable and would yield the belief p (on the occasion).
> So p belongs to a reference class of propositions most of which are true.
> Therefore, probably, p.

The first premise of the inference is the evaluation, and the inference is arguably justifying (assuming the evaluation is justified, the output of the process is believed sufficiently broad, and the reliability attributed is sufficiently high).

Surrogate processes, being native, do not directly add processes to those we exercise or have the capacity to exercise and so do not directly increase reliability or power (unless they are narrowly individuated). But they may increase the number and proportion of true beliefs by saving effort.[2] For they enable us to arrive at the justified belief p without exercising the process R, thus saving resources for other business, though we must weigh against this the cost of less practice in exercising R.

Unfortunately, surrogate processes are very limited in their ability to increase the number and proportion of true beliefs. Indeed, they often reduce them. One limitation derives from the fact that it is difficult to be justified in believing that looking at the sunset will yield the belief that the sunset is crimson *without actually looking*. And of course if one looks, then one does not need the surrogate process. Still there are cases in which one can be justified without looking at the sunset. For example, one can *simulate* looking at the sunset by imagining what it would be like to look at the sunset. Simulation may obviate the need for a surrogate process, but simulation by the imagination would not normally produce belief without an additional inference like the one formulated above, since the imagination does not by itself normally command belief. There are also cases in which one forms the belief that the sunset is crimson as a result of *remembering* that this belief resulted from a previous look. However, it is frequently the case that when one remembers that the belief that the sunset is crimson resulted from looking, one can also simply remember *that the sunset is crimson*. Remembering *p* is frequently a less costly alternative to a surrogate process.

A second limitation of surrogacy is that in many cases in which one is justified in the premise of the surrogate process, there is an alternative inference yielding the belief *p* that does not involve an evaluation. For example, when I am justified in believing that looking will reveal a crimson sunset without actually looking, this is often because I have observed the weather and am inductively justified in believing that weather of this sort is correlated with crimson sunsets. But in this case, I can simply infer that there is a crimson sunset from my observation of the weather and the correlation. This inference does not involve an evaluation of looking. Since the surrogate inference I might make would be based on this inference, it would be a superfluous appendage.

These limitations seem enough to deflate substantially the utility of surrogate processes.

(3) *Evaluation as part of a justifying belief-revising process.* Evaluations of the reliability of processes and the justification of beliefs may also serve in the justified *revision* of belief – i.e., the retraction of old beliefs and the formation of new beliefs. They may in this way enhance the number and frequency of true beliefs. (It is worth noting that on the most sophisticated psychology of belief-revision we now have, that of Einhorn and Hogarth (1984), the revision of degrees of confidence *always* involves a judgment of the evidence for the proposition.) I will focus on belief-retraction rather than formation. It will be convenient to assume at first that there is such a thing as justified belief-retraction, where belief-retraction is an act or process that leads to belief-withholding. This assumption may, however, be discharged in favor of the view that there is only justified belief-withholding – just replace "the belief *p*-retraction is justified" with: "the belief *p*-withholding is justified."

Let us assume for the moment a rigid tie between justified belief and justified retraction: the retraction of a belief *p* is justified if and only if the belief *p* is not justified. Then it is not difficult to see how evaluation might serve in our efforts at justified belief-retraction: we attempt to retain all beliefs we evaluate positively and retract all those we do not evaluate positively. Of course our evaluations are not always correct, and so we are not always able to make justified retractions; but on reliabilism, we are not always able to hold justified beliefs either.

There is, however, some question whether evaluation will not be too costly for this purpose, if indeed it is feasible at all. Gilbert Harman (1986) has recently argued that revision ought not always or even very often to involve evaluations of justified *belief* as understood on foundationalism (reliabilism will lead to similar trouble). For making use of such evaluations is often too costly or impossible. Evaluations of justified belief involve remembering the basing relations (in our terminology, the exercises of the processes) that originally give rise to beliefs, and remembering such things entails a high cost in storage and retrieval. Harman has in mind situations in which a belief on which many other beliefs are based is discovered unjustified, but the subject has lost track of which beliefs depend on the unjustified belief:

> Consider Karen, who has taken an aptitude test and has just been told her results show she has a considerable aptitude for science and music but little aptitude for history and philosophy. This news does not correlate perfectly with her previous grades. She had previously done well not only in physics, for which her aptitude scores are reported to be high, but also in history, for which her aptitude scores are reported to be low . . . .
>
> After carefully thinking over these discrepancies, Karen concludes that her reported aptitude scores accurately reflect and are explained by her actual aptitudes . . . .
>
> Some days later she is informed that the report about her aptitude scores was incorrect! The scores reported were those of someone else whose name was confused with hers. Unfortunately, her own scores have now been lost. How should Karen revise her views, given this new information?
>
> The foundations theory says she should abandon all beliefs whose justifications depend in part on her prior belief about her aptitude test scores.
>
> (Harman 1986: 33–4)

Harman admits that foundationalism is in accord with our intuitions about justified retraction here, but he nevertheless favors a coherence theory because it is sometimes too costly or impossible to recall basing relations or retract beliefs in conformity with them. Harman's remarks about cost and feasibility suggest that he rejects the rigid view that beliefs that are no longer justified are to be retracted in favor of the more lenient view that justified retraction is the subject's *best effort* to retract such beliefs. For subjects cannot be expected to employ costly evaluations to make revisions even when they make their best efforts. But, for reasons parallel to those I gave earlier against a coherence theory of epistemically responsible belief (chapter V), the lenient view does not support a coherence theory of justified retraction. Nevertheless, the lenient view does allow the justified retraction of justified beliefs, as well as the justified maintenance of unjustified beliefs.

In my view, Harman exaggerates the cost of remembering which beliefs depend on a given belief. On a global historical coherence theory of justified belief, our memory of basing relations is indeed in considerable jeopardy, since the basing relations are myriad. But on foundationalism or reliabilism, memory does not face such a formidable burden. It seems that we can remember which processes and inputs formed many beliefs. And even when we cannot remember, we can often make accurate conjectures about these matters. We remember the circumstances in which we formed beliefs. Or we can conjecture what the circumstances were on the basis of our knowledge of correlations between the topic of a belief and its circumstances of formation, and infer the process on the basis of our knowledge of correlations between processes and circumstances. Karen can retrace the beliefs that ensued from her acceptance of the aptitude test score.

Still, there remains some warrant for Harman's alarm. His worry about the cost of evaluating justified beliefs cannot be summarily rejected. The evaluation of justified beliefs does consume substantial memorial and inferential resources, and there is quite a bit of error in our judgments about which processes are exercised to form specific beliefs. One reaction to the problem is to follow Harman in abandoning the rigid tie between justified belief and justified revision in favor of an approximate tie. We might, as Harman does, define justified retraction as the subject's best effort to retract beliefs that are not justified. Alternatively, we might modify our account of justified belief by discounting the effect of the past on justified belief in proportion to its temporal or causal distance. Perhaps it would be more natural for a reliabilist to say that justified retraction is retraction that results from a reliable retracting process (i.e., a process with a high proportion of false to total beliefs retracted). Such an account is bound occasionally to allow the retraction of justified beliefs and disallow the retraction of unjustified beliefs. A different reaction is to maintain the rigid tie between justified belief and justified retraction by modifying the accounts of both justified belief and justified retraction. Let justified retraction amount to the subject's best effort to retract beliefs that are no longer justified. And let justified belief be undermined by counterevidence, when it arrives, if the subject would retract the belief as a result of his or her own best effort to retract beliefs for which there is counterevidence.

However, I prefer another reaction: maintain the rigid tie by making justified belief the result of a *longitudinal* reliable belief-forming process which both forms beliefs and withholds them when counterevidence arrives. The reliability of such a process would be defined longitudinally: false beliefs for which there are withholding provisions would count less against reliability than false beliefs for which there are no such provisions (and vice versa for true beliefs?). It might be that in calculating reliability earlier products should be discounted in favor of later ones. In any case, the retraction of a belief would be justified just in case the belief is withheld in virtue of undermining by counterevidence. The Salience Constraint would need to be modified to require only that pertinent (presumably temporally or causally recent) temporal parts of the process generally be salient, since it is too much to suppose that whole longitudinal processes would generally be salient. For purposes of retraction we would then evaluate recent temporal parts of longitudinal processes, not whole processes, and these evaluations would themselves be part of the longitudinal whole. I believe this proposal for dealing with retraction would be optimal, though working out the details would require a book-length effort. For present purposes, it suffices to observe that on any of the accounts we have mentioned, justified retraction often employs negative evaluation of justified beliefs. Employing evaluation here will enhance the number and proportion of true beliefs.

(4) *Evaluation as cause of the exercise of justifying processes.* There are two ways that the evaluation of processes may lead to the formation of justified beliefs and increase the reliability and power of processes, apart from figuring in justifying belief-forming and belief-retracting processes and metaprocesses.

(i) *Regulating beliefs*. The evaluation of processes may figure in regulating beliefs with respect to justification (see chapter IV, note 12). It is plausible that regulating beliefs with respect to justified belief entails telling, and thus justifiably believing, that the conditions of justified belief are satisfied – or in other words, it entails (doxastically) justified positive evaluation. But for this very reason, regulating belief with respect to justification is a costly route to justified belief. Justified positive evaluation is costly, and *telling* that a belief is reliably formed is even more costly. Nor may we, as Pollock (1986) proposes to do in order to avoid a regress of regulative justification, reduce the cost by requiring only that conditions of justified belief be detected without the subject's being justified in believing, or telling, that the conditions of justified belief are satisfied. A performer doesn't regulate her piano playing with respect to the norms of piano playing unless she *tells* that her performance conforms to these norms.

(ii) *Developing belief-forming habits and traits*. The most far-reaching way the evaluation of processes may lead to justified beliefs is through the development of belief-forming habits and traits. Habits and traits are highly desirable for exercising reliable processes of most kinds. Some habits are, or entail, dispositions to exercise processes more reliable than those that would typically be exercised without them, and some traits entail such dispositions. Thus they greatly enhance the number and proportion of true beliefs. Evaluation undoubtedly plays an essential role in facilitating the development of these habits and traits. This seems to be true of stylistic habits. Subjects will not develop or maintain the habit of perceiving or inferring carefully, thoroughly, systematically, etc., without monitoring their belief-forming behavior, and part of this monitoring must be the evaluation of processes and beliefs. No doubt we develop the habit of care by making it a point to form beliefs carefully, and while we may initially do so only because of the pressure to conform to socially given norms of habit development, we are able to maintain our resolve in developing the habit only by assessing the degree of reliability contributed by styles of belief-formation. And the pressure to conform exists only because we make a practice of assessing the reliability of these styles. It is true that habits save resources because they are dispositions to exercise more reliable processes without assessing the reliability of processes on each occasion of exercise. They enable us to get the effect of evaluation – exercising reliable processes – without the cost of consulting our list of reliable or unreliable processes, still less calculating the reliability of any processes, on many occasions of exercise. But despite this, many valuable habits come about and persist only through evaluation.

The same is true of many doxastic character traits, including many epistemic virtues – especially those developed through belief-forming habits (e.g., the virtue of carefulness). Traits require more effort for their development than habits do, but they are correspondingly more persistent in the absence of reinforcement. There are epistemic virtues – wisdom, for example – that need not come about as a result of evaluation, but entail it as part of their *manifestation*. The manifestation of such traits is more costly than that of traits whose manifestation does not entail evaluation. It should be noted that epistemic virtues that bring about large numbers rather than a high frequency of true beliefs do not depend on the evaluation of processes as reliable for their development or manifestation. For example, intellectual diligence brings about large numbers of true beliefs and serves that end, but its development makes no use of the evaluation of any relevant processes as reliable. Rather, it results from, or is maintained by, the recognition that diligence (or certain strategies that make for diligence) increases power.

We have considered how the various uses of evaluation enhance the number and proportion of true beliefs and occasionally the average reliability and power of the processes we actually exercise. While evaluation has considerable utility and is essential for certain purposes that greatly enhance the number and proportion of true beliefs, as in the case of the development and persistence of habits and traits, the utility of some of its uses is not quite as great as many have supposed. Its use in surrogate processes and in regulating belief with respect to justification does not have the utility it might at first seem to have. It remains to consider a chief threat to the utility of evaluation, the *inaccuracy* of evaluations.

2 The accuracy of evaluation

If our evaluations of justified belief and the reliability of processes are to increase the number and proportion of true beliefs, they must generally be accurate (within certain tolerances, and modulo their use for exercising processes, as I will explain below). There is, however, a deluge of recent work in empirical psychology that might be thought to challenge our accuracy here. Though I have so far urged caution about the utility of evaluation, I would like now to resist the idea that these recent empirical results support pessimism about our accuracy. My ulterior motive in resisting the charge of inaccuracy is to protect the Salience Constraint. That constraint does not entail the accuracy of our evaluations, since it holds only ceteris paribus, and it is a maximizing, not a satisficing constraint. Nevertheless, sufficient pessimism about accuracy would undermine the application of the constraint to cases by preventing us from balancing considerations of accuracy against the considerations embodied in the other constraints.

(1) *The accuracy of beliefs about whether processes are exercised.* Evaluating a justified belief involves judging whether the belief results from a reliable process, and that in turn generally involves judging which process is exercised on that occasion. An accurate judgment of which process is exercised on an occasion entails an accurate judgment of which sense impressions and beliefs are inputs and which perceptual or inferential process is in fact exercised on the occasion. Do subjects generally judge such things accurately? Though the classical answer is that introspection yields accurate beliefs about cognitive states and processes, there are few living enthusiasts of introspection. I doubt whether there ever was a time when the introspectibility of the mind was completely taken for granted, but in any case we long ago lost our naive confidence in the accuracy of introspection.[3] Two large trends in the history of psychology put an end to it. One was the expansion of the realm of the unconscious, the other the recognition of introspection as a process and the consequent appreciation of its fallibility even when applied to conscious mental states. A good deal of psychology since Freud and James converges on the conclusion that there are unconscious cognitive states and processes that are not reliably introspectible, either concurrently or retrospectively. Recent information-processing psychology, beginning with Donald Broadbent's classic unattended channel experiments in the 1950s, has accumulated an overwhelming body of evidence for this conclusion, which has accordingly become central to information-processing explanations of cognitive and bodily behavior. The

acceptance of unconscious mentality has by now trickled down to folk psychology. It has indeed become difficult to imagine scientific or folk psychological explanations of behavior and mentality anywhere near as rich and satisfying as those we now possess that do *not* postulate a vast unconscious mental life. Perceptual and inferential processes, sense impressions, and beliefs are among the states and processes now deemed unconscious. Yet it is implausible that unconscious mental states and processes are introspectible, though it may be possible to bring many unconscious mental states and processes to consciousness and then introspect them. Just as importantly, the recognition that introspection is a process susceptible to interruption and interference, as well as to computational error, has led to the appreciation of its fallibility even in its traditional sphere of operation, the sphere of conscious mental states. And it is recognized as well that judging by introspection whether a state obtains or a process is exercised can utilize resources required for the state to obtain or the process to be exercised and thus can interfere with and distort it in such a way as to lead to erroneous judgments. Finally, it is appreciated that a great deal of apparent introspection for purposes of explaining cognitive or bodily behavior is really rationalization of that behavior. When subjects are asked to explain how they inferred a conclusion from premises, they often appeal to a rule of inference by which subjects would normally or conventionally abide, and they disregard the actual causes of their behavior.

Some psychologists even go so far as to deny that there are *any* processes the exercise of which can be accurately introspected. In a notorious article on the accuracy of subjects' verbal reports of their processes, Richard Nisbett and Timothy Wilson (1977) argue for this extreme view. They survey a vast collection of empirical findings and conclude that verbal reports of processes are in general highly inaccurate (though they allow that reports of mental *states* are often accurate). Nisbett and Wilson's arguments have been fiercely criticized on methodological grounds (Smith and Miller 1978, White 1980), though I believe their conclusions are more defensible than many suppose. Partly in response to Nisbett and Wilson, K.A. Ericsson and Herbert Simon (1983) propose very sensible conditions under which subjects' verbal reports of mental states and processes are likely to be accurate. But whatever the outcome of this debate, its bearing on the accuracy of judgments of the exercise of relevant processes is uncertain.

To begin with the completely obvious, it is unclear whether the fact that experimental subjects' verbal *reports* of processes are inaccurate shows that their *beliefs* about processes are inaccurate. We may waive one objection to inferring the latter from the former: that experimental subjects are asked to make retrospective reports, and loss of memory might stand in the way of reporting the results of accurate introspections. If loss of memory explains subjects' inaccurate reports, then subjects will be unable to make accurate evaluations involving a memory of the exercise of processes; yet virtually all evaluation involves this, since it involves beliefs about the reliability of processes and hence about which processes have formed which beliefs. A more telling objection emerges from an observation that we have already made in connection with the effort involved in evaluation: much evaluation may be unconscious and automatic. In this case, beliefs about the exercise of processes need not even be reportable to play an effective role in forming justified beliefs. Our inability to make accurate verbal reports of the exercise of processes need not entail the unavailability of accurate beliefs for justified revision, regulating beliefs with respect to justification, and developing belief-forming habits and traits. Of course unconscious evaluation entails not only unconscious beliefs about the exercise of processes but also about their reliability. But reliabilism can accept the latter, so long as they result from sufficient inputs from long-term memory.

It must also be observed that even if Nisbett and Wilson are right that subjects do not accurately introspect their processes, the bearing of this result on our own concerns is tenuous. For the authors allow that subjects use, in place of introspection, an alternative method of forming beliefs about processes: causal theorizing on the basis of introspective beliefs about states and observational beliefs about behavior. And this causal theorizing may be accurate in a variety of circumstances. Such theories utilize conventional rules of behavior ("I came to a stop because the light started to change"), standard explanations of mental states ("I'm pleased because I received flowers today"), and observations of the covariation of external conditions and mental states ("I'm grouchy today. I'm always grouchy when I don't break one hundred in golf"). Perhaps subjects similarly theorize about the exercise of the cognitive processes that produce their beliefs on the basis of conventional rules about processes. When asked how they arrived at a generalization from singular premises, they might employ the rule "Generalizations from singular premises result from induction." Nisbett and Wilson themselves note that verbal reports may be accurate when subjects incidentally employ a correct theory of the processes that form their beliefs. If the processes identified by such rules are common enough, then subjects will generally be accurate in their verbal reports and their beliefs about the processes they exercise. We can expect many false positives under these conditions, but just how many will depend on how thoroughly the rules take introspected circumstances into account. It is worth noting, too, that cautious beliefs about processes made on the basis of observations of covariation are plausibly inductively justified, whether or not they are correct.

The case studies Nisbett and Wilson cite as instances of inaccurate verbal reports for the most part involve uncommon processes that result from experimental manipulation and could not be expected to occur naturally. Subjects could not be expected to attend to the right features of the cases to judge the processes. Nor do the experimenters focus on epistemologically relevant processes. Thus Nisbett and Wilson offer no reason as yet to suppose that subjects have erroneous beliefs about natural and relevant processes. They do not show that beliefs about processes are not generally accurate *in situ*. This is not to deny that their article raises troubling questions about the value of verbal reports for *experimental* purposes. Nor is it to deny that there are serious questions about the accuracy of our beliefs about processes. I regard the accuracy of such beliefs and the introspectibility of some processes as an open question. But for now there is no easy way to make epistemological capital of the Nisbett–Wilson findings, largely because the experiments they cite do not address the epistemologically interesting questions about the introspection of processes. We have no empirical reason yet to despair that subjects often have accurate beliefs about the exercise of processes.

(2) *The accuracy of beliefs about the reliability of processes.* There is a good deal of literature in empirical psychology that bears on the accuracy of our assessments of the reliability of processes. Especially pertinent here are two branches of cognitive psychology: research on metacognition (i.e., cognition about cognition), conducted mostly by developmental psychologists (Flavell 1985), and

research on the calibration of confidence (Lichtenstein, Fischhoff, and Phillips 1982). I will focus on the latter, which offers clearer and better established results. Our ultimate concern is the accuracy of our assessments of *reliability*, but the calibration literature concerns in the first instance the accuracy of our assessments of *degrees* of reliability.

The calibration literature is concerned with how well subjects' degrees of confidence in their beliefs correlate with frequencies of truths in certain classes of their beliefs. When psychologists speak of the calibration of confidence, they usually have in mind the extent to which the degrees of confidence a subject assigns her beliefs on a given topic match the actual frequencies of truths in the classes of beliefs assigned those degrees of confidence. For a particular degree of confidence c (between 0 and 1), there is a perfect match between these when the frequency of true beliefs in the class of beliefs assigned degree of confidence c is exactly c. We can measure a deviation from the perfect match for a particular degree of confidence by taking the absolute difference between c and the actual frequency of true beliefs assigned c. We can then measure the overall calibration of the subject on the given topic by taking the average of these absolute differences for all degrees of confidence c assigned to beliefs on the given topic, weighted by the relative sizes of the classes of beliefs assigned each degree of confidence c. A subject is said to be *well calibrated* when this average is low and *poorly calibrated* when it is high.

The literature on calibration brings unsettling news about subjects' calibration. The primary result is that subjects are overconfident – i.e., assign higher degrees of confidence than their frequencies of true belief – on tasks involving common knowledge that are of moderate or extreme difficulty (Fischhoff, Slovic, and Lichtenstein 1977; Lichtenstein and Fischhoff 1977, 1980). These tasks require subjects to solve a problem or make an inference that relies only on common knowledge and to assign a degree of confidence to their answers. It turns out that when the questions are difficult, subjects generally assign degrees of confidence to their answers that are on average higher than the frequency of truths in the class of their answers. We must ask what implications this finding has for the accuracy of our assessments of the degrees of reliability of the processes we exercise.

Clearly the calibration of a subject's degrees of confidence in his answers to questions concerning a topic is closely related to the accuracy of his assessments of the degrees of reliability of processes which have outputs on that topic. It might seem that the literature on calibration should lead to a pessimistic conclusion about the accuracy of assessments of the degrees of reliability of processes – that we should infer from the fact that subjects are poorly calibrated that their assessments of degrees of reliability are inaccurate and thus that subjects ought not to use these assessments to exercise processes, regulate belief, or develop belief-forming habits or traits.

But first, we cannot readily infer the inaccuracy of the assessments of degrees of reliability from poor calibration. Second, and more importantly, even if the assessments of degrees of reliability are inaccurate in the way suggested by the finding of overconfidence, it does not follow that they cannot be used effectively for purposes of exercising reliable processes. Let us take these points in turn.

Poor calibration does not entail inaccurate assessments of degrees of reliability. There are several reasons why it does not. First, most calibration experiments are designed to check the calibration of given subjects' answers to questions on specific topics. But we cannot infer inaccurate assessments of the frequencies of subjects' true beliefs on the topics from the poor calibration of such answers. For the classes of answers to which the subject assigns a specific degree of confidence are certainly not the same as the classes of beliefs in the output of relevant processes the subject assesses as reliable. For one thing, calibration experiments do not generally observe sufficient controls to infer from the fact that a subject gives an incorrect answer that she has an incorrect belief, or even that she has any belief at all on the topic. Similarly, calibration experiments generally lack sufficient controls to ensure that the degree of confidence assigned an answer or reported as assigned is the same as the degree of confidence that would be assigned a belief. They do not rule out the possibility that the subject has a motive for assigning a different degree of confidence – e.g., the subject's desire to appear confident. We cannot expect the calibration of degrees of confidence to be equivalent to the accuracy of the assessments of the degrees of reliability of relevant processes.

Second, we cannot infer the inaccuracy of assessments of the degrees of reliability of *processes* from the inaccuracy of assessments of the frequencies of true beliefs on the topics. For processes are individuated *across* subjects and topics. Moreover, it is unclear whether the degrees of confidence elicited by researchers are assessments of the reliability of processes. On the one hand, calibration experiments are usually set up so as to elicit degrees of confidence in the *subject* on the topic (i.e., estimates of the subject's frequency of true answers). These degrees of confidence seem to be the intended target of much calibration research. On the other hand, researchers sometimes assume that the degrees of confidence elicited *are* assessments of the degrees of reliability of processes or at least of methods. For the explanation of overconfidence would seem to require such an assumption, and this would seem to show that researchers really are uncovering assessments of the reliability of processes, not of the subject's answers.

The best proposed explanation of overconfidence (Pitz 1974) assumes that subjects report degrees of confidence of a kind that is pertinent to the accuracy of their assessments of the degrees of reliability of processes. Pitz explains overconfidence by the hypothesis that subjects oversimplify because of information-processing limitations in the early part of problem-solving, and then they forget that they have oversimplified. This explanation assumes that subjects assess the degree of reliability of an initial segment of their problem-solving *process* and identify the degree of reliability of the whole process with that of the initial segment. More generally, it would seem that *any* explanation of the correlation of overconfidence with task difficulty would have to advert to confidence in processes, and not merely to confidence in the subject on the topic. Task difficulty, even when measured by the frequency of true answers, is a variable that must be explained in part by differences in processes. Where tasks differ in difficulty because of differences in processes, differences in subject overconfidence must be due to differences in the accuracy of assessments of the degrees of reliability of the processes. So the fact that calibration varies with task difficulty suggests that what is measured by calibration is to some extent the accuracy of assessments of degrees of reliability. If the accuracy of these assessments were not what is measured, there would be no reason why calibration would differ with task difficulty. It should also be mentioned that there are researchers who explicitly measure confidence in processes because they are concerned to use differences in confidence as evidence of differences in processes (Wagenaar 1988). The fact remains, however, that we cannot easily use evidence of the poor calibration of degrees of confidence as evidence of inaccurate assessments of the degrees of reliability of processes. The calibration literature is less useful than it might be for epistemological purposes, and we will have to await more circumspect epistemologically oriented empirical research into degrees of confidence before we can draw secure, precise, detailed conclusions concerning our accuracy about the degrees of reliability of processes from findings about calibration. The literature on calibration, like most psychological literature, lacks clear import for epistemology because it fails to address the epistemologically significant questions.

Even though poor calibration does not entail inaccurate assessments of the degrees of reliability of processes, it does in the end suggest that subjects are likely to make errors about the degrees of reliability. Certainly if most subjects overestimate the frequency of their own correct answers on difficult tasks, this strongly suggests that they will overestimate the frequencies of their own true beliefs in large classes of beliefs and thus ultimately overestimate the frequencies of true outputs of processes. Indeed, to avoid doing so, they would either have to indulge in an equal and countervailing underestimation of the frequency of their correct answers on easy tasks, or exhibit a countervailing stinginess in estimating the frequencies of other subjects' true beliefs. And neither of these alternatives seems likely. The findings of calibration research do suggest a tentative and vague conjecture of inaccuracy in our assessments of the degrees of the reliability of certain processes.

One might look for solace in the finding that overconfidence is more pervasive and pronounced for difficult tasks. And one might offer the advice that we ought to avoid relying on the assessment of degrees of reliability of processes in regulating our performance of difficult tasks, using it only in easy tasks. Of course this is possible only if subjects can discriminate easy from difficult tasks. But even if subjects can do this, the proposal is hardly consoling. It seems the opposite of common sense to regulate beliefs in easy rather than hard tasks. It ought to be the other way around.

One might respond to poor calibration in a different way. One might hope that subjects are at least capable of *improving* their poor calibration. The explanation of overconfidence offered by Pitz suggests that there is no inherent inaccuracy in our assessments of degrees of reliability. We make mistakes because we assess the degree of reliability of an initial segment of our process and as a consequence of forgetting or inattention transfer the assessment to the whole process. If this is the cause of erroneous assessments, we may hope to correct it by improved memory or attention, for which attention to the source of error might suffice.

Unfortunately, attempts at improvement have had mixed results. Some researchers have found that feedback about overconfidence improves calibration (Adams and Adams 1958, 1961; Lichtenstein and Fischhoff 1980), but others have found that it does not (Lichtenstein, Fischhoff, and Phillips 1982). Explicit warnings against overconfidence do not significantly improve calibration (Fischhoff and Slovic 1980). Moreover, we must contend with the fact that experts in real life situations are rarely well calibrated, the few exceptions being experienced professional weather forecasters. The most plausible explanation of this fact would seem to be that good calibration results from frequent feedback of information about calibration over a long set of trials on a repetitive task, and weather forecasters are among the few experts who frequently receive such feedback – perhaps among the few experts for whom success is easily enough defined and evaluated to make feedback routine and decisively effective. The prospects for comparably successful feedback about calibration for nonexpert subjects on most topics are small. Perhaps we get such feedback about the calibration of simple perceptual processes. It would not be surprising to discover that we are well calibrated here. But we get less feedback for memorial processes and still less for inferential processes, especially on complex or abstract topics. One might hope that subjects at least have the *capacity* to become well calibrated by using feedback when they receive it. But merely having the capacity to become well calibrated given feedback will not do us any good if we are unable to obtain feedback, or if it is too costly for us to do so, or too costly to use the feedback we receive to recalibrate.

There are, however, two potentially saving objections to concluding from poor calibration that subjects cannot rely on the assessment of the degrees of reliability of processes. Even if overconfidence entails that assessments of the degrees of reliability of processes are inaccurate, this does not by itself prevent us from relying helpfully on these assessments in regulating beliefs or developing cognitive habits or traits. For what matters is not quite whether these assessments are correct but how subjects use them. First, if overconfidence is systematic and generally a monotonic function of reliability, then *ordinal comparisons* of degrees of reliability will remain unaffected. The inaccuracy of our assessments of degrees of reliability will not undermine the accuracy of such comparisons. Moreover, in these circumstances, it is possible to infer from inaccurate assessments of degrees of reliability assessments of *absolute* reliability that are effectively equivalent to the assessments we would infer from *accurate* assessments of degrees of reliability. All that is required is that we compensate for our inaccurate assessments of degrees of reliability by setting the lower bound on the degree of reliability necessary for absolute reliability sufficiently higher than it would be under the inference to absolute reliability we would otherwise make given inaccurate assessments of degrees of reliability. In this case, the effect of overconfidence will be cancelled by the higher lower bound on absolute reliability. As you might expect from what has already been said, the current state of calibration research does not afford any certain judgment whether overconfidence is a monotonic function of reliability.

But even if subjects are incorrigibly overconfident and do not adequately compensate for their overconfidence by setting a higher lower bound on absolute reliability, evaluation may still be helpful. For though overconfidence entails inaccurate evaluations, it does not entail completely inaccurate ones. Our evaluations may still enable us to purchase more processes that are reliable, and processes that are more reliable, than we could do without them, even if accurate evaluations would enable us to do better.

Finally, it is worth noting that reliabilism is not obviously in worse shape than some versions of mental internalism, and in particular, global coherentism, in its implications for the accuracy of the evaluation of justified beliefs. There is no reason to think that we are more accurate about the global coherence of our beliefs than about whether we exercise reliable processes. Judging whether a belief coheres with other beliefs requires judging the (rough) consistency of, and explanatory and inferential relations among, a vast array of beliefs, and that is bound to be difficult.

Hilary Kornblith (1989) has objected to BonJour's (1985) claim that coherence is *accessible* on the ground that one can make grand mistakes about the consistency of even a small and explicit set of beliefs, despite one's best efforts, as Frege did in his Basic Laws of Arithmetic, which were shown inconsistent by Russell. Kornblith is surely right that in formulating his Basic Laws Frege was as careful about consistency as a human being can be expected to be. And the difficulty of detecting inconsistency is certainly multiplied many times when we turn to something as massive and inchoate as a substantial fragment of a mature subject's system of beliefs. Whether this shows that coherence is inaccessible depends on just what is meant by "inaccessible" and how much consistency coherence requires. If accessibility entails being able to tell that the conditions of justification are satisfied, and the required consistency is perfect, then the example of Frege suggests that the consistency of a large body of beliefs is rarely if ever accessible; for it is quite possible for us to err in our judgments of consistency, whatever precautions we take. But if accessibility entails only being justified in believing that our beliefs cohere, or if the required consistency is less than perfect, then the example does not obviously argue against accessibility. Kornblith does, however, succeed in showing that rough explanatory coherence is often inaccessible even in a weak sense that entails only being justified on the basis of reflection alone. For we often need to communicate with others (in the case of the sciences, by reading journal articles) in order to judge which potential explanations are available, and this goes beyond the resources of reflection alone. Nevertheless, it is doubtful that BonJour needs to defend the accessibility of coherence, or even merely being justified in believing that our beliefs cohere. I suspect his inclination to do so derives from confusing perspectival internalism (justification from the subject's standpoint (1985: 41)), which is central to both his attack on reliabilism and his argument for coherentism, with accessibility internalism (grasping justification), which is peripheral to his concerns and should probably be irrelevant. He attacks reliabilism by appeal to perspectival internalism, but then apparently confuses the latter with accessibility internalism and concludes that fairness requires him to submit coherence, as well as reliability, to the constraint of accessibility. There is no need for him to do so. Coherentism is for BonJour a consequence of perspectival internalism and thus need not be submitted to accessibility internalism.[4]

What matters for our purposes, however, is whether we are any less accurate about reliability than coherence. The inaccessibility of coherence, in a sense of accessibility that entails being justified by reflection alone, does not yet entail the *inaccuracy* of our beliefs about it. While Frege's failure to judge accurately the consistency of his arithmetic suggests that it is quite *possible* that we err in our judgments of consistency, it does not suggest that we are generally mistaken in these judgments. We find Frege's case poignant precisely because he had such monumentally bad luck: he fell into error despite his impressive efforts to be consistent. And that shows that we do not expect people who take such precautions to end with massive and blatant inconsistency.

There are points of comparison between the evaluation of justified belief on reliabilism and its evaluation on coherentism. According to reliabilism, evaluating an inferential belief involves judging whether a chain of processes is exercised. On global coherentism, it involves judging whether a great many inferential relations obtain and thus whether inferential processes are exercised. In place of the reliabilist requirement of judging the reliability of a chain of processes, coherentism requires judging the pattern of a great many inferences. Of course if the evaluation of large numbers of beliefs is in question, reliabilism requires beliefs about the exercises of many processes. It also requires a systematic assessment of the reliability of processes. But without a more precise account of the pattern of inference necessary for justified belief on coherentism – an account coherentists have yet to supply – it is difficult to say whether the evaluation it requires is more or less costly than that required by reliabilism.

I have resisted the claim that there is decisive empirical evidence against the accuracy of our evaluations. Of course my defense leaves us with no reason to believe that our evaluations are accurate. That judgment could only come from comparing our actual assessments of the reliability of processes in the field with our best assessments in epistemology, using the Humean evaluative procedure outlined in chapter III, which judges the reliability of processes in light of our output and correlation beliefs. Of course we have no guarantee that such a comparison reaches the correct conclusion about our evaluations, for the same reason we have no guarantee that the Humean procedure reaches a correct conclusion about the reliability of our processes. While the nature of the Humean strategy limits the possible divergence of our field assessments from our best assessments, it does not prohibit a negative view of our actual assessments. And it is possible that we should dismiss a negative conclusion with the admission that the comparison can go radically awry, just as we may stand ready to dismiss the Humean evaluation of reliability. But we have no reason yet to suppose that the comparison of our field evaluations with the Humean evaluations will lead to such a negative view. Though on reliabilism evaluation plays a less significant role in forming justified beliefs than one might at first think, we have no reason to bar it on grounds of inaccuracy from the role it does play.

223

Notes

Introduction

1 For opposition to the view that knowledge entails *belief*, see Hanfling (1985). Popper (1979) famously opposes the view that knowledge entails *true belief*.

2 The claim that knowledge entails justified true belief is currently widely accepted. Support for this claim may be found in Swain (1981), BonJour (1985), and Lehrer (1990). See Adams (1986) and Alston (1989a) for objections to the claim that knowledge entails justified belief.

3 See Swain (1981) for an elegant defense of an indefeasibility account of knowledge. See Shope (1983) for an extensive review of the Gettier problem. Elsewhere I offer a reliabilist version of an indefeasibility account of knowledge (Schmitt 1983, 1985b), one which naturally extends the account of justified belief offered here.

4 So far as I can tell, the term "justified" was introduced to epistemology by Hume in *A Treatise of Human Nature*, but treatments of the concept go back to Plato.

5 The term "epistemically good end" is implicitly defined by its role in characterizing justified belief, and its meaning therefore varies widely from one account of justified belief to another. In general, however, it is not to be taken as referring to an intentional aim in cognition or as imposing the requirement that justified belief results from the motive of reaching the epistemically good end. The claim that the epistemically good end is true belief may be developed in a variety of ways: the end is all and only true belief, believing a proposition if and only if it is true, holding a large number and high proportion of true beliefs, relief from agnosticism plus the avoidance of false belief, and so on. These can be competing ends only in the presence of a characterization of justified belief. It is sometimes said that the epistemic end must be believing truths now, not in the long run (Foley 1987; Feldman 1989). But there is no reason to think that these ends can be distinguished in the characterization of justified belief: perhaps the only way to contribute to the end of believing truths now is to exercise a reliable process, and that entails contributing to the end of believing truths in the long run, at least in the sense that it contributes

to the exercise of the process, repetition of which would bring about true beliefs in the long run.

6 One might protest that making true belief the epistemic end introduces a circularity into the characterization of justified belief, since plausible theories of truth are epistemic. Putnam lodges this complaint: "Truth, in the only sense in which we have a vital and working notion of it, is rational acceptability" (1983: 231). It is tempting for the proponent of a truth-based epistemology to answer Putnam by defending a realist, correspondence conception of truth (Goldman 1986). But that is unnecessary. There are many other responses available that do not commit one to a realist or correspondence theory: (1) One might say that two can play at this game: justified belief, in the only sense in which we have a vital and working notion of it, is defined in terms of truth. In this case, there is no more to Putnam's point than a taste for defining semantical notions like truth in terms of epistemological notions, rather than the other way around. (2) If truth were definable in terms of rational acceptability, then rational acceptability would have to differ radically from justified belief, since justified beliefs can be, and frequently are, false. The difference would have to be so great that we would have no reason to expect that rational acceptability can be defined as the limit of the use of justifying methods, or indeed, that it can be defined in any ordinary epistemic terms at all. Yet once rational acceptability is nonepistemically defined, we can employ its nonepistemic characterization to characterize justified belief in terms of truth without fear of circularity. (3) We need not employ the notion of true belief in characterizing the epistemic end or justified belief. We may employ the notion of belief that is the case – belief p such that p. A reliable process may be defined as one that tends to yield beliefs that are the case. Truth enters the epistemological picture only because it is assumed that true belief is belief that is the case. If truth is instead rational acceptability, then we must return to characterizing justified belief in terms of belief that is the case. Thus the alleged failure of definitions of truth in nonepistemic terms does not imply that we must reject taking true belief (or belief that is the case) as the epistemic aim, or that we must reject reliabilism. It goes without saying that I am not denying here a correspondence theory of truth or favoring a deflationary or epistemic theory. I am only denying that there are specifically epistemological (as opposed to metaphysical or semantical) reasons for favoring such a theory.

7 I will assume throughout the book that a belief is justified only if it results from the exercise of a relevant belief-forming *process* meeting certain conditions – or as I will say, a justifying belief-forming process. Such a process account of justified belief is a species of causal account. One can in fact argue against various forms of internalism on the basis of a process account, but I will not do so here. The case for a process account is well known and widely accepted (Kornblith 1980; Swain 1981; Goldman 1986), so I will be brief. To be justified in believing p, it is not enough to have sufficient reason for believing p (or sufficient

evidence for *p*), or even to believe *p for* sufficient reason (i.e., to believe on the basis of a sufficient reason). Consider this example (Firth 1978): Holmes and Watson have the same sufficient reason for believing that the jeweler hid the pearls, and indeed both believe this for that reason. Yet Holmes and Watson differ in how they arrive at their beliefs. Holmes arrives at his belief via induction and Watson at his via a fallacious line of reasoning. In one sense of "justified" – the *doxastic* sense – Holmes is justified and Watson is not. The explanation is that they differ in the inferential processes by which they arrive at their beliefs.

There is, however, another sense of "justified" in which both are justified – the *propositional* sense. Propositional justification does not require merely *having* evidence: we have evidence for all the logical consequences of our doxastically justified beliefs, but we are not propositionally justified in believing all these consequences. It is natural to characterize propositional justification as requiring the availability of the exercise of a belief-forming process that would yield the belief *p* (Goldman 1979; Schmitt 1984). An opponent of the process theory might object that one is propositionally justified in believing a proposition one recognizes to follow from what one is doxastically justified in believing, regardless of whether there is an available process that would yield the belief. But the point of approving propositions by deeming them propositionally justified is to enable or encourage subjects to form beliefs in those propositions, and this cannot be done unless there are available processes. I do not assume the availability of the exercise of a process entails the feasibility of its exercise under the circumstances, but presumably available processes must generally be feasible if evaluating propositional justification is to promote doxastically justified belief. In general the difference between doxastic and propositional justification will not matter for our purposes, but I will flag the difference whenever confusing them would lead to trouble.

The opponent of a process account of doxastic justification may reply that Holmes and Watson differ in whether they believe *for* a sufficient reason, and thus we do not need to explain the difference in justification by appealing to any difference in the processes they exercise. This seems to require saying that Holmes and Watson differ in reasons that represent rules of reasoning associated with induction and fallacious reasoning – call these *second-order* reasons – and that one of these reasons is good and the other bad (Foley 1987). It is not hard to see, however, that we can iterate the case by giving Holmes and Watson the same first and second-order reasons but different processes, a justifying and a fallacious process respectively (Alston 1989b). Lehrer (1974) has offered a counterexample to any causal requirement – the well known case of the gypsy lawyer – but Swain (1981) replies to this example persuasively.

Foley (1987) has tried to explain why the absence of a causal connection might be judged unfavorably, despite not entailing the

absence of doxastically justified belief: it entails an epistemic flaw
of character (or epistemic irresponsibility), or at least the behavioral
manifestation of such a flaw. But first, it should be noted that there is
something wrong with the absence of a causal connection even when it
is not a flaw of character. There is something wrong when one fails to
arrive at one's belief from one's reasons via the right kind of process
even when one fails to do so as a result of unavoidable interference,
lapse of attention, or lack of cognitive energy. Second, it must be said
that the causal theorist can agree that this diagnosis explains what is
wrong with the absence of a causal connection in many cases: there
is a kind of epistemic flaw in the subject's practice. The practice of
exercising processes is valuable because it is the only way we have
to ensure a typical coincidence of what we believe and what we are
propositionally justified in believing. This diagnosis is correct as far as
it goes. But that very fact raises doubts about the noncausal account
of doxastically justified belief. If the practice of exercising processes
is valuable because it is our way of ensuring a typical coincidence
of these conditions, then each instance of exercising processes is
valuable too – in virtue of its contribution to this practice. So we
ought to laud not only the practice of exercising processes, but the
exercises of the processes as well, and the beliefs that result from
them. And this is just what we do, on the causal account. Moreover,
on the noncausal account, doxastically justified belief is not obviously
something deserving of favor. Looked at from one perspective – that
of propositional justification – it is a chimaera, combining in an
arbitrary way both propositional justification for *p* and for the rules
associated with inferences, while from the perspective of a causal
account, it fails to include what would be minimally needed for praise
beyond propositional justification: the actual exercise of the process.
Foley's explanation is unconvincing.

8 Innate beliefs will be an exception if they are formed only by
   noncognitive evolutionary, genetic, or neurodevelopmental processes.
9 See Dretske (1989) for insightful development of this point.
10 Other versions of externalism include Popperian epistemology
   (Popper 1979; Watkins 1984); explanationism (Harman 1973, 1986;
   Thagard 1988); and biological epistemology (Millikan 1984; Lycan
   1985; Plantinga 1988).
11 The issue between internalism and externalism in epistemology is
   closely analogous to that between those who deny and those who
   affirm moral luck in ethics (Nagel 1979; B. Williams 1981). For an
   excellent comparison of moral and epistemic luck, see Slote (1990).
   Foley (1987) has used the term "epistemic luck" to refer to a condition
   almost the opposite of what is analogous to moral luck.
12 I say *nearly* uncontroversial because I for one deny that knowledge
   must be possessed in this sense (Schmitt 1985a, 1987, 1989a, 1989b,
   forthcoming b; see also Coady 1973). I subscribe to *epistemological
   socialism*: a subject may be justified by reasons that are states of
   other individuals. Extant versions of internalism are inconsistent

with epistemological socialism. It is an interesting question, however, whether there could be versions of internalism consistent with it. Could there be a socialist internalism on which a subject is justified in virtue of reasons possessed by a group of individuals to which the subject belongs? I am inclined to doubt it. Such a view would require a socialized notion of accessibility or perspective – accessibility of the reason to the group, or a group epistemic perspective. But what is it to be accessible to a group, and how might the mutually inconsistent epistemic perspectives of the individual members of the group be summed to make a group epistemic perspective? Lacking answers to these questions, we would have to take any argument for epistemological socialism as an argument against internalism.

13 This way of explaining antecedent skepticism was first explicitly formulated by Hilary Kornblith (1985). Here I develop and defend Kornblith's insight.

14 Can the force of antecedent skepticism be explained by appeal to externalist conditions of knowledge alone, without adverting to accessibility internalism? Robert Nozick (1981) has argued that skepticism arises from requiring *tracking* for knowledge, an externalist condition, on the assumption that knowledge is closed under (known) logical implication (see also Dretske (1971) and Goldman (1976)). Suppose I must know the (known) logical implications of what I know. Then if I know that this is a table (p), then I must also know the implication that I am not deceived by a demon into believing falsely that this is a table (q). But suppose also that knowing q requires tracking the truth of q – i.e., if it were not the case that q, then I would not believe q. Then I do *not* know q, since I do not track the truth of q. So I do not know p. But in my view, this skepticism does not derive entirely from externalist conditions. The closure principle is a disguised internalist principle, so that Nozick's challenge depends on identifying a proposition q for which tracking clearly fails and the failure of tracking derives entirely from q's implication that my experience would be the same even if there were a demon (so that I would still believe q if there were a demon). Indeed, the portion of q that is an implication of p – that I do not falsely believe p – is irrelevant to ensuring that I do not track the truth of q. But q's implication here guarantees that q is a consequence not merely of p, but of *knowing* p: if I know p, it must be false that my experience would be the same even if there were a demon. At least, this is so if knowing p requires tracking the truth of p. This seems to show that Nozick's skeptical challenge is equivalent to one that rests on the principle of closure under (known) *knowledge-implication*: if I know p and I know that my knowing p implies q, then I know q. I fail to know p because I would still believe an implication, not of p, but of my knowing p (that my belief is not produced by a demon) even if this implication were false. The apparently purely externalist challenge turns out to be a partly internalist challenge like Barry Stroud's (1984).

15 In making this claim, I do not mean to say that historically important

epistemologists are self-consciously externalist, or even that they are aware of what is at issue between internalism and externalism, or indeed that they possess the conceptual resources to frame the issue. I mean to claim only that they are practicing externalists – that their views are partly driven by externalism.

I Greek Skepticism

1 In interpreting Plato's remarks in the *Theaetetus* I rely exclusively on what he has to say there. I am mainly interested in aspects of Plato's epistemology that were picked up and transmitted by the skeptical tradition, and from what I can tell, the ideas of the first third of the *Theaetetus* play a far greater role in subsequent epistemology than Plato's ideas elsewhere. For my purposes, then, I need not deny that Plato anywhere adopts internalism, only that internalism plays a role in his skeptical worries in the *Theaetetus*. Nevertheless, I regard his views elsewhere (in the *Meno*, *Republic* V–VII, and *Philebus*) as externalist and largely consistent with his remarks in the *Theaetetus*. Inconsistencies would most likely arise with *Republic* V–VII, where Plato is usually supposed to claim that knowledge and belief are disjoint, knowledge is of the forms only and of necessary truths (Vlastos 1985). I do not think that these claims deeply contradict the views I attribute to Plato here, but I also doubt whether he subscribes to them (Fine 1990). For simplicity of exposition, I will assume that knowledge is a certain kind of belief. I do think Plato holds such a view, at least in the *Meno* and *Theaetetus*, but nothing I want to say here depends on attributing this view, and readers who reject it are invited to translate what I say by replacing all occurrences of "belief" with a term designating what they take the bearer of knowledge to be. I follow McDowell's translation of the *Theaetetus* (1973), with slight modifications where it is contradicted by enough other translations and I am unsatisfied with his philosophical reasons for translating as he does. Possessing essentially no Greek, I must rely on a comparative study of the translations and commentaries.

2 Liddell and Scott translate *apseudes* as "unerring" (1968: 298). McDowell has "as if it's knowledge" where most translations have "as being knowledge." I find his ground for this nonstandard translation unconvincing.

3 I have appropriated the Epicurean term "criterion" because I find it convenient in describing Plato's position. Plato uses *kriterion* at 178b, though only to refer to Protagorean perspectives (not, so far as I can tell, to faculties, as Striker (1990) claims). Plato's criteria, in my usage, bear more resemblance to Epicurean than Stoic criteria, the latter being considerably narrower than Plato's, encompassing only exactly similar impressions.

4 Theaetetus does say that it is difficult to see what evidence (*epideixai*) one should use to prove that we are not dreaming. But what he lacks

is not a proof of the reliability of a criterion, or even a proof at all. He simply lacks evidence that he is awake. The proposition that he is awake is a paradigmatic instance of a proposition for which there is no criterion because it is clearly false when he is dreaming. (In this, it differs from such propositions as "There is a table in my house" and "Two plus two equals four.") As Socrates says, "there is plenty of room for doubt, when we even doubt whether we are asleep or awake" (159c–d). It is true that Socrates speaks of their having confidence that they are awake whether they are dreaming or awake, and this might be taken as an observation that they lack a proof that they are awake by which they might prove the reliability of the criterion. But it is more plausibly taken as a defense of the claim that their criterion is the same in waking and in dreaming: they cannot distinguish the criterion they employ in the two cases by appeal to their psychological state of confidence, since they are equally confident. One might retort that having a proof of the proposition that one is awake is a necessary condition of having a proof of the reliability of the criterion, and indeed that the reference to the proposition that one is awake is designed to indicate what evidence might constitute a proof of reliability. I will suggest a similar interpretation of Descartes' dream and demon challenges in the *Meditations*. But I do not see Plato as treating a proof of the proposition that one is awake as a necessary condition of a proof of reliability or as an indication of what counts as a proof of reliability. Rather, he treats the proposition that one is awake as one among many propositions that render it doubtful that there are criteria because they are false while one is dreaming.

5 There is an alternative, though less plausible, explanation of why Plato asks whether truth is to be decided by length of time that is consistent with my approach: Plato wishes to turn from raising the skeptical challenge, which he has done well enough by appeal to dreaming, to the Protagorean defense of Theaetetus' claim that knowledge is perception. That defense involves appealing to the Protagorean doctrine of relativism about truth, and truths may be relative to various conditions of the subject – normality or disorder, sanity or madness. At this point in the discussion, Socrates begins to speak on behalf of Protagoras, suggesting that beliefs that arise from disorders or madness may be no less true than beliefs that arise from normality or sanity. A few lines later (158e) Socrates formally introduces the Protagorean defense. The trouble with this explanation is that before the formal introduction, Socrates refers again to criteria of truth in asking about "certain marks."

6 Another possible response on the skeptic's behalf is to insist that individuating factors be quite general ones, more general than dreaming, disorders, and madness, so that these do not count as individuating factors. One reason to insist on quite general individuating factors is that we must be able to assess the reliability (and thus judge the individuation) of criteria if we are to employ

the criteria in arriving at beliefs on specific topics. But then our judgments of the individuation of criteria must not depend on our beliefs about these specific topics. I am not convinced, however, that dreaming, disorders, and madness are specific enough to be ruled out by generality. I am inclined to think that individuating factors will in the end conspire to distinguish dreaming and waking and thus foil an externalist dream challenge. This is not to say that an internalist dream challenge fares better, since it rests on a vulnerable form of internalism – a matter to which we will return in the next chapter.

7 Or it may be understood as externalist in virtue of the fact that when there are equal reasons for contrary propositions, there are opposing criteria that are equally reliable.

8 Rist (1969) identifies apprehension and knowledge, but, as Annas (1980) observes, this is inconsistent with Zeno's simile. Rist also attributes both a coherence theory of knowledge and a coherence theory of truth to the Stoics – a combination designed to ensure that knowledge entails truth. Annas suggests that the Stoics fail to distinguish clearly between knowledge and truth. But I see no evidence of this. They may well hold a coherence theory of knowledge, but I see no evidence of a coherence theory of apprehension or of truth.

9 It is worth noting that Stoic epistemology also resembles Cartesian epistemology in key respects – indeed, Descartes probably derives his basic epistemological concepts from Cicero's description of Zeno's epistemology in *Academica* (*LS* I 254; *Acad.* I 41–2). Stoic cognitive impressions may be compared with Descartes' clear and distinct perception, while Stoic cognition is like Descartes' *cognitio* (i.e., judgment resulting from clear and distinct perception – usually translated "knowledge"), and Stoic knowledge (*episteme*) parallels Descartes' *scientia* (i.e., cognition secured against the demon challenge by the validation of clear and distinct perception). But of course there are profound differences between Stoic and Cartesian epistemology: for the Stoics cognitive impressions are not compelling by themselves, as clear and distinct perception is for Descartes; cognitive impressions are sensory, while clear and distinct perception is intellectual; and the Stoics do not say, as Descartes does, that knowledge requires a validation of cognitive impressions. Rist (1969) has argued that the Stoics hold a coherence theory of knowledge, and there is considerable plausibility in that claim; but Descartes also plausibly holds a coherence theory of sensory cognition. Yet here too there is an important difference: for the Stoics, at least the early ones, cognitive impressions are already reliable before they cohere with beliefs, while for Descartes coherence is part of what is required for sense to *be* reliable. On the Stoic view, it is not so clear why coherence *is* necessary – why reliability does not suffice – while on Descartes' view it is quite clear.

10 I follow Cicero's translation of *pithanos* as "probable," rather than "convincing," as in *LS*. One reason for doing so is that *pithanos* is clearly normative and not merely a psychological status. Another is that the Stoics seem to accept a relative frequency theory of *pithanos*.

11 To make matters even less clear, Cicero describes cognitive impressions as being "of a kind of which a false mark could not be." If a "kind" is broader than the criterion defined by the given cognitive impression, then the mere existence of a single impression of that kind for which there is a similar false impression will be enough to prevent impressions of that kind from being cognitive.

12 I have said that this account of the Academics' challenge is equivalent to the preceding account. It is equivalent if the probability that a criterion is reliable is simply the actual relative frequency of reliable criteria of that kind, and the kind is defined in the same way as it is in the preceding analysis (and if reliability is perfect reliability).

13 What constitutes proof? Sextus discusses the nature of proof in the Stoic sense and argues against its existence (*LS* I 214–16; *M* VIII 429–34, 440–3), but I do not find that the Stoic definition or Sextus' objections to the existence of proof illuminate the skeptical modes.

14 As I have said, the circularity argument (*Et.* 62–3; *PH* I 114–17) comes to much the same thing as the regress argument. Indeed there is no circularity here, since Sextus does not show that the criterion used to prove the reliability of the initial criterion is the same as that criterion (or, more generally, that some criterion used in the regress of proofs is the same as some criterion used earlier in the regress). If Sextus wishes to avoid the assumption that some criterion must repeat because our minds are limited, he must retreat to the idea that we run out of criteria because all the criteria we might employ are called into question. Clearly this way of prosecuting the argument also depends on a comprehensive doubt (and in just the same way as the regress argument did).

II Descartes' Skepticism

1 The interpretation I propose here is perhaps closest to Curley's (1978) among recent interpretations.

2 The central aim of Descartes' inquiry is true belief. There is evidence, however, that Descartes is also concerned with *stable* or *irrevisable* belief. Stable belief is presumably belief that tends not to be retracted (and thus belief that tends to withstand the addition of further beliefs). Irrevisable belief is belief sufficiently justified that there could be no reasons that would (in conjunction with the reasons one already possesses) no longer justify the belief. Descartes expresses a concern with stable belief at the outset of *Meditation* I:

I realized that it was necessary, once in the course of my life, to demolish everything completely and start again right from the foundations if I wanted to establish anything at all in the sciences that was stable and likely to last.

(II 12; VII 17)

Alternatively, one might urge that the aim of true belief is merely instrumental to the aim of stable belief: if science contains true beliefs, it will be stable. Or one might argue, citing the perplexing passage at *CSM* II 103; *AT* VII 144–5 as Frankfurt (1970: 25) has done, that Descartes simply *defines* human truth as irrevisability (whereas divine truth is correspondence with reality). But as B. Williams (1978) has pointed out, this passage does not say that a proposition could be clearly and distinctly perceived and divinely false, but only that someone could *pretend* that it is divinely false. Moreover, Descartes' validation of reason is surely intended to do more than this proposal can allow. If human truth is simply that which is irrevisable, then the validation is an argument from God's nondeception to the conclusion that clear and distinct perception is irrevisable (since its conclusion is that clear and distinct perception is perfectly reliable). According to the proposal, then, the conclusion of the validation is that God does not lead us to believe *human* falsehoods. Then the premises of the validation say that God does not compel assent and later provide reason for revision. They say, in other words, that God is constant. While constancy is a virtue, orthodox theology ascribes a more robust virtue than that: God is a nondeceiver in the sense that he does not compel us to believe *God's* falsehoods. It must also be said that stable belief is a less plausible ultimate epistemic aim than true belief. The aim of stable belief could be satisfied by a system of stable but false beliefs – beliefs whose falsity we have no possibility of uncovering, as in the case of deception by a demon. But surely if, contrary to his claim to foreclose the possibility of a demon, Descartes were to countenance the possibility of such a system, he would not regard it as fulfilling our ultimate epistemic aims. The aim of true belief, on the other hand, seems to entail a certain stability, given the limitations of human cognition. We cannot maintain the number and proportion of our true beliefs if we tend to lose the beliefs we have, unless at the same time we continue to acquire true beliefs in the same number and proportion as we lose them. Many beliefs are of course of ephemeral value, and we may lose them with impunity. We maintain our number and proportion of true beliefs by replacing them with other beliefs of similar value by exercising reliable processes. But beliefs of lasting value we wish to retain, especially when they are costly to acquire, and the stability of these beliefs contributes to the maintenance of the number and proportion of our true beliefs.

3 Descartes assumes that a belief is tainted by its association with false beliefs. He initially suggests that *any* false belief casts doubt on all sensory beliefs: "from time to time I have found that the senses

deceive, and it is prudent never to trust completely those who have deceived us even once" (*CSM* II 18; *AT* VII 12). Descartes has been charged here with the mistake of inferring invalidly from the premise that some sensory beliefs are false to the conclusion that all sensory beliefs might be false (Rescher 1959). But whether this inference is invalid depends on what "might be false" means. If it means "falling under a principle that is unreliable," then the inference is valid, so long as the beliefs that are false also fall under the principle. Descartes' remark here suggests that his principle casts a very wide net – covering all the senses. But he does not maintain this position long. His subsequent remarks show that he does not regard sensory beliefs as undermined here to an extent that would warrant withholding assent from all sensory beliefs. For he turns immediately to more powerful reasons for withholding assent.

4 Descartes offers a *practical* motivation for judging beliefs by the reliability of principles: it "would be an endless task" to assess beliefs individually. But this practical motivation is certainly not his real motive for turning to the reliability of principles. For it is otiose: one *cannot* assess beliefs individually, since the grounds for retracting them depend on judging other beliefs (or propositions) to be false. One may retract a belief falling under a principle only if other beliefs falling under the principle are false. Accordingly principles must be individuated in such a way that they fail to justify the beliefs that fall under them when they yield false beliefs. Equivalently, beliefs resulting from a principle must be justified in virtue of the overall reliability of the principle.

5 The requirement of perfect reliability might be warranted by appeal to the idea that a process that yields a false belief would not be a genuine criterion of truth, any more than a genuine algorithm for square roots can sometimes yield cube roots (Burnyeat 1982). B. Williams (1978) argues that the requirement of perfect reliability is warranted because Descartes is engaged in pure, not practical, inquiry, and the practical costs of maintaining perfect reliability are not relevant. But maintaining perfect reliability has pure as well as practical costs: perfect reliability is purchased at the cost of forgoing exercising many less than perfectly reliable processes – at the cost of many true beliefs. Yet believing truths is as much a pure cognitive aim as avoiding believing falsehoods. To insist on perfectly reliable processes is to give undue weight to avoiding falsehoods. Such an insistence would seem to derive either from a deluded epistemological optimism or a kind of epistemic prudery. In addition to this reason for denying that Descartes requires perfect reliability, there are two further points: (1) Descartes treats hypothetico-deduction as justifying, even though it is clearly not perfectly reliable; (2) Descartes is troubled primarily by *extensive*, not occasional false belief, as the opening sentence of *Meditation* I shows.

6 Descartes imposes this requirement in his Replies to Bourdin's uncomprehending Seventh Objections:

it is wholly false that in laying down our foundations in philosophy there are corresponding limits which fall short of complete certainty, but which we can sensibly and safely accept without taking doubt any further. For since truth is essentially indivisible, it may happen that a claim which we do not recognize as possessing complete certainty may in fact be quite false, however probable it may appear. To make the foundations of all knowledge (*scientiae*) rest on a claim that we recognize as being possibly false would not be a sensible way to philosophize.

(*CSM* II 374; *AT* VII 548)

Descartes makes explicit in this passage what is implicit in the opening sentence of *Meditation* I: we must avoid false foundations because an erroneous foundational belief may well lead to the use of highly unreliable principles, and thus to extensive falsehood in the remainder of our beliefs (Schmitt 1986).

7   Our account contrasts with a common interpretation: that Descartes rejects sensory beliefs on the ground that they are *revisable* (Tlumak 1978); sensory reasons are not sufficiently justifying to exclude the possibility that these reasons, conjoined with counterreasons, no longer justify the belief. Thus Descartes observes that when I view a tower from a distance, I may judge it to be round because it appears so, but subsequently revise my belief when I approach and it appears square. On the revisability interpretation, Descartes' point is that my sensory reason – the tower's seeming round – is not sufficiently justifying to prevent my subsequent sensory counterreason – the tower's seeming square – from undoing my justification for believing that the tower is round. Descartes can be made to fit this interpretation only with violence. It is not plausible to suppose that one can show a belief revisable by pointing out that it is possibly false. For there are ways that beliefs can be false that do not plausibly entail that the belief's degree of justification is insufficient to overcome future counterreasons. And these ways are precisely the ways to which Descartes subsequently appeals in rejecting sensory beliefs: the possibility of dreaming or deception by a demon. Moreover, if Descartes were concerned only to reject sensory beliefs on grounds of revisability, his job would be easy: all sensory beliefs are obviously revisable, so they should all be rejected if revisability is a sufficient ground for rejection. My belief that the tower is square is no less revisable than my belief that the tower is round (though my sensory reason for this belief provides a higher degree of justification and would withstand more counterevidence). Yet Descartes does not reject my belief that the tower is square on grounds of revisability, but turns to the prima facie possibility of dreaming or deception by a demon. And such possibilities are not naturally construed as counterreasons against the belief that the tower is round, since as mere possibilities they do not indicate that my belief is false. Nor can they be weighed against my sensory reason in judging whether

the tower is square, in the way that the tower's seeming round can be weighed against the tower's seeming square. Nor would rejecting beliefs on grounds of revisability be in keeping with Descartes' aim of true belief. If stable belief were the ultimate epistemic aim, then we might expect irrevisability (or, more plausibly, a weakened version of it: having reasons that are sufficiently justifying to outweigh all actual or likely future counterevidence) to be a plausible candidate for justification. But if, as I argued in note 2, stable belief is a mere consequence of fulfilling the epistemic aim, irrevisable belief will be at best a consequence of fulfilling this aim: highly reliable belief-forming processes may lead to irrevisable beliefs by supplying reasons that are sufficiently justifying to outweigh actual or likely counterreasons. (See chapter VII for related discussion of the reliabilist treatment of counterevidence.)

A second familiar interpretation sees Descartes as rejecting sensory beliefs on grounds of *underdetermination*: there are contrary propositions that are consistent with and offer a sufficiently good account or explanation of the reasons for sensory beliefs – the reasons being sensory experiences. Thus my initial sensory reason, the tower's seeming round, is consistent with the tower's being round (as I initially believe) or its being square, and, to take Descartes' subsequent doubt, the totality of my sensory reasons (my whole sensory experience) is consistent with my experience's being produced by bodies, dreaming, or a deceiving demon. This interpretation is preferable to the revisability interpretation in accommodating Descartes' skeptical use of the possibility of dreaming or deception by a demon. Indeed, it treats his use of these possibilities as similar to – on the same logical level as – his use of the tower case. It must also be said that Descartes is familiar with and engaged by problems of the underdetermination of scientific theories by observations (e.g., *Principles* IV.204 (*CSM* I 289; *AT* VIII 327)). And Descartes attempted to answer such doubts, though obliquely, through his theological validation of reason. On the underdetermination interpretation, Descartes' rejection of sensory beliefs is assimilated to the Academic opposition of propositions. But I do not think Descartes rejects sensory beliefs on grounds of underdetermination. When he rejects his belief that the tower is round, he does not do so by observing that his reason (the tower's seeming round) is consistent with and equally well explained by the contrary proposition (or fact) that the tower is square. There is no evidence that he thinks this reason is equally well explained by the latter proposition. He clearly regards his later sensory reason (the tower's seeming square) as better supporting the proposition that the tower is square than the contrary proposition that the tower is round; so he must think that sensory reasons sometimes support one sensory belief better than a contrary belief, and it is plausible to suppose that he thinks such reasons are better explained by the proposition (or fact) belief in which they support. This leaves no basis for thinking that he regards all sensory reasons as equally explained by contrary propositions. Nor, when he restores his sensory beliefs against the demon and dream possibilities in *Meditation* VI, does he argue that bodies better explain my sensory reasons than the dream or demon hypotheses. Similarly, on the underdetermination interpretation of the skeptical challenges, Descartes would have no motivation to establish the reliability of clear and distinct perception, only to show that the demon hypothesis is an inferior explanation of his sensory reasons. Descartes' skeptical challenge is not the charge that sensory beliefs are underdetermined by sensory reasons. Though the skeptical charge of underdetermination is a significant one, it raises a derivative rather than a fundamental challenge. If the epistemic aim is true belief, what matters fundamentally is whether our processes yield true beliefs. Underdetermination raises a significant challenge for either of two reasons: sensory processes that yield beliefs underdetermined by sensory reasons are in fact unreliable – they have no means of selecting true sensory beliefs from among contrary beliefs in the presence of sensory reasons; or sensory and other reasons are prima facie possibly unreliable.

8 On either interpretation, the discriminate sensory process must include only the purely *cognitive* component of what occurs under normal sense, and not environmental conditions – otherwise it could not occur in cases of madness, dreaming, or deception by a demon. Note that Descartes' criticism of sensory processes is not merely that they are possibly less than *perfectly* reliable, but that they are possibly *massively* unreliable. For madness, dreaming, and deception by a demon entail massive unreliability.

9 Many commentators have assumed that when Descartes poses the dream challenge, he challenges each particular sensory belief in isolation by raising the prima facie possibility that this belief is false – a possibility raised, at least for many indexical beliefs, by considering that I might be dreaming only at this moment. Such an interpretation fits naturally with the view that, for Descartes, a belief is indubitable only if I can rule out the prima facie possibility that it is false. Wilson (1978) shows that this interpretation is countertextual.

Proponents of the interpretation have typically been driven by the desire to steer Descartes around an alleged problem for an interpretation like mine, on which Descartes challenges sense by raising the prima facie possibility that our sensory process is unreliable much as if we were always dreaming: we cannot be justified in believing that dream experiences are illusory unless we rely on sense, so that the claim that sense is prima facie possibly unreliable is justified only if sense is reliable. One response to this objection is that we do not have to rely on sense to be justified in believing that sense is prima facie possibly unreliable, since we do not have to be justified in believing that dream experiences are illusory – only in believing that it is prima facie possible that sensory experience is the way we believe dream experience to be. A second response – one which also defends the claim that we could conclude the massive unreliability of our sensory processes from the analogous objection that any such conclusion would depend on sense and thus be justified only if sense is reliable – is that we need not be justified in the beliefs on which we base a skeptical attack, so long as those beliefs are at least as justified as any others on which the respondent may rely.

10 Does knowledge require *actually* answering the antecedent skeptical challenge – showing the belief-forming process reliable – or merely being in a position to show this? Early in the *Meditations* Descartes leaves it ambiguous whether knowledge requires answering the skeptic. For example, at the outset of *Meditation* III he describes his list of certainties ambiguously as "everything I truly know (*scio*), or at least everything I have so far discovered that I know" (*CSM* II 24; *AT* VII 35). The first disjunct implies the demanding view that knowledge requires that one already have answered skepticism, while the second implies the lenient view that knowledge does not require this. By the end of *Meditation* V, however, Descartes honors the pull of both views by abdicating a choice between them, assigning them to different concepts of knowledge. *Scientia* "depends uniquely on my knowledge (*cognitione*) of the true God" (*CSM* II 49; *AT* VII 71). That is, it requires that one actually have answered the antecedent skeptical challenge. *Cognitio*, on the other hand, is "the kind of knowledge (*scientiam*) possessed by the atheist" (*CSM* II 289; *AT* VII 428). It does not require that one actually have answered skepticism, though of course it does require that one be in a position to answer it. Descartes refuses to favor one concept over the other, but he does insist that answering skepticism deepens our knowledge (*CSM* II 22; *AT* VII 33). Somehow answering skepticism is supposed to impart an insight into the nature of knowledge that affects the knowledge itself.

11 Loeb (1986) has raised an interesting objection to the view that the demon challenge in *Meditation* I is intended to show the prima facie possible unreliability of sensory processes. Loeb thinks Descartes considers this type of skeptical challenge and consciously rejects it in the madness passage, where he declines to imagine that he is like those "whose brains are so damaged by the persistent vapours of melancholia" (*CSM* II 13; *AT* VII 19). In *Meditation* I the demon is imagined to deceive me by causing each of my sensory experiences individually, rather than by implanting in me a defective process or faculty. In reply, I would urge that we need not choose between this interpretation and my own. On the contrary, if, as I claim, Descartes wishes to raise the possibility of the unreliability of my sensory processes by imagining the demon to produce in me defective processes, he will still have to suppose that the demon does so by falsifying each of the beliefs that result from the processes. The processes must indeed be the same as those I actually exercise – otherwise Descartes will not have imagined a case in which those very processes are unreliable. But then Descartes must imagine that the processes are the same when they are cognitively just like the processes I actually exercise, and he must also imagine that the demon deceives

me, not by producing in me some cognitively different processes, but by arranging my environment so that my sensory beliefs are false. As I have suggested in the text, Descartes may reject the madness hypothesis precisely because it involves imagining a case in which my processes are rather different from the way they actually are.

12 It is typically assumed that "I exist" is indubitable because it is the conclusion of an inference with the premise "I think," or of a syllogism with the major premise "Whatever is a thinking thing exists" or "Whatever has attributes exists." This reading requires that "I think" is already assumed indubitable. In favor of this reading is the fact that Descartes occasionally formulates the cogito as an inference from "I think." In these passages Descartes seems concerned to say what sort of inference the cogito is supposed to be. But even if "I exist" is supposed to be inferred from "I think," it does not follow that "I exist" is *indubitable* because it is so inferred, or that "I exist" is justified on the basis of "I think," or that "I think" must first be assumed or shown indubitable if "I exist" is to be indubitable. In the *Search for Truth*, Descartes explains the cogito this way: "I exist, and I know the fact because I am doubting, i.e. because I am thinking" (*CSM* II 415; *AT* X 521). This remark suggests that for Descartes I can tell that I exist, not because I *infer* it from "I think," but because *I think*, hence exist, even in the situation of entertaining the skeptical challenge, or in the situation described by the skeptical challenge (that is, the situation in which I am deceived by a demon). What makes "I exist" indubitable is the *fact* that it is true in the demon situation. We infer "I exist" from "I think" in the sense that we recognize that "I exist" is true in the demon situation. But I do not tell that I exist on the basis of telling that I think. There is a sense in which "I think" must be first assumed or shown indubitable: it obviously describes part of what is true in the situation of entertaining the demon challenge – and it is from this description that "I exist" is inferred. But the situation might have been described without describing it as a situation in which I think. It might have been described directly and simply as a situation in which I exist. That may be why Descartes shows no sign of worry when he admits at *Principles* I.10 that he needs the major premise "Whatever is a thinking thing exists" to make the inference of the cogito. Some have interpreted Descartes here as exempting our knowledge of the meanings of terms from the skeptical challenge (see also Descartes' remark in the "Sixth Replies" that we know what thought and existence are by "internal awareness" rather than "the kind of knowledge that is acquired by means of demonstration" (*CSM* II 241; *AT* VII 422). But that does not fit with the generality of the demon doubt, which would seem to encompass any propositional knowledge at all, including analytic knowledge deriving from our knowledge of the meanings of terms. (And anyway, as a proponent of the Ontological Argument, Descartes cannot treat the proposition "Whatever is a thinking thing exists" as analytic, since having an attribute cannot analytically entail existence if the Ontological Argument is to avoid begging the question.) A

philosophically preferable position is that a premise is indubitable when it is true in the situation in which I entertain the demon challenge, or in the situation described by the challenge.

13 We should mention two other arguments for independent accessibility internalism:

(1) Stroud has suggested that independent accessibility internalism is a consequence of the project of epistemology itself, and in particular of the general character of the explanation of knowledge attempted by epistemology:

> If we start by considering a certain domain of facts or truths and ask how anyone could come to know anything at all in the domain, it will seem that any other knowledge that might be relevant could not be allowed to amount to already knowing something in the domain in question. Knowledge of anything at all in that domain is what we want to explain and if we simply assume from the outset that the person has already got some of that knowledge we will not be explaining all of it. Any knowledge we do grant to the person will be of use to him only if he can somehow get from that knowledge to some knowledge in the domain in question.
>
> (Stroud 1989: 34–5)

That is, epistemology seeks a general explanation of how knowledge in a domain is possible, and we are therefore barred from relying on such knowledge to explain this possibility; the premises on which we rely in explaining knowledge must be known independently of our knowledge in the domain. This argument has two striking defects: (i) It has overkill, for it assumes that we have knowledge only if a general epistemological explanation is possible. But then the argument leads immediately to the conclusion that it is *logically* impossible for anyone to know anything. Yet neither Descartes nor any historical skeptic ever intended to challenge the *logical* possibility of knowledge or thought the victory of skepticism so easily secured. If the assumption that we have knowledge only if a general epistemological explanation is possible leads immediately to so extreme a form of skepticism, we should reject the assumption. (ii) Stroud's argument begs the question by assuming that we can know the propositions that explain how knowledge is possible in a domain only independently of knowledge in the domain. Surely this is just what is at issue when we ask for an argument for independent accessibility internalism.

(2) A second argument for the relevance of the demon challenge to knowledge is suggested by Descartes' insistence that doubt has no implications for action (Stroud 1984). The demon challenge is distinguished from challenges we regard as relevant to knowledge by its improbability or dissimilarity to actual circumstances. According to the argument, we treat the difference as significant only because we import practical considerations into the conditions of knowledge. If we consider knowledge from a purely theoretical vantage, we will

240

no longer import these practical considerations into the conditions we assign knowledge. (Stroud also suggests the rather different line that practical considerations bear only on the conditions of *appropriate* knowledge attribution, not the conditions of *correct* attribution which are at issue here, but he offers no argument for this suggestion.) In response, I would question whether there is a theoretical vantage from which the difference in the probability of contraries is insignificant. For there are theoretical concerns that may limit the relevant doubts to those that are probable. There are two components in the epistemic end of believing truths – having true beliefs and avoiding having false beliefs. It is a commonplace in epistemology that these components are in competition with one another. The fact that we cannot answer the demon challenge entails that making that challenge relevant favors the second component at the expense of the first. And favoring the second component in this way is by no means a mandate that emerges from a theoretical vantage once practical concerns have been bracketed. On the contrary, the theoretical vantage does not by itself favor the second component. At best, one might argue that whether subjects have knowledge is always relative to a particular weighting of the components, a weighting that is determined by the evaluator's purposes in evaluating (whether theoretical or practical).

III Hume's Skepticism

1 Here I rely almost exlusively on *A Treatise of Human Nature*, largely because it offers a deeper and more extensive treatment of skepticism than the *Enquiry Concerning Human Understanding*.

2 Hume's most explicit account of suppositional representation appears in his theory of relative ideas. He explains that we have no proper idea of an external existence, such as a body, since that would require conceiving of something existent that is qualitatively different from what is represented by the idea; yet the idea of existence cannot be abstracted from ideas of qualities. Hume adds: "The farthest we can go towards a conception of external objects, when suppos'd *specifically* different from our perceptions is to form a relative idea of them, without pretending to comprehend the related objects" (*T* 68; cf. *T* 242). We may treat the relative idea as a demonstrative the reference of which is fixed by ideas of qualities: it is the idea of whatever it is that is related in a certain way to our ideas of qualities. Hume's doctrine of relative ideas is a broad generalization (to all external existences) of Locke's treatment of our ideas of causal power, substance, and real essence. But Hume's relative ideas are not quite his suppositions, since we cannot truly have an idea of a relation abstracted from its relata, and such an idea would be required if we were to have a relative idea of an existence which is not the archetype of our idea. Suppositions are demonstrative representations involving representations of relations of which we

have no true idea. It is clear that Hume thinks we can understand suppositions only through corresponding relative ideas, which are the closest to suppositions we can approximate. These relative ideas play a regulative role in our suppositions: we have no idea what we are talking about in making a supposition except to the extent that we have a corresponding relative idea, and we must therefore restrict our suppositions to those representations that are close to relative ideas. Though suppositions have considerable conceptual liabilities, it is plain that Hume thinks that we are determined to make them and moreover that we need them for the conduct of life.

So far as I have been able to discover, there are only a few points in the *Treatise* where Hume appears to link conceptual skepticism directly with epistemological skepticism. The most striking passage is at *T* 172 (see also *T* 74, 218): "we can never have reason to believe that any object exists, of which we cannot form an idea." Is Hume really saying that conceptual skepticism about *x*s entails epistemological skepticism about *x*s? It is possible that Hume has in mind here his official view that a belief is an idea – in which case the claim he makes is literally true but does not amount to the claim that conceptual skepticism entails epistemological skepticism, since he also employs an extended notion of belief on which it is not an idea, allowing, for example, belief in (philosophical) body even though we have no idea of body. On the other hand, Hume's remark may be a slip intended to make the more modest claim that we can never have reason to believe that *x* exists unless we can at least make a supposition of *x* (suitably tied to a relative idea) – which again does not amount to the claim that conceptual skepticism entails epistemological skepticism.

In admitting suppositions, Hume might appear to lose the Lockean motivation for concept empiricism: if suppositions can represent external objects without being derived from an external archetype, why do ideas need to be tied to impressions and thus external archetypes in order to represent things? Hume might try to answer: suppositions are able to represent things only in virtue of being suitably tied to ideas. But this answer seems to be undermined by Hume's denial that ideas do represent external existences – a denial which is, after all, the very basis for his introduction of suppositions. If ideas do not represent external existences, and so are not derived from external archetypes, how is it possible to secure the accuracy of suppositions by tying them to ideas? Hume's very reason for introducing suppositions might seem to undermine his original motivation for tying ideas to impressions. I believe that Hume can maintain the Lockean motivation for concept empiricism against this line of objection. It is true that for Hume, ideas do not strictly represent external objects; consequently they do not have archetypes and the question of their accuracy does not arise. But ideas are nevertheless *occasioned* by external qualities of objects – ideas of certain colors are occasioned by certain reflectancies of light. On the Lockean view, our suppositions about external objects (about bodies and primary qualities) must tend to be accurate if they are to represent these objects. Such a tendency to accuracy could be secured by tying suppositions to ideas even if these ideas do not represent external objects, so long as the ideas are occasioned by external qualities. These ideas will be occasioned by external qualities only if they are tied to impressions. In this way, Hume can maintain the Lockean motivation for concept empiricism while admitting nonrepresenting ideas and suppositions without external archetypes.

3 Hume maintains an ambiguous attitude toward hypothetico- deduction. He in fact uses hypothetico-deduction: the whole of the *Treatise* might be regarded, with some major qualifications, as a hypothetico-deduction in favor of concept empiricism. On the other hand, he clearly thinks hypotheses must be closely tied to experience: he accuses the ancient philosophy "of being entirely Hypothetical, and depending more upon Invention than Experience" (letter probably to Cheyne, 1734 (*L* ii: 16)); and he applauds Newton for his tentative hypothesis of aether as an explanation of gravity (*EU* 67n). However, Hume regards analogical inference as more central to thought than hypothetico-deduction.

4 In addition to the term "operations," Hume uses the Cartesian terms "principles" (*T* 98), "methods" (*T* 104), and "foundations" (*T* 117, 143, 146). Hume does sometimes speak (as Descartes also does) as if his main focus of attention were belief-forming *faculties* – reason, sense, imagination – rather than processes. It may appear that he applies epistemic epithets directly to faculties. But this appearance is an artefact of his presentation, in which he begins with unqualified talk of a faculty, and gradually specifies a particular function of the faculty – an operation. There is, however, one claim that Hume makes that might be taken to betray confusion about the implications of an operational account: that the wise man proportions his belief to the evidence. This may be taken to claim that justified belief is belief proportioned to the evidence – a claim inconsistent with an operational account of "evidence" (see chapter VII). But as I suggest in the text it is not clear that Hume means by "evidence" what is now meant. And anyway he probably intends here not an account of justified belief but a regulative ideal – hence the reference (with its Stoic overtones) to the "wise man." In any case, Hume is quite clear about one implication of a focus of operations: it excludes a straightforward identification of justification with conformity to or guidance by logical (*T* 181) or probabilistic (*T* 143–55) principles.

5 Here are examples of Hume's use of "justify" in application to experience and operations: "what experience will justify" (*T* 113); "how can we justify to ourselves any belief we repose in them?" (*T* 218). And of "just" in application to operations, arguments, and standards: "reason justly" (*T* 74); "this reasoning seems just and obvious" (*T* 88); "just argument" (*T* 186; see also *T* 135); "We have no just standard, by which we can decide any dispute" (*T* 262). Applied to ideas and definitions, "just" means exact or accurate: "just idea of the taste of a pineapple" (*T* 5); "just and consistent idea" (*T* 228); "just definition" (*T* 170). Hume's use of the terms "unjust"

and "justify" in successive sentences at *T* 225 makes it clear that he sometimes treats them as contradictories.

6 In opposition to the proposal that operations confer epistemic status on beliefs, it might be observed that in his discussion "Of Unphilosophical Probability" (*T* 143–55), Hume says that some unreasonable assignments of probability are derived from the same principles as reasonable assignments. That appears to contradict my claim that beliefs are justified in virtue of resulting from the exercise of justifying operations, since that claim entails that all outputs of a justifying operation are justified. But in fact Hume's interest here is in part to produce a more subtle classification of principles, distinguishing subprinciples by features associated with a higher incidence of error. Thus, a statistical causal inference tends to err when based on a small number of instances or when the instances are contrary. Similarly, a reliance on general rules, such as that "An *Irishman* cannot have wit, and a *Frenchman* cannot have solidity" is apt to lead to error (*T* 146). In some cases, our own belief-forming tendencies reduce the likelihood of error: we are apt to assign a probability only in proportion to the number of instances. But in other cases, our tendency does not vary with avoidance of error.

7 We should not assume that by "fallible," Hume means merely possibly erroneous. He may mean actually unreliable.

8 The following objection to the claim that Hume assigns justification on the basis of reliability worries me. Hume distinguishes evidence from knowledge and from proofs, and yet assigns certainty to both; so the degrees of evidence are not all distinguished solely by the degree to which operations avoid error. It might be proposed that evidence from knowledge and evidence from proofs differ in that evidence from knowledge *necessarily* avoids error, while evidence from proofs does so only de facto. Hume even makes a remark which suggests such a view at *T* 181: "knowledge and probability are of such contrary and disagreeing natures, that they cannot well run insensibly into each other." This remark may refer, however, to the difference between unity and less than unity. Certainly, Hume should allow that the operations of categorical causal inference on the basis of a huge number of observations do not *always* avoid error, so proof does not always avoid error.

9 There is another example at *T* 113. Hume claims that experience, not mere testimony, is what justifies our beliefs on the basis of testimony. I take him to be arguing for this claim. If so, his complaint against mere testimony is that there often fails to be a connexion between the ideas in the minds of others and the facts represented by these ideas – in other words, mere testimony is unreliable. Hume prefers experience to testimony as a justifier on grounds of reliability. The alternative interpretation is that Hume takes experience as justifying by definition and is arguing that people are unjustified in accepting testimony because they overrate the reliability of testimony. This interpretation works only if Hume is claiming not merely that people

mistakenly overrate testimony, but *unjustifiably* do so – and Hume does not make that claim.

10 Nor is there a convincing *general* argument that indirect perception by itself entails skepticism about body. The general argument from indirect perception to skepticism about body would seem to come to this: indirect perception leaves open the possibility of error: if our impressions are distinct from body, then they do not guarantee the existence and features of body. The denial of a guarantee might amount to the claim that the existence and features of impressions do not entail the existence and features of body – in which case it assumes a variant of epistemological deductivism – that knowledge or justified belief requires reasons that entail the belief, an unlikely assumption for a probabilist like Hume. Or the denial of a guarantee might amount instead to the claim that there is no independent operation that yields a belief in the reliability of sense. But then the attribution of skepticism assumes that Hume accepts independent accessibility internalism, contrary to his professed interest in consequent skepticism. Reid's and Kant's claim that Hume's indirect realism gives rise to skepticism may well confuse antecedent and consequent skepticism.

11 Hume is traditionally interpreted as a skeptic, not only about body, but about induction and deduction, but I see him as arguing rather that rationalist and empiricist accounts of induction and deduction lead to skepticism (see Beauchamp and Rosenberg (1981) on induction).

12 Hume does make the fantastic claim that the vulgar think of body as a set of perceptions with a continued and distinct existence. This claim seems to be a consequence of attributing to the vulgar two claims: the vulgar claim that colors, tastes, smells, sounds, heat, and cold exist in bodies; and the Berkeleian claim that these things are merely perceptions. In attributing the latter claim, Hume is taking extravagant liberties with the vulgar. A more palatable, though still mistaken, view might be that it never occurs to the vulgar to distinguish bodies from perceptions.

13 The difficulty Hume ponders here is similar to one that he faces in the searching Conclusion of Book I, though he adds there two other difficulties. He recognizes the unreliability of bright fancy: "if we assent to every trivial suggestion of the fancy; beside that these suggestions are often contrary to each other, they lead us into such errors, absurdities, and obscurities, that we must at last become ashamed of our credulity" (*T* 267). Bright fancy not only leads to inconsistent beliefs; it is thoroughly unreliable. Yet it is continuous with the very operations (e.g., causal inference) that lead us to reject it as unreliable (*T* 267). Hume is worried about making a principled distinction between bright fancy and causal inference. But he is also worried by a second difficulty not noted in I.IV.II: whether we can legitimately reject bright fancy in the absence of such a distinction, since we must rely on causal inference to justify our rejection. The problem is not simply that our beliefs in body are unjustified, or our causal inferences are unjustifying, because the operations that yield

them are continuous with bright fancy. It is that we cannot judge bright fancy itself unjustifying without employing operations called into question by their continuity with bright fancy. And Hume notes yet a third difficulty. Bright fancy is continuous with an operation that alone prevents reason from judging itself unreliable – namely, our difficulty with remote views. Hume accordingly doubts whether we can eliminate bright fancy without losing our justification for reason (or perhaps even our ability to arrive at beliefs by reason). He cites in particular his conclusion from *Treatise* I.IV.I: one trivial imaginative operation, our difficulty with remote views, is essential to prevent reason from judging itself unreliable, and so must be considered a virtual constituent of reason. Clearly it is a tricky task to characterize the individuation of operations in an intuitively plausible way. Hume expresses some pessimism about whether it can even be done in the present case.

14 There is a superficially different reading of Hume's skeptical worries: that he seeks, but does not find, a way to limit the imaginative galley so that its frequency of true output within that limit is sufficiently high, despite its low frequency elsewhere. There is a good deal of evidence for this interpretation. But such a view cannot really be distinguished from the one I am proposing if Hume is a reliabilist. If what makes a belief justified is the reliability of the operation that yields it, then the high frequency of truths in a suboutput of an operation can make it justifying only if there is a suboutput of it that counts as a relevant operation under the correct individuation of operations. Thus, if Hume is a reliabilist, the interpretation here collapses into my own. On the other hand, it might be urged that Hume is not a reliabilist but a proponent of what might be called *truncated reliabilism*: that a belief is justified when it results from an operation that has a high frequency of true output in some suboutput to which the belief belongs (and that we are – or the subject is – justified in believing to have a high frequency?). But if Hume's skepticism traces to this view, it would then derive from a worry analogous to the one he confronts on my interpretation. Such a view faces a problem of individuation analogous to the one faced by reliabilism, since we cannot say that just any suboutput, no matter how small, will do. And the skeptical worry of how to find a principled way to limit the operation would then be closely analogous to the problem of individuation on reliabilism.

15 A strong operation is one that yields beliefs with high average strength or vivacity. Note that strength psychologism defines justified belief in terms of the strength of operations, not beliefs. It would be implausible to characterize justified belief as strong belief, since beliefs that are less than vivacious can be justified. We might add to strength psychologism the condition: there is no equally strong operation that would yield a contrary belief.

16 One version of psychologism that has been attributed to Hume says that a belief is justified just in case it is psychologically irresistible.

This version of psychologism is typically motivated by appeal to the principle that "ought" implies "can" (see chapter IV for further discussion). The motivation is supposed to be this. Since "ought" implies "can," it follows by contraposition that "cannot" implies "ought not." Hence, "cannot fail to believe *p*" implies "ought not fail to believe *p*." Or in other words, its being irresistible to believe *p* implies that it is permissible to believe *p* – i.e., that the belief *p* is justified. The trouble with this motivation is that the principle that "ought" implies "can" applies, to a first approximation, only to what we may call the *guiding* "ought." The claim that we ought to do something implies that we can do it only if the point of saying that we ought to do something is to get us to do it. And equally, on the guiding conception, the point of saying that it is permissible to believe *p* is to afford us the opportunity to believe it. If we cannot fail to believe it, there is no point to affording us the opportunity to believe it. If a belief is irresistible, the guiding "ought" does not apply to it, and neither does the principle that "ought" implies "can." It is therefore clear that an account of justification that makes irresistible beliefs justified must utilize a nonguiding conception of justification. Now, it is true that such an account might explain the justification of irresistible beliefs by appeal to the guidance of *other* beliefs – fostering the use of irresistible beliefs as a basis for or constraint on the formation of the remainder of our beliefs. But such a move has its dangers. For it opens the possibility that irresistible beliefs be treated *negatively*, instead of positively – i.e., ignored or segregated from the remainder of our beliefs. It cannot be assumed that on such a conception all irresistible beliefs will be deemed justified. We have no argument here for saying that all irresistible beliefs are justified.

IV Accessibility Internalism

1 At one point Ginet formulates a yet weaker constraint: "A position that gives one justification for being confident of a proposition must be such that, given sufficient intelligence, one could acquire an ability to recognize that position whenever one is in it" (1974: 35). Being able to acquire an ability to recognize, given sufficient intelligence, does not entail actually being able to recognize, given the concept of justification.

2 Ginet makes the following disclaimer:

The requirement on justification of direct recognizability does *not* mean that one who can recognize a certain sort of position as justifying confidence that *p* and discriminate it from any other sort of position that does not do so . . . must be able to describe all the factors that go to make it a justifying position, or even that he must have concepts of them all . . . A child can learn to discriminate and identify square figures before he realizes that a square has to have four equal sides forming four equal angles, even before he has a concept of what an angle is.

(Ginet 1974: 37)

I find the latter claim implausible. Perhaps one can discriminate squares from other things without having the concept of figure with four equal sides or figure with four equal angles, but if so, discriminating squares does not entail telling that something is square. If, on the one hand, discriminating squares entails having the concept of square, then, since the child can discriminate not only squares but figures with four equal sides and four equal angles, it follows that she has the concepts of figure with four equal sides and figure with four equal angles, since these latter concepts are simply constituents of the former, and to possess a concept is to possess its constituents, together with a capacity to apply them conjointly. If, on the other hand, discriminating squares does not entail having the concept, then it is not obvious that a child who can discriminate without the concept of figure with four equal sides has the concept of square. Perhaps Ginet would say that direct recognizability only entails discriminating. But then it no longer obviously entails justification, and accessibility internalism so understood does not obviously require epistemic access. Moreover, the deontic argument is lost, since on the deontic argument, the sense in which one must tell that one is justified would seem to be one that does entail justification for believing that one is justified – how else could one be warranted in taking it that one's belief is justified? To tell that anything is square, one must tell that it possesses some property Q sufficient for being square, and that requires the concept of Q. Ginet is right, however, that the subject need not be able to *describe* Q.

3 It should be noted that Ginet also introduces a qualification like Chisholm's: "S would fail to know that [the condition of justification] obtains . . . through . . . failure to consider sufficiently carefully the question whether or not it obtains . . ." (1974: 35). Chisholm endorses versions of accessibility internalism concerning *knowledge*, as well as justified belief (1977: 114, 116).

4 It has also been taken to define the various ordinary concepts that constitute the beliefs that are justified according to the rules (Pollock 1974).

5 Strong foundationalism entails accessibility internalism on both the inclusive and exclusive readings *if* it is assumed that a subject must be able to tell that her belief is justified.

6 It is worth noting that reliabilism is ruled out by the mere requirement that one be able to tell, by reflection *or any other means*, that one's belief is justified. Such a requirement rules out many nonexternal conditions as well – e.g., most versions of perspectival internalism and coherentism.

7 My discussion of the deontic argument is deeply indebted to Alston's (1989a) astute critique. I find his objections convincing, but I add new ones here. See also Goldman (1980).

248

8 Here I substitute "is justified" for "has justification," by which Ginet means propositional justification (1974: 28). I have simplified Ginet's presentation by omitting his qualification "or entailed by something directly recognizable," which merely indicates that Ginet takes his argument to establish only that the condition of justified belief must supervene on what is accessible, not that it is itself accessible. The deontic argument would, however, seem to show (if successful) that the condition itself must be accessible.

9 Schematically Ginet's argument for (e) is this:

(g) Suppose some part of S's justification were not always accessible to S (or not entailed by what is accessible).

(h) Then S's position would change from being justified to not being justified without any change in what is accessible.

(i) But if there is no change in what is accessible, then S cannot always tell that his justification has changed.

(j) Therefore, if S can always tell whether he is justified, then S's justification is always accessible.

The conclusion (j) is identical with premise (e) of the deontic argument. The trouble with Ginet's argument here is that it begs the question in premise (i). No one who doubted premise (e) would accept (i) without further argument. And (i) is again mistaken, for the same reason (e) is: *S can* tell whether his justification has changed even if the change is not accessible.

10 The proponent of the claim that "ought" implies "can" might admit that these "ought" claims do not entail "can" claims but insist that some "ought" claims nevertheless do. It might be said that these "ought" claims do not entail "can" claims because they are merely *hypothetical* "ought" claims. The claim that one ought to turn the handlebar to the left when the bicycle leans to the left is plausible only when prefaced by the hypothesis "to ride a bicycle." The fact that such hypothetical "ought" claims do not entail "can" claims is not inconsistent with the position that *categorical* "ought" claims entail "can" claims. But I would say in response that epistemic "ought" claims might well be hypothetical: the claim that one ought epistemically to believe p might be interpreted as the claim that, to believe the truth, one ought to believe p. What is more, it is far from clear that the suppressed hypothesis in the hypothetical "ought" claims is necessary to explain why they do not entail "can" claims. For not only does the hypothetical "ought" claim not entail a "can" claim. The "can" claim is not entailed by the "ought" claim even when both are governed by the hypothesis.

11 Nor is there any prospect for an argument for accessibility internalism understood as requiring a *broad*, rather than narrow, ability to tell. Clearly, on the broad understanding of ability, we will lose the argument that we must be able to tell by reflection because we must be able to tell on all occasions and thus on the occasion of our first justified beliefs: the argument requires that we show that

we must be narrowly able to tell on the first occasion, but broad ability does not entail narrow ability. Moreover, once we have turned to the rationale that a broad ability to tell is needed for cultivating dispositions, habits, and traits that lead to justified beliefs, it becomes more pressing to say just why *justified belief* requires having such an ability. Why does it not simply require the dispositions, habits, and traits for which the ability is useful?

12 Our objections to accessibility internalism and the deontic argument apply, a fortiori, to *access* internalism and the parallel *regulative* argument for it. According to access internalism, the subject must not merely be able to tell that the conditions of justified belief are satisfied, but must *actually tell* by reflection that they are (a view closely related to Moser's (1989) awareness internalism and Pollock's (1986) internalism). It is natural to argue for this view by appeal to a regulative conception of justified belief, on which it is belief justified in virtue (in part) of being *regulated* with respect to justification. I doubt whether there is regulatively justified belief. Compare: there is no regulatively grammatical speech – no speech that is grammatical in virtue (in part) of the subject's regulating speech with respect to grammaticalness. Rather, there is only regulation of speech with respect to grammar; speech is grammatical in virtue of conforming to the norms of grammar. Similarly, there is no regulatively justified belief; there is only belief that is regulated with respect to justification, and justified belief is belief justified in virtue of conforming to the norms of justification. Access internalism faces a difficulty additional to the ones faced by accessibility internalism: it gives rise to an infinite regress of justification. Pollock (1986) tries to avert the regress by appeal to the idea that regulating belief with respect to justification requires only knowing how to reason, not being justified in believing that one is justified in believing *p*. But it seems pretty clear that knowing how will entail being justified in believing one is justified if it suffices for regulating belief with respect to justification (as regulating one's piano playing with respect to the norms of piano playing requires being justified in believing one conforms to the norms). Thus, the idea that the only justified belief is regulatively justified belief entails an unacceptable regress of justification.

13 The second constraint is consistent with reliabilism, as Alston notes. And both are consistent with the denial of what I take to be the weakest version of internalism, mental internalism (see chapter V), so I am disinclined even to call them versions of internalism.

V Perspectival Internalism, Mental Internalism, and Epistemically Responsible Belief

1 In effect, he exempts certain beliefs from reliabilist iterativism.
2 Lehrer (1974, 1990) proposes a theory that bears some resemblance to Foley's in characterizing justified belief in terms of an idealized

epistemic perspective, but Lehrer's theory is awfully complex, and we cannot deal with it here.

3 BonJour does seem to assume that a subject must have access to her belief's being sanctioned by her perspective. But this assumption seems to derive from confusing accessibility with perspectival internalism (see chapter VIII). Pollock (1986: 133) seems to assume that subjects must have access, not to the condition of justified belief (the belief's conforming to a guiding norm), but to the fulfillment of the condition specified by the norm. But he confuses access to the fulfillment of the condition specified by the norm with detection by automatic processing of some internal condition in virtue of which one fulfills the condition specified by the norm. Pollock may be right that a belief can conform to a guiding norm only if there are conditions detected by automatic processing prior to any judgment. But it does not follow from this that the subject must have access to the fulfillment of the condition specified by the norm. For the conditions detected by automatic processing need not be anything like the conditions specified by the norm. And it would seem that subjects must have access to conformity to the norm if they are to *possess* justification in a sense required by accessibility internalism: automatic detection is not enough for possession. Guidance psychologism does not entail accessibility internalism.

4 We might summarize the advisory argument this way. Reliabilism cannot characterize proper epistemic advice, since we cannot take reliabilist advice (the advice to believe what is reliable). Two reasons for this might be given: we cannot always judge correctly whether the belief *p* is reliable; and reliabilist advice generates a regress of advice, since it rests on a judgment of reliability, and this in turn on a judgment of the truth of the outputs of the process, and hence on further reliabilist advice as to whether these outputs are true. In reply to the first reason, it is true for many types of advice (financial, culinary, etc.) that we cannot always judge correctly whether the advised condition obtains. This even seems true of *perspectival* advice. In reply to the second reason, it is also true of perspectival advice that it generates a regress of advice. An alternative argument for perspectival internalism would claim that even if reliabilist advice is proper, the subject must conform to perspectival advice in taking reliabilist advice, since taking advice requires relying on one's perspective. But even if this is so, it does not follow that there is any epistemic status of taking perspectival advice, and so it does not follow that perspectival internalism characterizes an epistemic status. It is worth noting, too, that perspectival internalism might be supported on the ground that it assimilates justified belief to belief that manifests epistemic integrity, where the latter involves sticking to one's epistemic principles. This is an intriguing idea that we will have to leave for another occasion.

5 It is doubtful that BonJour's talk of belief it is epistemically responsible to "accept" makes literal sense. Belief is not generally under direct voluntary control. We speak of *actions* as responsible, but not

dispositions, habits, traits, or other items that are not under direct voluntary control. BonJour's use of the term "accept" reveals his (perhaps subliminal) sensitivity to this point. Acceptance is ambiguous between *judgment*, which is a form of action, and to which epistemic responsibility directly applies, and *belief*, which is not a form of action. If by "accepting a belief" BonJour means judging that the proposition believed is true, acceptance may be epistemically responsible – but then of course epistemic responsibility differs from justification in not being a property of the belief. If, on the other hand, by "accepting a belief" BonJour simply means holding it, then acceptance cannot be epistemically responsible. However, this dilemma need not prevent epistemic responsibility from being a significant epistemic status. Rather than speak of epistemically responsible belief, we may speak, with Kornblith (1983), of epistemically responsible cognitive action (see also Code (1983). There is nothing wrong with using the term "epistemically responsible belief" to refer to belief that results from epistemically responsible action. But we must recognize that it is by no means clear which beliefs deserve this epithet, since we have not yet specified the appropriate way in which a belief must result from epistemically responsible action to count as an epistemically responsible belief. Thus the claim that justified belief is epistemically responsible belief conceals a difficult problem – specifying which beliefs do appropriately result from epistemically responsible action.

Alston (1989a) has gone so far as to urge that the causal component of the notion of epistemically responsible belief renders it an unsuitable basis for a pure perspectival internalism, since whether a belief is epistemically responsible is now a matter of whether it results in an appropriate way from epistemically responsible action – and that is not a purely perspectival matter. Certainly the causal conception of epistemically responsible belief is an unsuitable basis for extant versions of perspectival internalism, since these versions do not require that a belief have a certain causal history – only that the subject be justified in believing that the belief is reliable. Nevertheless, I do not see that the causal conception is patently unsuited to support any perspectival internalism. For I see no reason why perspectival internalism cannot include a causal component. The core idea of perspectival internalism is that a belief is justified just in case it is sanctioned by the subject's perspective. The notion of a subject's perspective is not a causal notion, but the notion of being sanctioned might be. On the simplest view of sanctioning, a belief's being sanctioned is a matter of there being some proposition in the subject's perspective according to which the belief is reliable. Even on such a simple view, whether a belief is sanctioned is not something *specified* by the subject's perspective and so can accommodate a causal component. I see nothing to bar incorporating a causal component into the notion of being sanctioned.

6 Here I modify an example that Alston (1989a) uses to argue that the deontic conception of justified belief and perspectival internalism

diverge, but for the reasons given in the preceding chapter, I do not think that this and the other examples offered by Alston show what he wants.

7 Similarly, it is possible for me to have good reason to believe that my reliable beliefs are *unjustified* – hence condemned by my perspective, where a perspective is defined by beliefs about justification – even though they turn out to be irresistible and thus not irresponsible. In this case, it might be necessary for me not to realize that my religious beliefs are irresistible – otherwise I would infer that they are not irresponsible, assuming I realize that irresponsibility entails resistibility. If so, the example depends on the assumption that irresistibility entails nonirresponsibility when the subject does not realize that the belief is irresistible. And one might balk at this assumption.

8 Access internalism (chapter IV, note 12) is an exception to these claims because any condition meeting it entails that the subject does tell that she is justified in believing *p*, hence that she is justified in believing *p*. But this very fact calls into question whether any condition meeting access internalism can characterize epistemically responsible belief understood on (a). For there do not seem to be any conditions that the subject is necessarily right about when she does the best she can to ascertain whether she is justified in believing *p*. One might say that she is necessarily right because in forming the belief *p* a norm guides her only if she tells and thus correctly believes that her belief *p* conforms to that norm (as must be so if guidance psychologism is a version of access internalism). But even if this is true, it does not entail that she is right when she does her best to ascertain whether her belief is justified.

9 Steup (1988) has objected that in Alston's example the subject does not fulfill his obligations, so Alston has not established that it is possible to fulfill one's obligations and yet not be justified. I do not wish to side with Alston here. If Steup's point is correct, then in my view it follows that there are instances in which a subject does his best, yet does not fulfill his obligations. Alston's example still shows that a belief can be epistemically responsible and not justified on the deontic conception. My point below, that it is possible to be justified in believing that one is justified in believing *p* and not be justified in believing *p*, is consistent with Steup's claim that the subject does not fulfill his obligations, so long as it is possible to be justified in believing that one is justified and yet not fulfill one's obligations, as I believe it is.

10 The example tells even more obviously against Foley's view; for the student would on reflection judge his interpretation reliable. There are also counterexamples to guidance psychologism: imagine a subject who is actually guided by norms like the gambler's fallacy, hasty generalization, or wishful thinking. Suppose that these are basic norms for the subject – there are no other norms from which they derive or with which they conflict. Surely we would deny that the

subject is justified in beliefs that conform to them, despite her being guided by them. One might protest that the guiding norms determine the content of our beliefs so that it would not be possible to conform to different norms and retain the beliefs we do. But the most likely source of support for such a view is an implausible verificationism on which the norms of justification determine the content of our concepts and beliefs (see Pollock (1986)).

11 It is tempting to try to avert this counterexample to reliabilism by retreating to a version of reliabilism that purports to characterize *nomologically* rather than logically necessary conditions of justified belief (or by claiming that nomologically and logically necessary conditions coincide). This temptation should be resisted. One problem is that there is no canonical answer to the question which laws govern the universe, and thus we must specify under which laws this version of reliabilism attempts to characterize justified belief. If we could make sense of the idea that there are epistemological laws, we would have a ready answer to our question – though we would still face the ticklish task of saying which specific laws are epistemological without begging the question in favor of reliabilism. But there are no epistemological laws. The second problem is that the laws of psychology and biology – natural candidates here – do not rule out the brain-in-a-vat counterexample. If we could add semantical laws, we would, in my opinion, avert the counterexample, but are there any semantical laws?

12 There is one objection to reliabilism based on the vat example (mentioned by Goldman (1979)) that I think can be answered straightaway. This objection asks us to consider, not some possible world in which our justifying processes are unreliable, but the actual world, and we are asked to consider what we would say if in the actual world our processes were, unbeknownst to us, unreliable because we are in fact deceived by a demon. Surely, the objection goes, we would say that our beliefs are justified. The fact that we are deceived has no effect on our judgment that our beliefs are justified. This counterexample turns on the claim that it is possible that the actual world is in fact a demon world. But in what sense is this possible? There are two options for an answer: *metaphysically* possible and *epistemically* possible. To claim that it is metaphysically possible is to claim that there is some possible world in which the actual world is a demon world. But if there is some possible world in which this is the case, then the actual world actually is a demon world, since, for possible world w and property F, if it is possible that w has F, then w actually has F. But of course no one would allow that the actual world actually is a demon world. So the claim cannot be that it is metaphysically possible that the actual world is a demon world. This leaves epistemic possibility. To say that it is epistemically possible that the actual world is a demon world is presumably to say that for all we know (or are justified in believing) the actual world is a demon world. The claim is that it is consistent with what we know that this

world is a demon world. But one problem with this claim is that it simply assumes either that reliabilism is false or that we do not use reliable processes. For if we do use reliable processes, then on reliabilism it is *not* consistent with what we know that the actual world is a demon world. We know many of the propositions we take ourselves to know – that we live on earth, that the sky is blue, and so on – and these propositions are not consistent with the actual world being a demon world. But of course the objector cannot assume that reliabilism is false without begging the question at issue, and there is no warrant for denying that we use reliable processes. (Nor will it help to retreat to the claim that we do not know that we know that the actual world is a demon world. For the preceding reliabilist response can be iterated.) Perhaps the objector can introduce some special interpretation of epistemic possibility that avoids these assumptions. For example, the objector might insist that the proposition that the actual world is a demon world is consistent with certain epistemically privileged beliefs. It is consistent with a description of our experiences. I am inclined to agree that in this sense it is epistemically possible that the actual world is a demon world. But to say this is only to admit that we have no way of answering antecedent skepticism. If epistemic possibility is defined this way, the question becomes whether it is important for a theory to imply that we *are* justified in the demon world. And this is equivalent to the question whether the antecedent skeptical challenge is one we must meet in order to be justified in our beliefs – to which we have already given an answer in chapter II.

13 For arguments in favor of externalism about mental representation, see Burge (1979, 1982).

14 There are various versions of reliabilism that entail that the vat subject is justified – versions that also entail mental internalism:
    S is justified in believing p in world w just in case:

    (a) *Optimal world-indexed reliabilism* (ORI reliabilism): S's belief p results in w from a process of a sort that would be reliable in w if there were any process that is both reliable and available to S for exercise in w.

    (b) *Actual world-indexed reliabilism* (AWI reliabilism): S's belief p results in w from a process that is reliable in the actual world (A) (Goldman 1979).

    (c) *Normal worlds-indexed reliabilism* (NWI reliabilism): S's belief p results in w from a process that is reliable in *normal worlds*, where a normal world is one which is like what we believe the actual world A to be like (Goldman 1986).

(There is yet another version similar to (a) suggested by Luper-Foy (1985).) ORI reliabilism is perhaps the most natural of these versions. These three versions of reliabilism are similar in a number of important respects. (i) They all save our intuition about the vat example and entail mental internalism. (Since these are all versions of externalism, it follows that mental internalism is consistent with externalism.) (ii) If we are *right* in what believe about the actual world, as of course we believe we are, then they are necessarily coextensive. Moreover, (iii) when we *apply* them to examples, we end up with the same evaluations. There is no pragmatic difference between the versions. Despite these similarities between the versions, AWI reliabilism is superior to ORI and NWI reliabilism because the latter afford no way of seriously doubting whether we are right in our judgments as to which processes are justifying. ORI reliabilism affords no way of doubting this beyond the extent to which we can doubt that perception is reliable if anything is reliable and available – or equivalently, no way of doubting this beyond the extent to which we can doubt that the actual world as we believe it to be is the epistemically best possible world. NWI reliabilism affords no way of doubting beyond the extent to which we can doubt which beliefs we have and which processes are reliable in the world as we believe to be. AWI reliabilism, on the other hand, does leave room for doubt about our judgments as to which processes are justifying and it makes the business of determining this a matter of investigating the nature of the actual world. ORI and NWI reliabilism implausibly leave no room for doubting our judgments of justification once we have relied on our beliefs about *A* to judge which processes are reliable. It seems that our judgments of justification *are* at risk in a respect these versions of reliabilism rule out: our judgments could be based on false beliefs about the actual world.

The mental internalist might argue that, from the standpoint of the epistemic end of true belief, reliabilism has no advantage over AWI reliabilism, since these theories evaluate justified beliefs in the same way in the actual world. But for purposes of judging the consequences of actions in different states of nature, it is advantageous to be able to treat justification differently in other possible worlds, depending on differences in reliability. So reliabilism has an advantage over AWI reliabilism. (Let it also be noted that AWI reliabilism has a drawback that reliabilism does not have: it is incapable of assigning justification to beliefs that result from processes that are not exercised in the actual world, since the reliability of such processes in the actual world is undefined.)

15 Despite the frequency with which opponents of reliabilism trot out the vat example, it is not quite as obvious as one might think that perception is completely unreliable in the vat world. The easy presumption that perception is unreliable results from ignoring the role of nearby possible worlds in the calculation of reliability (see chapter VI, note 1.) If reliability is the average frequency of true output of a process in the world of the case *and* nearby worlds, then we must consider what happens in nearby worlds. Here are some worlds that are similar to the vat world: (1) worlds in

which vat brains are *veridically* stimulated by the computer – the computer turns honest, informing the brains of their situation and stimulating them appropriately (with no input?); (2) worlds in which the computer embodies brains; (3) worlds in which there are naturally occurring embodied exercises of perceptual processes in addition to vat exercises; (4) worlds where there are disembodied (and perhaps even subjectless) exercises of perceptual processes; and (5) worlds in which there are stray brains unconnected to the computer. In worlds of kinds (1)–(3), perceptual processes would have a high frequency of true output (though perhaps not as high as in the actual world). And in worlds of kinds (4) and (5), perceptual processes may also have a high frequency. Can there be disembodied and stray exercises of perceptual processes with no input and thus no output? Would such exercises count for or against the frequency of true output of the process? I doubt whether there are intuitive answers to these questions, but there are answers that entail that the frequency of true output is fairly high in such worlds. As long as these questions remain unanswered, it will not be obvious that the frequencies in these worlds are low. Nor is it entirely obvious whether such worlds count as nearby.

16 I doubt whether reliabilists need to use the technique against the example of reliable wishful thinking, in which a benevolent demon fulfills all of our wishes. It might be claimed that intuitively the subject is not justified in these wishful beliefs despite their reliability. We might respond that our intuition is a carryover from our real life evaluative habits. But I doubt whether we need to make this response. For I doubt whether we really do or should have this intuition. The appearance that we do quite likely derives from the fact that in the actual world we are always justified in believing that wishful beliefs are unreliable. We covertly assume that the same is true in the benevolent demon world. If it is true, then reliabilism can explain the failure of justification by appeal to undermining by justified negative evaluation (see chapter VII). If on the other hand justification is not undermined here, then I think a vivid picture of the reliability of wishful thinking will lead us to view it much as we would reliable clairvoyance – as justifying (chapter VII).

I would add that the technique does not disarm just any counter-example to just any view. Consider again the Coherent Fantasy Objection to coherentism: coherentism entails the counterintuitive result that every coherent fantasy is justified. A coherentist could not easily disarm this example by saying that our intuitions are forged in evaluations of actual examples, and for evaluative efficiency we focus on features of actual examples in fact correlated with coherence, so that we automatically (and mistakenly) think that input from experience or the world is necessary for justification. The trouble is that such input is not obviously closely enough correlated with coherence to afford this explanation of our intuition.

VI Reliability, Relevant Processes, and Metaprocesses

1   There are numerous difficult issues of detail in formulating reliabilism. Here are several important issues I have not yet mentioned:

(1) How much reliability is necessary for justified belief? The answer is: as much reliability as justification, since the degree of reliability is the degree of justification. (But see note 5 below for qualification of this answer.) Presumably there is no precise answer to the question how much justification is required for justified belief, and there may be no noncontextual answer either. How much is required may depend on the likelihood of the subject's relying on the belief in inferring other beliefs (the greater the likelihood, the greater the required justification) and on how easy it is for the belief to be corrected if mistaken (the easier, the less the required justification).

(2) Should some output beliefs count more than others in calculating the reliability of a process – i.e., should reliability be a *weighted* average of the truth-values of the output beliefs? For example, should we weight beliefs in proportion to the amount of semantical information they carry? Or should we define reliability not as the average of the truth-values of the beliefs but as the ratio of true to total semantical information contained in those beliefs? The issue is closely related to the question of how we should individuate beliefs. Should Newtonian mechanics count as a single belief or as many thousands of beliefs? The answer will matter on an unweighted assessment of reliability. Defining reliability as the ratio of true to total information has an advantage over the frequency of true beliefs (whether narrowly or broadly individuated): it averts the charge (Thagard 1988: 132) that reliability makes inference to the best explanation unjustifying because this process has yielded mostly false scientific theories in the past; for these theories contain more true than false information.

(3) Should a belief count less if the process repeatedly yields beliefs with the same propositional content – i.e., should we calculate reliability by averaging the truth-values of the *propositions* belief in which it yields, or by averaging the truth-values of the *beliefs*?

(4) We have said nothing about how reliabilism would account for justified degrees of belief, subjective probabilities, degrees of confidence, and the like. Let us focus here on degrees of belief, which we will think of as representations of the extent of the subject's credence in a proposition, rather than as degrees of confidence (i.e., representations of the amount of evidence for the proposition believed or the degree of justification for the belief – a matter to which we will return in chapter VIII) or as subjective probabilities (which are assumed to conform to the probability calculus). An account of justified degrees of belief is clearly needed to complete an account of justified belief, since degrees of belief are sometimes input to

258

belief-forming processes, and the justification of the beliefs that result from such input depends on the justification of the input. Goldman (1986) has suggested a calibrational account of justified degrees of belief. I find the approach congenial, though the condition Goldman suggests is clearly too strong. On his account, a degree of belief is justified just in case it results from the exercise of a well-calibrated degree-of-belief-forming process, where a process is well-calibrated when, for each degree d, the proportion of true propositions it assigns d is (approximately) d. This is a very strong requirement, since it tolerates no deviations of the degree of confidence from the frequency for any degree d. We should retreat to the more lenient requirement that the process is *fairly well calibrated* – its total error does not exceed a specified upper bound u. That is, the average difference between degree d and the proportion of true propositions assigned d is less than u. We should also note that Goldman's requirement assigns equal weight to each degree d. But weight should be assigned in accordance with the ratio of the propositions the process assigns d in the total output of the process. Making these modifications, we should say that the pertinent average is the average difference mentioned above, weighted by the ratio of propositions assigned degree d in the total output. Then we end up with the measure of calibration standardly used by psychologists – the second, calibrational component of Murphy's expansion of the Brier score (Murphy 1973). The individuation of degree-of-belief-forming processes is clearly crucial for the plausibility of the calibrational approach. The problem of individuation is equivalent to the problem of specificity discussed in the calibrational literature. It is doubtful that all propositions assigned d by a process should be grouped together in assessing calibration – unless processes are individuated in a way that makes this natural. If, for example, we were to apply the present proposal to weather forecasters, rather than processes, we would end up saying that the fact that a weather forecaster does poorly in assigning a twenty percent chance of rain after cloudy days impugns his forecasting of a twenty percent chance of rain after partly cloudy days, even if the latter forecasts are accurate, since all assignments of twenty percent are grouped together in figuring calibration. It is natural to individuate the forecasts in such a way as to distinguish the two kinds of forecast. We will want to individuate processes in a similar way. The resulting constraint on individuation is an analogue of the Frequency Similarity Constraint discussed below.

(5) Do deductive inferences have reliability one, as their corresponding argument forms have, or reliability less than one, to take into account the degrading effect of interference? I doubt whether our intuitions clearly favor one of these alternatives.

(6) Ideally the reliability of a process would simply be its frequency of true belief in the actual world. But there is an impediment to this simple view: evaluators have quite different and conflicting beliefs about the actual world and accordingly arrive at different

assessments of the frequency of true belief in the actual world. Presumably substantial agreement about reliability is necessary if our system of evaluation is to work. The remedy is to average frequency across nearby possible worlds. We must let the range of nearby worlds extend far enough to ensure a rough agreement on frequency. This range may vary from process to process.

2 The two tasks are equivalent if, as I will assume for the time being (see note 5 below), for each belief there is at most one relevant process and the relevant processes must be individuated in such a way that they have disjoint output mutually exhaustive of all beliefs that are assigned an epistemic status (justified or unjustified). Under these assumptions, an individuation of processes determines a unique process relevant to a given belief assigned an epistemic status – namely, the one epistemically relevant process that produces the belief. In practice, we must assess reliability by looking not only at the output of the beliefs, but at the psychological description of the process, since only that will pinpoint the output in nearby worlds. We need not assume that every belief is assigned an epistemic status, or – equivalently – that for every belief there is a relevant process. It is possible that there are beliefs that are not even formed by cognitive processes (e.g., innate beliefs, if they derive from a genetic or neurodevelopmental process that does not involve a cognitive process). Such beliefs cannot be justified on reliabilism, since only cognitive processes are justifying. Consequently, it is impossible for there to be justified innate belief or innate knowledge, if these do not derive from a cognitive process – though no doubt there is a status analogous to justification that may be assigned in virtue of the reliability of the genetic or neurodevelopmental process. On the other hand, we need not treat such beliefs as *unjustified* either – any more than images or, for that matter, tables and trees, are unjustified just because they are not justified. Nor need we assume that there is a single individuation of processes for all evaluative purposes.

3 It should be noted that *any* process theory of justified belief will face a problem of individuation.

4 The constraints are tuned to the actual world – that is, they describe the pragmatic conditions of evaluation and the conditions necessary for facilitating true belief in the actual world. There is little helpful to say about how to facilitate true belief in a world like the vat world: here evaluation can do nothing to ensure that our beliefs are often true, though there may be common necessary conditions of feasible evaluation. We might try to extend the account of relevant processes to the vat world by applying the constraints tuned to the actual world or by applying only the conditions of feasible evaluation common to both the vat world and the actual world. (Either way, subjects will come out unjustified in the vat world, since perceptual processes are mostly unreliable on all the evaluatively feasible individuations.)

5 The introduction of conditional reliability and chains of inferences raises a number of difficult questions, though in my view these are

questions that ought to arise, and are bound to be difficult to answer, on any plausible account of justification. So long as we assumed a single relevant process for any given belief, the degree of justification assigned the belief was unambiguous, as was the reliability associated with the belief. But once chains of inferences are introduced, the degree of justification becomes ambiguous, and the question how much justification is required for the belief to be justified no longer has the simple answer: a high degree of justification. (There is an additional ambiguity introduced by multiple simultaneous inputs to an inferential process, where these inputs derive from processes with various reliabilities.) On any plausible account of justification, the degree of justification afforded by an induction will vary to some extent with the degree of justification of its premises, and the degree of justification of these premises will in turn be affected by the degree of justification of the premises from which they are inferred, and so on. And this fact entails that the range of degrees of justification possessed by justified beliefs must vary beyond the range of degrees of justification admissible for noninferential justification, if the range of degrees of conditional justification of an inferential process (i.e., the range of degrees of justification of its output given perfect justification of its input) is the same as the range of degrees of noninferential justification. For the lowest degree of conditional justification admissible will be discounted yet further when the inputs are less than perfectly justified. Many proposals for defining the degree of justification of a belief come to mind. One natural proposal is to define it as the frequency of true beliefs in a restricted portion of the output of the final inferential process – the output that results from input that is the output of the penultimate inferential process that is in turn output that results from input that is output of the preceding process, and so on up to the initial perceptual process. The trouble with this proposal is that it is extremely difficult to identify that restricted output or to know its frequency of true beliefs. There is no reason at all to think it will bear much resemblance to the reliabilities of any of the processes in the chain or to any average of these reliabilities. Another idea is to define the degree of justification as an average of the reliabilities of the processes in the chain. Neither an arithmetical average nor a geometrical average seems right. The arithmetical average has the counterintuitive consequence of raising the reliability of induction beyond its conditional reliability when the inputs issue from more reliable processes. The geometrical average will make the degrees of justification very low for long chains of inferences, and that is surely counterintuitive. It seems that what we need is a weighted geometrical average where the weights discount the effect of earlier processes in the chain in proportion to their distance from the final process. Earlier processes will be discounted more than later processes. If the discounting is steep enough, the degree of justification of the belief will not converge to zero as the chain gets longer, even when the reliabilities of the processes are relatively low.

6 There are other plausible constraints on relevance worth mentioning:
(6) *Frequency Polarizing Constraint*. One way to promote the exercise of very reliable processes is to set the degree of reliability required for a process to be justifying very high. But another way is to individuate processes so that they are either assigned a very high frequency of true beliefs or a very low frequency. That is, we individuate them so as to maximize their polarization (i.e., the average differences between the frequencies of processes with reliability greater than one half and reliability less than one half). Thus we arrive at the Frequency Polarizing Constraint:

> Ceteris paribus, relevant processes are individuated so as to maximize the polarization of the frequencies of true beliefs in their outputs.

This constraint does not by itself favor a broader or narrower individuation of processes, since it does not distinguish between individuating processes into as many distinct processes as there are beliefs, and individuating them into two processes, one with all true and the other all false outputs.
(7) *Control Constraint*.

> Ceteris paribus, relevant processes are individuated so as to maximize the proportion of reliable relevant processes subjects are able to bring it about that they exercise and the proportion of unreliable relevant processes they are able to bring it about that they do not exercise.

This constraint ensures that subjects can make use of epistemic evaluation to form true beliefs.
7 I would like to survey briefly three other proposals for individuation:

(1) Millikan (1984) proposes that processes be individuated by the features of the process the subject uses in forming the belief. Talk of use here is odd, since the subject does not use features of the process to form the belief except in the trivial sense that the features enter into the causation of the belief – in which case Millikan's criterion collapses into Goldman's Narrowest Process Criterion.
(2) In his interesting critique of reliabilism, Pollock (1984) proposes individuating processes at the narrowest process the subject is justified in believing to be exercised in forming the belief. Such a criterion seems way out of kilter with our intuitions about cases. A subject who is myopic and nevertheless forms beliefs about the details of distant objects is unjustified, even if he is not justified in believing he is myopic but on the contrary is justified in believing that he exercises a normal visual process. The narrowest process the subject is justified in believing to be exercised is in fact reliable, so that Pollock's proposal yields the mistaken conclusion that the subject's belief is justified.
(3) In an earlier article, I proposed an *indicator* criterion: we individuate processes on the basis of what their frequency of true

output indicates about the truth-value of the belief in the given case (Schmitt 1984). Let the relevant process be one such that the truth of the belief p is (objectively) probable (but not too probable), given a high frequency of true beliefs in the output. (The qualification "not too probable" is needed to prevent the output from being identical with the belief p.) The point of the indicator criterion is to make the assessment of reliability immediately relevant to the task of assessing the truth-value of the belief. Thus the criterion differs from others that have been proposed in having a clear rationale in the epistemic end of true belief. The criterion faces various difficulties that can probably be surmounted: it makes it difficult to determine which process is relevant to a given belief, since determining this requires determining the conditional (objective) probability of the belief p's being true given a high frequency of true beliefs in the output; it does not specify a unique process for a given belief (we will have to judge the justification of the belief by taking an average of the reliabilities of the processes); and necessarily true beliefs are trivially probable given a high frequency of true beliefs. A serious difficulty, however, is that it runs afoul of the same intuitions that oppose Goldman's Narrowest Process Criterion: in the example of the degraded template, it assigns justification to beliefs that result from low matches, since it makes relevant the process that yields beliefs that result from low matches (it is probable that such a belief is true given a high frequency of true beliefs among those resulting from a low match), and this process is reliable. Like the Narrowest Process Criterion, the indicator criterion is too narrow.

8 It is unclear whether the methods of which Goldman speaks – the square root algorithm, etc. – are *folk* processes. This might be sufficient to rule them out as justifying by themselves, if Gertrude is not suitably related to a community of evaluators who are able and liable to evaluate in terms of such processes. More generally, the Folk Process Constraint may simulate the effects that Goldman seeks by adding the requirement of a metaprocess. If the methods are not folk processes, they must be fitted into folk processes in the right way. In this case, the reason reliable methods are not sufficient is not that they are not native but that they do not have the right evaluative properties. Still, Goldman is right that Gertrude is unjustified so long as she does not arrive at the use of the method in the right way.

9 Goldman (1986: 93–4) proposes that a subject may fail to be justified in virtue of having failed to acquire a correct method, given the opportunity. The suggestion may be that a belief is justified in virtue of having resulted from a method (or process) only if the metaprocess that acquires the method acquires correct methods when it has the opportunity. This seems to me too strong. The subject need not employ a metaprocess that acquires correct methods when it has the opportunity, so long as the metaprocess that leads to the use of a method leads to correct methods. On the other hand, Goldman may be suggesting only that a subject who uses an

incorrect method or a process in lieu of a correct method may be unjustified. This is true, but it follows from the requirement that methods be correct and processes reliable.

VII Justification and Evaluation

1 It is worth noting that there are other forms of negative evaluation that might be taken to undermine justification – most importantly, the evaluation that the subject is not *justified* in his belief. This raises the question whether the undermining power of the latter form of negative evaluation derives from that of the form we discuss in the text. If reliabilism is true, then the two forms of evaluation are equivalent. A different question is whether there are conditions that undermine other than being justified in a negative evaluation. I see two candidates: (1) It might be said that justification is undermined by what the subject *should* be justified in believing, or by what he *would* be justified in believing had he formed only justified beliefs in the past, or had he formed all justified beliefs he was in a position to form that bear on *p* or on the reliability of the process. Suppose, for example, that Burl believes *p* as the result of the exercise of a process, as above. Suppose he does not have evidence that his process is unreliable. Nevertheless, there is much evidence that he has overlooked. One might claim that Burl is unjustified. This claim has some intuitive punch. (2) It might be said that Burl's justification for believing *p* would be undermined by his belief that the process he exercises is unreliable even if he were not justified in believing this. I confess I do not find this intuitive: why should mere unfounded belief have such an undermining effect? However this may be, intuitions (1) and (2) may be accommodated in ways that parallel closely the reliabilist explanation of undermining I develop. But I will not venture to say here whether the parallel accommodation is ultimately defensible.
2 Nonnegative iterativism also has the disadvantage of introducing a circularity into the characterization of justified belief. This and the last objection to iterativism in the text apply as well to Kornblith's (1980) proposal that *S* is justified only if *S*'s process is reliable, not only in the actual situation, but in relevant counterfactual situations as well – where the latter are determined by *S*'s background beliefs. The undermining background beliefs are specified by content, raising the problems we have mentioned.
3 Goldman's (1986) reliabilism is a localized version of holistic reliabilism, though Goldman does not develop its holistic aspect.
4 Holistic reliabilism might accommodate BonJour's case of Norman (discussed above) in an analogous fashion.
5 Perhaps comparative reliabilism should restrict the undermining processes to belief-withholding processes that withhold the belief *p in virtue of* withholding the exercise of the process *R*, or perhaps it should refer instead to *R*-exercise-withholding processes, rather than *belief-*

264

withholding processes. Comparative reliabilism might be formulated without employing belief-withholding processes by requiring only that there be no process at least as reliable as *R* that takes the input of the belief *p*-forming exercise of *R* as input and fails to yield the belief *p*. This is essentially Goldman's view (1979).

6 Feldman has argued that comparative reliabilism imposes too strong a condition on introspective justification of beliefs about belief:

> I might know, and be justified in believing, that I believe *q*. But suppose that my belief in *q* results partly from my failure to consider all relevant evidence (a reliable process). Were I to use that reliable process, I would not believe *q* and thus not believe that I believe *q*. So (G5) implies, incorrectly, that I am not justified in believing that I believe *q*.
>
> (Feldman 1985: 166)

This objection fails because the process that leads to withholding my belief *q* (or to not believing *q*, as on the version that Feldman attacks here) is not a process that undermines my justification for the belief that I believe *q*. It is not a process that leads to a withholding of the belief that I believe *q*. For the belief *q* is not an *input* to the process that forms the belief that I believe *q* in the manner in which beliefs are inputs to inferential processes. Rather it is an *object* of introspection. For the same reason, the process that leads to the belief *q* is not part of an inferential chain that leads to the belief that I believe *q*, any more than the process that forms an apple is part of the perceptual process that forms my belief that this is an apple. (Nor does my exercising the process that leads to not believing *q* entail my exercising a process that leads to my not believing that I believe *q*.) The process that withholds my belief *q* simply brings about conditions in which I fail to exercise a process that leads to the belief that I believe *q*. That does not show that there is an available process at least as reliable that leads to my withholding the belief that I believe *q* (or that fails to form the belief that I believe *q*).

7 We can give a reliabilist account of justified belief-withholding correlative to our reliabilist account of justified belief by interchanging the roles of belief-withholding and belief-forming processes in our account. Justified belief-withholding is of course not the same as justified belief-retraction.

8 Does the requirement that the negative evaluation that is input be justified inject a circularity into comparative reliabilism, as Fumerton (1988) has claimed? No, we can easily avoid a circularity by formulating comparative reliabilism recursively.

9 Nor will it help to individuate *R'* more broadly, so that its withholdings include not only the withholdings of *R*, but also those of other processes – e.g., to individuate it broadly enough to include the withholdings of processes whenever there is a justified negative evaluation, so that the frequency of false beliefs withheld by *R'* will equal the additive inverse of the average reliability of all the

processes withheld. That would greatly increase the frequency of false beliefs withheld, since the processes exercised when subjects are justified in believing that their beliefs are not reliably formed are generally unreliable. But even if our constraints on relevance could be made to motivate this seemingly ad hoc individuation of R', the increase in the frequency of false beliefs withheld by R' will still not be enough in some cases to increase its reliability to that of R. It will not be enough to increase the reliability of R' to equal that of R if R's frequency of true beliefs on occasions of justified negative evaluation is at least as great as the additive inverse of the average reliability of the processes withheld. And that will surely be true of some highly reliable process R.

10 Does reliabilism handle our intuition that counterevidence the subject acquires *after* forming the belief p can undermine her justification (Walker 1986; Pappas 1987)? I believe the best approach is to conceive of the process that yields the belief p longitudinally, as one that makes provisions for retracting beliefs in the presence of counterevidence (see chapter VIII).

11 We are now in a position to say a word about how knowledge might differ from justified true belief. Justified belief requires that there be no counterevidence available to the subject sufficient to outweigh the subject's evidence for p, where "available" means roughly "already possessed by." On a defeasibility account of knowledge of the sort to which I subscribe (1983, 1985b), knowledge requires that there be no such counterevidence available to the subject, where "available" includes evidence the subject does not already possess (though perhaps not all such evidence). The difference between knowledge and justified true belief is most naturally seen, on my version, as deriving from a difference in the individuation of the relevant processes. The processes relevant to knowledge will be individuated more narrowly: the process relevant to knowledge in a case will be the perceptual process in the absence of unpossessed as well as possessed counterevidence, while the process relevant to justification will be the broader perceptual process in the absence of possessed counterevidence. The advantages of such an account are exactly the converse of the advantages of a counterfactual dependency or reliable indication account of knowledge. The present account explains why knowledge entails justified belief: exercising the narrower process entails exercising the broader process. It does not, however, explain why knowledge entails *true* belief. Truth must be superadded to justification to get knowledge. The counterfactual dependency account, on the other hand, explains why knowledge entails true belief: "if it were not the case that p, then I wouldn't believe that p" entails "my belief p is true," assuming that I believe p. But it does not explain why knowledge entails justified belief, since satisfying the counterfactual dependency does not entail exercising a reliable process. Neither account gets us everything we would ideally have in an account of knowledge: why it entails both justification and truth. I know of no plausible account that

does that. We can only say that reliability accounts of knowledge are preferable to others (including nonreliabilist defeasibility accounts) in providing an explanation of one of these entailments. Which of the two accounts one prefers will depend on which entailment one thinks it more urgent to explain.

VIII The Value of Evaluation

1 I will look here at *self*-evaluation – i.e., the subject's evaluation of her *own* beliefs – but the same questions could be asked about other-evaluation.

2 Whether surrogate processes directly increase the frequency of true beliefs over exercising the processes for which they are surrogates depends on their individuation. If they are individuated in such a way that their output is identical with the output that the processes for which they are surrogates would have if exercised, then it is plausible to suppose that they have the same reliability as those processes. But I believe it is more plausible to individuate them broadly, to include outputs of other inferences – e.g., by being absorbed into a broader form of inference – and then their reliability could be either higher or lower than the reliability of the processes for which they are surrogates.

3 See Curley (1978) for doubts about whether Descartes regarded introspection as unproblematically reliable. See Lyons (1986) for an extensive and illuminating review of the subject of introspection.

4 The inaccessibility of coherence is no threat to BonJour's "Doxastic Presumption" (1985: 103), which simply claims (correctly) that we are dialectically entitled, in answering (antecedent) skepticism, to assume that our beliefs in fact have the propositional content, consistency, explanatory and inferential relations we take them to have.

Bibliography

Adams, F. (1986) "The function of epistemic justification," *Canadian Journal of Philosophy* 16: 465–92.

Adams, J. K. and Adams, P. A. (1961) "Realism of confidence judgments," *Psychological Review* 68: 33–45.

Adams, P. A. and Adams, J. K. (1958) "Training in confidence judgments," *American Journal of Psychology* 71: 747–51.

Alston, W. P. (1980) "Some remarks on Chisholm's epistemology," *Nous* 14: 565–86.

—— (1989a) *Epistemic Justification: Essays in the Theory of Knowledge*, Ithaca: Cornell University Press.

—— (1989b) "Foley's Theory of Epistemic Rationality," *Philosophy and Phenomenological Research* 50: 135–47.

Annas, J. (1980) "Truth and knowledge," in M. Schofield, M. Burnyeat, and J. Barnes (eds) *Doubt and Dogmatism: Studies in Hellenistic Epistemology*, Oxford: Oxford University Press.

—— (1990) "Stoic epistemology," in S. Everson (ed.) *Companions to Ancient Thought 1: Epistemology*, Cambridge: Cambridge University Press.

Armstrong, D.M. (1973) *Belief, Truth and Knowledge*, Cambridge: Cambridge University Press.

Audi, R. (1989) "Causalist internalism," *American Philosophical Quarterly* 26: 309–20.

Beauchamp, T. and Rosenberg, A. (1981) *Hume and the Problem of Causation*, Oxford: Oxford University Press.

BonJour, L. (1985) *The Structure of Empirical Knowledge*, Cambridge, Massachusetts: Harvard University Press.

Burge, T. (1979) "Individualism and the mental," in P.S. French, T.E. Uehling, and H.K. Wettstein (eds) *Midwest Studies in Philosophy: Studies in Metaphysics*, Minneapolis: University of Minnesota Press.

—— (1982) "Other bodies," in A. Woodfield (ed.) *Thought and Object*, Oxford: Oxford University Press.

Burnyeat, M. (1982) "Idealism and Greek philosophy: what Descartes saw and Berkeley missed," *Philosophical Review* 91: 3–40.

Chisholm, R. (1977) *Theory of Knowledge*, 2nd edn, Englewood Cliffs,

New Jersey: Prentice-Hall.
—— (1982) *The Foundations of Knowing*, Minneapolis: University of Minneapolis Press.
Cicero (1933) *Cicero* 28 vols, trans. H. Rackham, Cambridge, Massachusetts: Loeb Classical Library, Harvard University Press.
Coady, C.A.J. (1973) "Testimony and observation," *American Philosophical Quarterly* 10: 149–55.
Code, L. (1983) *"Father and Son*: A case study in epistemic responsibility," *The Monist* 66: 283–97.
Cottingham, J. (1986) *Descartes*, Oxford: Basil Blackwell.
Curley, E.M. (1978) *Descartes Against the Sceptics*, Cambridge, Massachusetts: Harvard University Press.
Descartes, R. (1964–76) *Oeuvres de Descartes*, 12 vols, ed. C. H. Adam and P. Tannery, Paris: Vrin/C.N.R.S.
—— (1970) *Descartes: Philosophical Letters*, trans. A. Kenny, Oxford: Oxford University Press.
—— (1976) *Descartes' Conversation with Burman*, trans. J. Cottingham, Oxford: Oxford University Press.
—— (1984) *The Philosophical Writings of Descartes*, 2 vols, trans. J. Cottingham, R. Stoothoff, and D. Murdoch, Cambridge: Cambridge University Press.
Dretske, F. (1971) "Conclusive reasons," *Australian Journal of Philosophy* 49: 1–22.
—— (1989) "The need to know," in M. Clay and K. Lehrer (eds) *Knowledge and Skepticism*, Boulder: Westview.
Einhorn, H. and Hogarth, R. (1984), "A contrast model for updating Beliefs," unpublished manuscript.
Ericsson, K.A. and Simon, H. (1983) *Protocol Analysis: Verbal Reports as Data*, Cambridge, Massachusetts: MIT Press.
Feldman, R. (1985) "Reliability and justification," *The Monist* 68: 159–74.
—— (1989) "Foley's subjective foundationalism," *Philosophy and Phenomenological Research* 50: 149–58.
Fine, G. (1990) "Knowledge and belief in *Republic* V–VII," in S. Everson (ed.) *Companions to Ancient Thought 1: Epistemology*, Cambridge: Cambridge University Press.
Firth, R. (1978) "Are epistemic concepts reducible to ethical concepts?" in A.I. Goldman and J. Kim (eds) *Values and Morals*, Dordrecht: Reidel.
Fischhoff, B. and Slovic, P. (1980) "A little learning . . .: Confidence in multicue judgment," in R. Nickerson (ed.) *Attention and Performance VIII*, Hillsdale, New Jersey: Erlbaum.
Fischhoff, B., Slovic, P., and Lichtenstein, S. (1977) "Knowing with certainty: The appropriateness of extreme confidence," *Journal of Experimental Psychology: Human Perception and Performance* 3: 552–64.
Flavell, J. (1985) *Cognitive Development*, 2nd edn, Englewood Cliffs, New Jersey: Prentice-Hall.

Knowledge and Belief

Fodor, J. (1983) *The Modularity of Mind*, Cambridge, Massachusetts: MIT Press.

Fogelin, R. (1985) *Hume's Scepticism in the Treatise of Human Nature*, London: Routledge.

Foley, R. (1987) *The Theory of Epistemic Rationality*, Cambridge, Massachusetts: Harvard University Press.

—— (1989) "Reply to Alston, Feldman and Swain," *Philosophy and Phenomenological Research* 50: 169–88.

Frankfurt, H. (1970) *Demons, Dreamers, and Madmen: The Defense of Reason in Descartes's Meditations*, Indianapolis: Bobbs-Merrill.

Fumerton, R. (1987) "Nozick's epistemology," in S. Luper-Foy (ed.) *The Possibility Knowledge: Nozick and His Critics*, Totowa, New Jersey: Rowman and Littlefield.

—— (1988) "Foundationalism, conceptual regress, and reliabilism," *Analysis* 48: 178–84.

Galileo (1967) *Dialogues Concerning the Two Chief World Systems – Ptolemaic and Copernican*, 2nd edn, trans. S. Drake, Berkeley: University of California Press.

Gettier, E. (1963) "Is justified true belief knowledge?" *Analysis* 23: 121–3.

Ginet, C. (1974) *Knowledge, Perception and Memory*, Ithaca: Cornell University Press.

Goldman, A.I. (1976) "Discrimination and Perceptual Knowledge," *Journal of Philosophy* 73: 771–91.

—— (1979) "What is justified belief?" in G. Pappas (ed.), *Justification and Knowledge*, Dordrecht: Reidel.

—— (1980) "The internalist conception of justified belief," in P. French, T.E. Uehling, Jr., and H.K. Wettstein (eds), *Midwest Studies in Philosophy* vol. V: *Studies in Epistemology*, Minneapolis: University of Minnesota Press.

—— (1986) *Epistemology and Cognition*, Cambridge, Massachusetts: Harvard University Press.

Hanfling, O. (1985) "A structural account of knowledge," *The Monist* 68: 40–56.

Harman, G. (1973) *Thought*, Princeton: Princeton University Press.

—— (1986) *Change in View: Principles of Reasoning*, Cambridge, Massachusetts: MIT Press.

Hume, D. (1969) *The Letters of David Hume*, 2 vols, ed. J.Y.T. Grieg, Oxford: Oxford University Press.

—— (1970) *Dialogues Concerning Natural Religion*, ed. N. Pike, Indianapolis: Bobbs-Merrill.

—— (1974) *Enquiries Concerning Human Understanding and Concerning the Principles of Morals*, ed. L.A. Selby-Bigge, 3rd edn, ed. P.H. Nidditch, Oxford: Oxford University Press.

—— (1978) *A Treatise of Human Nature*, ed. L.A. Selby-Bigge, 2nd edn, ed. P.H. Nidditch, Oxford: Oxford University Press.

—— (1987) *Essays Moral, Political, and Literary*, rev. edn, ed. E. Miller, Indianapolis: Liberty Classics.

270

Bibliography

Kahneman, D., Slovic, P., and Tversky, A. (1982) *Judgment Under Uncertainty: Heuristics and Biases*, Cambridge: Cambridge University Press.

Kant, I. (1929) *Critique of Pure Reason*, trans. N. Kemp-Smith, London: Macmillan.

Kemp-Smith, N. (1941) *The Philosophy of David Hume*, London: Macmillan.

Kornblith, H. (1980) "Beyond foundationalism and the coherence theory," *The Journal of Philosophy* 72: 597–612.

—— (1983) "Justified belief and epistemically responsible action," *Philosophical Review* 92: 33–48.

—— (1985)"Ever since Descartes," *The Monist* 68: 264–76.

—— (1989) "The unattainability of coherence," in J. Bender (ed.) *The Current State of the Coherence Theory: Critical Essays on the Epistemic Theories of Keith Lehrer and Laurence BonJour, with Replies*, Dordrecht: Kluwer.

Lehrer, K. (1974) *Knowledge*, Oxford: Oxford University Press.

—— (1990) *Theory of Knowledge*, Boulder: Westview Press, London: Routledge.

Lemos, N. (1989) "High accessibility and justification," *Philosophy and Phenomenological Research* 49: 463–76.

Lenz, J. W. (1964) "Hume's defense of causal inference," in V. C. Chappell (ed.) *Hume*, Garden City, New York: Anchor.

Lichtenstein, S. and Fischhoff, B. (1977) "Do those who know more also know more about how much they know? The calibration of probability judgments," *Organizational Behavior and Human Performance* 20: 159–83.

—— (1980) "Training for calibration," *Organizational Behavior and Human Performance* 26: 149–71.

Lichtenstein, S., Fischhoff, B., and Phillips, D. (1982) "Calibration of probabilities: the state of the art to 1980," in D. Kahneman, P. Slovic, and A. Tversky (eds) *Judgment Under Uncertainty: Heuristics and Biases*, Cambridge: Cambridge University Press.

Liddell, H.G. and Scott, R. (1968) *A Greek–English Lexicon*, Oxford: Oxford University Press.

Locke, J. (1894) *An Essay Concerning Human Understanding*, ed. A.C. Fraser, Oxford: Oxford University Press.

Loeb, L. (1986) "Is there radical dissimulation in Descartes' *Meditations*?" in A.O. Rorty (ed.) *Essays on Descartes' Meditations*, Berkeley: University of California Press.

—— (1990) "Stability, justification, and unphilosophical probability," unpublished manuscript.

Long, A. A. and Sedley, D. N. (1987) *The Hellenistic Philosophers* vol. I: *Translations of the Principal Sources with Philosophical Commentary*, Cambridge: Cambridge University Press.

Luper-Foy, S. (1985) "The reliabilist theory of rational belief," *The Monist* 68: 203–25.

Lycan, W. (1985) "Epistemic Value," *Synthese* 64: 137–64.

271

—— (1988) *Judgement and Justification*, Cambridge: Cambridge University Press.

Lyons, W. (1986) *The Disappearance of Introspection*, Cambridge, Massachusetts: MIT Press.

Millikan, R.G. (1984) "Naturalist reflections on knowledge," *Pacific Philosophical Quarterly* 65: 315–34.

Moser, P.K. (1989) *Knowledge and Evidence*, Cambridge: Cambridge University Press.

Murphy, A.H. (1973) "A new vector partition of the probability score," *Journal of Applied Meteorology* 12: 595–600.

Nagel, T. (1979) "Moral luck," in *Mortal Questions*, Cambridge: Cambridge University Press.

Neisser, U. (1976) *Cognition and Reality: Principles and Implications of Cognitive Psychology*, San Francisco: W.H. Freeman.

—— (1982) *Memory Observed: Remembering in Natural Contexts*, San Francisco: Freeman.

Nisbett, R. and Wilson, T.D. (1977) "Telling more than we can know: Verbal reports on mental processes," *Psychological Review* 84: 231–59.

Nozick, R. (1981) *Philosophical Explanations*, Cambridge, Massachusetts: Harvard University Press.

O'Neil, B.E. (1974) *Epistemological Direct Realism in Descartes' Philosophy*, Albuquerque: University of New Mexico Press.

Pappas, G. (1987) "Suddenly he knows," in S. Luper-Foy (ed.), *The Possibility of Knowing: Nozick and His Critics*, Totowa, New Jersey: Rowman and Littlefield.

Pitz, G. F. (1974) "Subjective probability distributions for imperfectly known quantities," in L.W. Gregg (ed.) *Knowledge and Cognition*, New York: Wiley.

Plantinga, A. (1988) "Positive epistemic status," in J. Tomberlin (ed.), *Philosophical Perspectives* II, Atascadero, California: Ridgeview.

Plato (1921) *Plato* 12 vols, trans. H. N. Fowler, Cambridge, Massachusetts: Loeb Classical Library, Harvard University Press.

—— (1973) *Theaetetus*, trans. J. McDowell, Oxford: Oxford University Press.

Pollock, J. (1974) *Knowledge and Justification*, Princeton: Princeton University Press.

—— (1984) "Reliability and justified belief," Canadian Journal of Philosophy 14: 103–14.

—— (1986) *Contemporary Theories of Knowledge*, Totowa, New Jersey: Rowman and Littlefield.

Popper, K. (1979) *Objective Knowledge*, Oxford: Oxford University Press.

Prichard, H.A. (1950) *Knowledge and Perception*, Oxford: Oxford University Press.

Putnam, H. (1983) "Why reason can't be naturalized," in *Realism and Reason*, Cambridge: Cambridge University Press.

Reid, T. (1969) *Essays on the Intellectual Powers of Man*, ed. B. A. Brody, Cambridge, Massachusetts: MIT Press.

Bibliography

—— (1983) *Inquiry and Essays*, Indianapolis: Hackett.

Rescher, N. (1959) "The legitimacy of doubt," *Review of Metaphysics* 13: 226–34.

Rist, J.M. (1969) *Stoic Philosophy*, Cambridge: Cambridge University Press.

Rogoff, B. and Lave, J. (eds) (1984) *Everyday Cognition: Its Development in Social Context*, Cambridge, Massachusetts: Harvard University Press.

Ross, W. D. (1939) *The Foundations of Ethics*, Oxford: Clarendon Press.

Russell, B. (1912) *The Problems of Philosophy*, London: Holt.

Schmitt, F. F. (1983) "Knowledge, justification, and reliability," *Synthese* 55: 209–29.

—— (1984) "Reliability, objectivity and the background of justification," *Australasian Journal of Philosophy* 62: 1–15.

—— (1985a) "Consensus, respect, and weighted averaging," *Synthese* 62: 25–46.

—— (1985b) "Knowledge as tracking?" *Topoi* 4: 73–80.

—— (1986) "Why was Descartes a foundationalist?" in A. O. Rorty (ed.), *Essays on Descartes' Meditations*, Berkeley: University of California Press.

—— (1987) "Justification, sociality, and autonomy," *Synthese* 73: 43–85.

—— (1988) "Descartes' consequent skepticism," unpublished manuscript.

—— (1989a) "On the road to social epistemic interdependence," *Social Epistemology* 2: 252–5.

—— (1989b) "Testimony and evidence," *Social Epistemology* 2: 323–6.

—— (forthcoming a) "How psychology is relevant to epistemology," *New Ideas in Psychology*.

—— (forthcoming b) "Social cognitive psychology and social epistemology," *Social Epistemology*.

Schneider, W. and Shiffrin, R. (1977) "Controlled and Automatic Human Information Processing: I. Detection, Search and Attention," *Psychological Review* 84: 1–66.

Sextus Empiricus (1933) *Sextus Empiricus*, 4 vols, trans. R.G. Bury, Cambridge, Massachusetts: Loeb Classical Library, Harvard University Press.

—— (1985) *Sextus Empiricus: Selections from the Major Writings on Scepticism, Man, and God*, ed. P.P. Hallie, trans. S.G. Etheridge, Indianapolis: Hackett.

Shope, R. (1983) *The Analysis of Knowing*, Princeton: Princeton University Press.

Siegler, R.S. (1981) "Developmental sequences within and between concepts," *Monographs of the Society for Research in Child Development* 46, 2, serial no. 189.

Slote, M. (1990) "Ethics naturalized," unpublished manuscript.

Smith, E.R. and Miller, F.D. (1978) "Limits on perception of cognitive processes: A reply to Nisbett and Wilson," *Psychological Review* 85: 355–62.

273

Sosa, E. (1985) "Knowledge and intellectual virtue," *The Monist* 68: 226–45.

Steup, M. (1988) "The deontic conception of justification," *Philosophical Studies* 53: 65–84.

Stich, S. (1978) "Beliefs and Subdoxastic States," *Philosophy of Science* 45: 499–518.

Striker, G. (1990) "The problem of the criterion," in S. Everson (ed.) *Companions to Ancient Thought 1: Epistemology*, Cambridge: Cambridge University Press.

Stroud, B. (1984) *The Significance of Philosophical Scepticism*, Oxford: Oxford University Press.

—— (1989) "Understanding human knowledge in general," in M. Clay and K. Lehrer (eds), *Knowledge and Skepticism*, Boulder: Westview Press.

Swain, M. (1981) *Reasons and Knowledge*, Ithaca: Cornell University Press.

Thagard, P. (1988) *Computational Philosophy of Science*, Cambridge, Massachusetts: MIT Press.

Tlumak, J. (1978) "Certainty and Cartesian method," in M. Hooker (ed.) *Descartes: Critical and Interpretive Essays*, Baltimore: Johns Hopkins University Press.

Vlastos, G. (1985) "Socrates' disavowal of knowledge," *Philosophical Quarterly* 35: 1–31.

Wagenaar, W. (1988) "Calibration and the effects of knowledge and reconstruction and retrieval from memory," *Cognition* 38: 277–96.

Walker, A. F. (1986) "Justified belief and internal acceptability," *Canadian Journal of Philosophy* 16: 493–502.

Watkins, J. (1984) *Science and Scepticism*, Princeton: Princeton University Press.

White, P. (1980) "Limitations on verbal reports of internal events: A refutation of Nisbett and Wilson and of Bem," *Psychological Review* 87: 105–12.

Williams, B. (1978) *Descartes: The Project of Pure Enquiry*, Harmondsworth: Pelican.

—— (1981) "Moral luck," in *Moral Luck: Philosophical Papers 1973–1980*, Cambridge: Cambridge University Press.

Williams, M. (1986) "Descartes and the metaphysics of doubt," in A.O. Rorty (ed.), *Essays on Descartes' Meditations*, Berkeley: University of California Press.

Wilson, M.D. (1978) *Descartes*, London: Routledge.

Wright, J.P. (1983) *The Sceptical Realism of David Hume*, Minneapolis: University of Minnesota Press.

Index

Foley, Richard 116, 123, 226–7, 253
folk psychology 143–52, 201
foundationalism 86–7, 109, 119, 206, 235, 248
Frankfurt, Harry 44–6, 49, 73, 78, 233
Frege, Gottlob 221–2
Freud, Sigmund 148, 211
Fumerton, Richard 8–10, 265

Galen 17
Galileo 30
Gassendi, Pierre 14
Gettier, Edmund 1, 134
Ginet, Carl 84–5, 90–8, 102–3, 106, 247–9
Goldman, Alvin 3, 146, 158, 163–74, 178–9, 248, 254, 259, 262–5

Harman, Gilbert 206–7
hasty generalization 75, 79, 80–2, 137, 149, 253
Hume, David 5, 36–7, 48–9, 53–83, 127, 135, 146, 162–3, 222–3, 241–7
hypothetico-deduction 54, 148, 234, 243

imagination 45, 54–83, 140, 192, 204, 243–6
independent accessibility internalism 39–52, 83, 245
indirect theory of perception 15, 50, 56–8, 245
individuation of processes 14, 59, 62–6, 126, 140–63, 167–74, 177–8, 183–4, 187–98, 203–4, 245–6, 259–66
indubitability 42–9, 239–40
induction 54, 73–4, 76, 87, 99–100, 102, 137, 140–1, 146, 153, 155, 162, 166, 180, 200–1, 205, 214, 245
inference to the best explanation 148, 258

introspection 56, 87, 89, 148, 150, 153, 157–8, 211–14
isosthenia 17, 19

James, William 211
justification: advisory conception of 167, 251; aretaic conception of 97–8; deontic conception of 90–8, 103, 248–9, 253; dialogical models of 111–15; doxastic 84, 98, 103, 130–1, 199, 209, 226–7; propositional 84, 91, 98, 103, 130–1, 175, 194, 199, 200, 226–7; regulative 209; supervenience of on nonepistemic properties 99, 120, 124, 127, 132, 250

Kames, Henry Home, Lord 48
Kant, Immanuel 15, 49–50, 56, 58, 245
knowledge: defeasibility account of 1, 266–7; reliability account of 266–7
Kornblith, Hilary 127, 221, 252, 264

Lehrer, Keith 226
Locke, John 54, 241–3
Loeb, Louis 238
Luper-Foy 149–50, 157, 255

Malebranche, Nicolas 54
memory 87, 113, 148, 150, 157–8, 203–7, 213, 219
mental internalism 120–9, 131–9, 220, 256
metacognition 214
metaprocesses 154–5, 163–74, 177, 185, 196, 198–9, 203, 263
methods 87; acquired 164–74, 196, 198–9, 203, 217, 263
Millikan, Ruth Garrett 262

Newton, Isaac 243
Nisbett, Richard 212–14

Williams, Bernard 233–4
Williams, Michael 26–7,
 29–30, 35–6
Wilson, Margaret 38, 46, 237
Wilson, Timothy 212–14

wishful thinking 137, 184–5,
 253, 257
Wright, John 57

Zeno 20